The Scientific
Revolution

PROBLEMS IN EUROPEAN CIVILIZATION SERIES

General Editor
Merry E. Wiesner

The Scientific Revolution

Edited with an introduction by

Lisa T. Sarasohn
Oregon State University

Houghton Mifflin Company   Boston   New York

Vice President and Publisher: Charles Hartford
Senior Sponsoring Editor: Nancy Blaine
Editorial Associate: Annette Fantasia
Project Editor: Reba Libby
Manufacturing Coordinator: Carrie Wagner
Senior Art and Design Coordinator: Jill Haber Atkins
Senior Composition Buyer: Sarah Ambrose
Senior Marketing Manager: Sandra McGuire
Marketing Assistant: Molly Parke

Cover image: The astronomer and his wife. Coques, Gonzalez: 1614–1684, Flemish.
Credit: The Art Archive/Musée des Beaux Arts Strasbourg/Dagli Orti

Printed in the U.S.A.

Library of Congress Control Number: 2003110186

ISBN: 0-618-05243-7

123456789-MP-08 07 06 05 04

Contents

v

Preface

When I first starting studying the Scientific Revolution over 30 years ago, under the able tutelage of Amos Funkenstein and Robert Westman at UCLA, there was no question of whether or not there had been a Scientific Revolution. The big questions were whether it was a continuous and organic development from an earlier period or something unique to the sixteenth and seventeenth centuries, and whether its causes arose from within the scientific enterprise or reflected external pressures. We read the classics of the historiography: Koyré and Hall, Dijksterhuis and Kuhn. On rereading these works for this volume, I was struck with how well they have held up, revealing perhaps my own attitudes as an intellectual historian. Still, the discipline has been enormously enriched by the many contextual and local studies appearing in the last two decades. Scientific Revolution studies have benefited by inclusion of personalities and pursuits outside the consideration of the founders of the field. To my thinking, these new approaches have deepened rather than dissipated the idea of a Scientific Revolution. Shining through all the new evidence and arguments is the reality that our sixteenth and seventeenth century forbears thought they were doing something new and different, and I think we have to take them at their word.

The changes in scholarship and interpretation of the Scientific Revolution reflect changes in the writing of history in general. In this book, and in the classes I teach on the Scientific Revolution, I emphasize themes drawn from the broader historiography of the discipline: intellectual history, women's history, material culture, popular culture, and social and economic history. The study of the Scientific Revolution can be a model for an expanding notion of what historians do, and I hope this book will be useful not only in courses dealing directly with the Scientific Revolution, but also in historiography classes and broader surveys of early modern European history and Western Civilization.

Many of the giants of Scientific Revolution scholarship have died very recently. Betty Jo Dobbs, Richard S. Westfall, Thomas Kuhn, I. Bernard Cohen, and Roy Porter all made enormous contributions to knowledge, and it has been a privilege to help bring their work and the work of others to the notice of the newest students of the subject. For that I wish to thank the editors of this series, Merry Wiesner for first thinking of me and Nancy Blaine at Houghton Mifflin for guiding and encouraging me. I would also like to thank the reviewers of my proposal for this volume for their many suggestions and insights: Roy J. deCarvalho, University of North Texas; Jan Golinski, University of New Hampshire; and those who remain anonymous. Annette Fantasia has been the best of editors, keeping me on task and on time. I also owe a debt of gratitude to my colleagues in the History of Science at Oregon State University, Paul Farber, Mary Jo and Bob Nye, Ron Doel, and Gary Ferngren, who have created a wonderful space to debate the nature and development of science. Finally, I could not do this project, or anything else, without the encouragement and editing of David Sarasohn, and the computer know-how and forbearance of our sons, Alex and Peter.

Lisa T. Sarasohn

Editor's Preface to Instructors

There are many ways to date ourselves as teachers and scholars of history: the questions that we regard as essential to ask about any historical development, the theorists whose words we quote and whose names appear in our footnotes, the price of the books that we purchased for courses and that are on our shelves. Looking over my own shelves, it struck me that another way we could be dated was by the color of the oldest books we owned in this series, which used to be published by D. C. Heath. I first used a "Heath series" book—green and white, as I recall—when I was a freshman in college and taking a modern European history course. That book, by Dwight E. Lee on the Munich crisis, has long since disappeared, but several Heath books that I acquired later as an undergraduate are still on my shelves. Those that I used in graduate school, including ones on the Renaissance and Reformation, are also there, as are several I assigned my students when I first started teaching or have used in the years since. As with any system of historical periodization, of course, this method of dating a historian is flawed and open to misinterpretation. When a colleague retired, he gave me some of his even older Health series books, in red and black, which had actually appeared when I was still in elementary and junior high school, so that a glance at my shelves might make me seem ready for retirement.

The longevity of this series, despite its changing cover design and its transition from D. C. Heath to Houghton Mifflin, could serve as an indication of several things. One might be that historians are conservative, unwilling to change the way they approach the past or teach about it. The rest of the books on my shelves suggest that this conservatism is not the case, however, for many of the books discuss topics that were unheard of as subjects of historical investigation when I took that course as a freshman thirty years ago: memory, masculinity, visual culture, sexuality.

Another way to account for the longevity of this series is that several generations of teachers have found it a useful way for their students to approach historical subjects. As teachers, one of the first issues we confront in any course is what materials we will assign our students to read. (This decision is often, in fact, paramount, for we have to order books months before the class begins.) We may include a textbook to provide an overview of the subject matter covered in the course and often have several from which to choose. We may use a reader of original sources, or several sources in their entirety, because we feel that it is important for our students to hear the voices of people of the past directly. We may add a novel from the period, for fictional works often give one details and insights that do not emerge from other types of sources. We may direct our students to visual materials, either in books or on the Web, for artifacts, objects, and art can give one access to aspects of life never mentioned in written sources.

Along with these types of assignments, we may also choose to assign books such as those in this series, which present the ideas and opinions of scholars on a particular topic. Textbooks are, of course, written by scholars with definite opinions, but they are designed to present material in a relatively bland manner. They may suggest areas about which there is historical debate (often couched in phrases such as "scholars disagree about . . .") but do not participate in those debates themselves. By contrast, the books in this series highlight points of dispute, and cover topics and developments about which historians often disagree vehemently. Students who are used to the textbook approach to history may be surprised at the range of opinions on certain matters, but we hope that the selections in each of these volumes will allow readers to understand why there is such a diversity. Each volume covers several issues of interpretive debate and highlights newer research directions.

Variety of interpretation in history is sometimes portrayed as a recent development, but the age of this series in its many cover styles indicates that this account is not accurate. Historians have long recognized that historical sources are produced by particular individuals with particular interests and biases that consciously and unconsciously shape their content. They have also long—one is tempted to say "always"—recognized that different people approach the past differently, making choices about which topics to study, which sources to use, which developments and individuals to highlight. This diversity in both sources and methodologies is part of what makes history exciting for those of us who study it, for new materials and new approaches allow us to see things that have never been seen before, in the same way that astronomers find new stars with better tools and new ways of looking.

The variety and innovation that is an essential part of good historical scholarship allow this series both to continue and to change. Some of the volumes now being prepared have the same titles as those I read as an undergraduate, but the scholarship on these topics has changed so much in the last several decades that they had to be completely redone, not simply revised. Some of the volumes now in print examine topics that were rarely covered in undergraduate courses when the series began publication, and a few former volumes are no longer in print because the topics they investigated now show up more rarely. We endeavor to keep the series up-to-date and welcome suggestions about volumes that would prove helpful for teaching undergraduate and graduate courses. You can contact us at http://college.hmco.com.

Merry E. Wiesner

Editor's Preface to Students

History is often presented as facts marching along a timeline, and historical research is often viewed as the unearthing of information so that more facts can be placed on the timeline. Like geologists in caves or physicists using elaborate microscopes, historians discover new bits of data, which allow them to recover more of the past.

To some degree, this model is accurate. Like laboratory scientists, historians do conduct primary research, using materials in archives, libraries, and many other places to discover new things about the past. Over the last thirty years, for example, the timeline of history has changed from a story that was largely political and military to one that includes the experiences of women, peasants, slaves, children, and workers. Even the political and military story has changed and now includes the experiences of ordinary soldiers and minority groups rather than simply those of generals, rulers, and political elites. This expansion of the timeline has come in part through intensive research in original sources, which has vastly increased what we know about people of the past.

Original research is only part of what historians do, however, in the same way that laboratory or field research is only part of science. Historical and scientific information is useless until someone tries to make sense of what is happening, tries to explain why and how things developed the way they did. In making these analyses and conclusions, however, both historians and scientists often come to disagree vehemently about the underlying reasons for what they have observed or discovered, and sometimes about the observations themselves. Certain elements of those observations are irrefutable—a substance either caught fire or it did not, a person lived and died or he or she did not—but many more of them are open to debate: Was the event (whether historical or scientific) significant? Why and how did it happen? Under what circumstances might it not have happened? What factors influenced the way that it happened? What larger consequences did it have?

The books in this series focus on just those types of questions. They take one particular event or development in European history and present you with the analyses of several historians and other authors regarding this issue. In some cases the authors may disagree about what actually happened—in the same way that eyewitnesses of a traffic accident or crime may all see different things—but more often they disagree about the interpretation. Was the Renaissance a continuation of earlier ideas, or did it represent a new way of looking at the world? Was nineteenth-century European imperialism primarily political and economic in its origins and impact, or were cultural and intellectual factors more significant? Was ancient Athens a democracy worthy of emulation, an expansionary state seeking to swallow its neighbors, or both? Within each volume are often more specific points of debate, which add complexity to the main question and introduce you to further points of disagreement.

Each of the volumes begins with an introduction by the editor, which you should read carefully before you turn to the selections themselves. This introduction sets out the *historical* context of the issue, adding depth to what you may have learned in a textbook account or other reading, and also explains the *historiographical* context—that is, how historians (including those excerpted in the volume) have viewed the issue over time. Many volumes also include a timeline of events and several reference maps that situate the issue chronologically and geographically. These may be more detailed than the timelines and maps in your textbook, and consulting them as you read will help deepen your understanding of the selections.

Some of the volumes in the series include historical analyses that are more than a century old, and all include writings stretching over several decades. The editors include this chronological range not only to allow you to see that interpretations change, but also to see how lines of argument and analysis develop. Every historian approaching an issue depends not only on his or her own original research, but also on the secondary analyses of those who have gone before, which he or she then accepts, rejects, modifies, or adapts. Thus, within the book as a whole or within each section, the selections are generally arranged in chronological order; reading them in the order they are presented will allow you to get a better sense of the historiographical development and to make comparisons among the selections more easily and appropriately.

The description of the scholarly process noted above is somewhat misleading, for in both science and history, research and analysis are not sequential but simultaneous. Historians do not wander around archives looking for interesting bits of information but turn to their sources with specific questions in mind, questions that have often been developed by reading earlier historians. These questions shape where they will look, what they will pay attention to, and therefore what conclusions they will make. Thus, the fact that we now know so much more about women, peasants, or workers than we did several decades ago did not result primarily from sources on these people suddenly appearing where there had been none, but from historians, with new questions in mind, going back to the same archives and libraries that had yielded information on kings and generals. The same is true in science, of course; scientists examining an issue begin with a hypothesis and then test it through the accumulation of information, reaching a conclusion that leads to further hypotheses.

In both history and science, one's hypotheses can sometimes be so powerful that one simply cannot see what the sources or experiments show, which is one reason there is always opportunity for more research or a reanalysis of data. A scholar's analysis may also be shaped by many other factors, and in this volume the editor may have provided you with information about individual authors, such as their national origin, intellectual background, or philosophical perspective, if these factors are judged important to your understanding of their writings or points of view. You might be tempted to view certain of these factors as creating "bias" on the part of an author and thus to reduce the value of his or her analysis. It is important to recognize, however, that every historian or commentator has a particular point of view and writes at a particular historical moment; very often what scholars view as complete objectivity on their own part is seen as subjective bias by those who disagree. The central aim of this series over its forty-plus years of publication has been to help you and other students understand how and why the analyses and judgments of historians have differed and changed over time, to see that scholarly controversy is at the heart of the historical enterprise.

The instructor in your course may have provided you with detailed directions for using this book, but here are some basic questions that you can ask yourself as you read the selections:

- What is the author's central argument?
- What evidence does the author put forward to support this argument?
- What is the significance of the author's argument?
- What other interpretation might there be of the evidence that the author presents?
- How does each author's argument intersect with the others in the part? In the rest of the book?
- How convincing do you find the author's interpretation?

These questions are exactly the same as those that professional historians ask themselves, and in analyzing and comparing the selections in this book, you, too, are engaged in the business of historical interpretation.

Merry E. Wiesner

Chronology of the Scientific Revolution

Introduction:
The Scientific Revolution

Does science have a history? The very idea may be alien to those who believe that science happens simply because smart people think up smart ideas. But putting science into a historical context does not diminish discovery. Instead, it demonstrates that people thought differently in different times. Seeing their different circumstances gives a deeper appreciation of what their ideas meant in their time, and our own. Demystifying the process of scientific development provides a richer understanding of the past and makes science part of the common human heritage. This volume depicts the ways historians have viewed the history of the investigation of nature, and how their interpretations were influenced by their own times.

As early as the eighteenth century, Enlightenment thinkers saw that a radical change in ideas about the natural world had developed during the preceding two centuries. Voltaire did the most to advance the view that changes in science were heroic, a story of great men throwing off the shackles of superstition and religion, and setting the stage for unlimited progress in the future. According to Voltaire, Isaac Newton was a greater man than Caesar or Alexander, "for if true greatness consists in having received from heaven the advantage of a superior genius, with the talent for applying it for the interest of the possessor and mankind, a man like Newton—and such a man is hardly to be found within ten centuries—is surely by much the greatest." In 1949, the historian Herbert Butterfield echoed this view, declaring,

> Since [the Scientific Revolution] overturned the authority in science not only of the middle ages but of the ancient world—since it ended in not only the eclipse of scholastic philosophy but in the destruction of Aristotelian physics—it outshines everything since the rise of Christianity and reduces the Renaissance and Reformation to the rank of mere episodes within the system of medieval Christendom.

"The Great Tradition," this book's first part, looks at traditional views of the Scientific Revolution. Authors in this tradition—including

1

Edwin Arthur Burtt, A. Rupert Hall, Alexandre Koyré, and Richard S. Westfall—assumed there was a major change in scientific thought in the sixteenth and seventeenth centuries, when the established Aristotelianism was rejected in favor of a new metaphysical and methodological approach to nature. This so-called "Whig" approach to the history of science concentrates on a central group of thinkers—including Copernicus, Kepler, Galileo, Descartes and Newton—and emphasizes changes in astronomy and physics, largely ignoring other disciplines such as chemistry, medicine, and natural history. This view sees the universe—and history—shifting when Copernicus developed the heliocentric model of the universe, Kepler discovered the Three Laws of Planetary Motion, Galileo turned his telescope on the heavens while mathematically determining how bodies really fall to the earth, Bacon and Descartes developed inductive and deductive methodologies (with Descartes thinking up the Law of Inertia in his spare time), and Newton brought it all together with the Law of Universal Gravitation and the discovery of the calculus. Relying on these assumptions about science, historians built a triumphalist "master narrative" in which science advances inexorably to the present. Their major argument debated whether science developed due to internal intellectual factors—that is, the very logic of the subject—or whether external religious, economic, social, or other cultural factors shaped the Scientific Revolution.

The next part, "Science and Religion," focuses more directly on the relationship between science and religion. No historiographical debate has changed more in tone and content. Nineteenth-century historians, sharing the Enlightenment's antipathy towards religion, assumed that it was hostile toward science. They believed that religion's only impact on science was obstructionist and detrimental, an attitude reflected in Andrew Dickson White's 1899 title, *A History of the Warfare of Science with Theology in Christendom*. The conflict was symbolized by the Catholic Church's persecution of Galileo and its condemnation of the Copernican Theory. Later, some historians modified this view by exempting the Protestant faiths, which, they argued, indirectly provided a stimulus or at least a sympathetic environment for scientific development. Robert K. Merton argued that Puritanism promoted the scientific enterprise, which explained why the greatest discoveries of the Scientific Revolution occurred in Protestant countries, especially England. Focusing on that country, Barbara Shapiro has argued that

Latitudinarian Anglicans were most receptive to the new science. Recent interpreters such as Margaret J. Osler argue that natural philosophers such as the Catholic René Descartes and Pierre Gassendi, and the Protestant Isaac Newton were inspired by religious motivations, shaping both their scientific thinking and the reception of their ideas. These historians see religion as not an enemy of science, but a contributor to it.

The next part, "Science and Society," deals with science in its time. Recent historians not only recognize and analyze how science is shaped by its society, but argue that context "makes" science. Thomas S. Kuhn began this trend with his enormously influential book, *The Structure of Scientific Revolutions*, arguing that scientific work is colored by prior assumptions and beliefs about the natural world, and that only a radical shift in perception allows scientists to perceive the world differently. Kuhn sees the Copernican revolution as a vivid example of this shift. When the scientific community starts practicing science differently, a new paradigm or conceptual scheme emerges. Although Kuhn sees some scientific principles as objectively true, later authors have almost discounted such ideas, seeing science as the product of a specific social context. Steven Shapin and Simon Schaffer, whose book *Leviathan and the Air-Pump* is a classic of recent literature on the Scientific Revolution, argue that "matters-of-fact" became scientific truths when they were accepted by the scientific community—such as the members of the Royal Society who served as witnesses to validate Robert Boyle's experiments with the air-pump. Other historians, most notably Mario Biagioli in *Galileo Courtier*, have examined the institution of patronage in early modern Europe and have emphasized its dominant role in shaping the development of science. Steven Shapin, in a later work, *A Social History of Truth*, has argued that scientific truth during the seventeenth century was linked with codes of gentlemanly behavior. Ultimately, for these scholars, the Scientific Revolution devolves into a series of social practices.

Historians who contest the very idea of a Scientific Revolution have turned to figures and practices outside traditional accounts, in order to depict the complexity of natural philosophy in the sixteenth and seventeenth centuries. In early modern times, students of nature considered themselves natural philosophers who studied all of nature; along with our modern sciences, their subjects included alchemy, astrology, medicine,

and natural magic. Figures such as the chemical philosopher and physician Paracelsus and the astronomer Kepler inhabited a natural landscape,
in which scientific activity commingled with esoteric and occult pursuits, as illustrated by Frances Yates in *Giordano Bruno and the Hermetic
Tradition*. Paula Findlen and William Eamon have shown that other,
less famous savants collected scientific wonders indiscriminately, seeking
to penetrate the secrets of nature, and sought knowledge in medieval
books of secrets. But such activities were not peripheral for the actors involved, including "real" scientists, whose work incorporated the insights
and assumptions of their esoteric studies in the rest of their natural
philosophies. The most important studies of this interaction of so-called
rational and esoteric factors have focused on Isaac Newton, whose investigations of alchemy, comets, and Biblical chronology provide an
alternate view of this canonical hero of the Scientific Revolution.

The next part—entitled "Did Women have a Scientific Revolution?"—looks at a group usually outside the boundaries of traditional
historians, and often ignored even in revisionist studies. Starting with
Carolyn Merchant, feminist historians have questioned women's place
in the Scientific Revolution. They ask how gender assumptions might
have colored the work of the canonical thinkers, especially the mechanical philosophers such as Descartes and Hobbes, who deprived
matter of any animating force—a force traditionally associated with the
female. Historians are also interested in women thinkers themselves
as a new object of study. Margaret Cavendish, whom I discuss in "A
Science Turned Upside Down: Feminism and the Natural Philosophy
of Margaret Cavendish," developed her own scientific vision. Other
women played a part in the history of science, either through participation in craft traditions, as Londa Schiebinger shows, or as participants
in salon society.

The last section of this volume examines the fundamental question
of whether there was a Scientific Revolution. Should historians discard
this idea, as Betty Jo Dobbs argues, as a hindrance rather than a help to
understanding the developments in science of the sixteenth and seventeenth centuries? Or should they, as Richard S. Westfall and I. Bernard
Cohen have urged, retain it, as a way of emphasizing the profound
qualitative change in views of the natural world occurring during this
period? Should the category be used merely as a research tool to order
and organize the study of this period, as Peter Dear has suggested? Dear,

in his introduction to *The Scientific Enterprise in Early Modern Europe*, argues, "The historian's choice of subject matter and the way of framing the questions to be asked of it are themselves always determined by reference to an existing historiographical picture. This means there is, of necessity, a certain conservatism built even into the most revisionist account." Consequently, whether one favors discarding the category or embracing it, historians cannot get away from it. The category of "Scientific Revolution" has been integrated into the academic curriculum, whether historians think it existed or not.

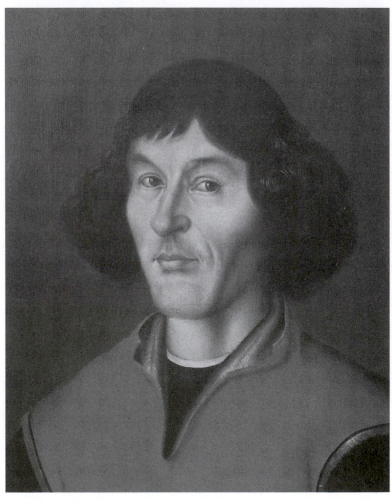

Copernicus, 1473–1543, Polish astronomer and mathematician whose work *De Revolutionibus* (1543) initiated the change to a heliocentric model of the universe. (© *Paul Almasy/CORBIS*)

PART

I

The Master Narrative

"Revolutions, too, need time for their accomplishment," wrote the eminent historian Alexandre Koyré in 1957, "revolutions, too, have a history." The historians included in this section believed that they were chronicling a fundamental change in the human perception of nature in the sixteenth and seventeenth centuries, and that this change was revolutionary. Starting from the assumption that scientific change involved a basic reconstituting of metaphysical assumptions, historians in the intellectualist tradition argued that during the period from Copernicus to Newton, both science and philosophy were transformed.

Edwin Arthur Burtt, A. Rudolf Hall, Alexandre Koyré, and Richard S. Westfall trace the transformation of thought during the Scientific Revolution. Whether through the rejection of the philosophy of Aristotle—either in its original ancient formulation or in its elaboration during the Middle Ages by scholastic philosophers—or because of the Renaissance exposure to Platonic and Pythagorean thought with its emphasis on mathematics, thinkers of the sixteenth and seventeenth century embraced a new worldview based on a new understanding of the aims and methods of natural philosophy.

Earlier students of nature, including Aristotelians and Renaissance naturalists, had assumed that nature was animated by occult forces and determined by some particular end or teleological design. Most of the central scientists of the Scientific Revolution, according to these historians, instead envisioned a mechanistic universe composed only of matter and motion, which could be understood either through rational thought or empirical observation. The universe could be measured, but not necessarily entirely understood.

Edwin Arthur Burtt, who originally wrote *The Metaphysical Foundations of Modern Physical Science* (first published 1924; revised edition 1934) as a doctoral dissertation in philosophy, did not believe that this change in worldview was necessarily a good thing. As the historian of science Lorraine Daston pointed out in 1991, Burtt assumed that science was informed by certain metaphysical assumptions, whether about the way knowledge is acquired (epistemology) or what constitutes the principles of being (ontology). He lamented that the qualitatively rich universe of the late middle ages had been stripped of its metaphysical warmth by the quantitative coldness of early modern science. Burtt's appeal to later historians of science, according to Daston, was his nostalgia for another age, a nonmodern age, "where human beings nestled in a womblike nature before a rude rebirth into an indifferent Nature."

Perhaps desire for an idealized medieval past was possible when Burtt wrote in the 1920s, but by the 1950s historians lived in a different world. One recent historian of science, Roy Porter, has linked the historiographical tradition associated with Alexandre Koyré and A. Rupert Hall with the attitudes of the West in the Cold War. The Scientific Revolution represented the unequivocal triumph of free thought over despotism: "Science had not chugged forward following [Soviet-style] Five Year Plans, but had been transformed in stupendous, unpredictable leaps of reason." Koyré, who in 1939 was the first historian to employ the term "Scientific Revolution," was a Russian emigré, who was then forced to flee from occupied France during World War Two. According to the historian of science, H. Floris Cohen, Hall argued for "the rational nature of the Scientific Revolution as opposed to the various brands of mysticism, magic, superstition and the like, which early modern science conquered and gradually outgrew."

Richard S. Westfall, a generation after Koyré and Hall, followed them in emphasizing the central importance of the Scientific Revolution. Westfall united both an intellectual and contextualist approach to the history of science. Although his award-winning biography of Isaac Newton, *Never at Rest* (1980), emphasized Newton's genius, it also placed the scientist in the context of his times. Westfall was fascinated by the religious and social factors influencing early modern science, but did not consider context the only approach. In one of his last statements on the subject, he proclaimed the "Whiggish" view of studying the past from the perspective of the present, maintaining that "the existence of modern science is the precondition for most of the central features of our society."

The transformation of fundamental categories of thought by individual geniuses was the theme uniting the historiographical approaches of Burtt, Hall, Koyré, Westfall, and all historians who adopted "The Master Narrative" of the Scientific Revolution.

Edwin Arthur Burtt

The Metaphysical Foundations of Modern Physical Science, 1924

Edwin Arthur Burtt's analysis of the Scientific Revolution begins with medieval physics and the medieval worldview, which he believed unified Greek philosophy and Judeo-Christian theology. He argues that Copernicus rejected the earlier picture of the universe because he had absorbed Platonic ideas that gave preeminence to simplicity and harmony as categories for evaluating the truth of cosmological systems. Copernicus, and later Kepler, embraced mathematics as the key to conceptualizing and understanding the universe. With Newton, medieval scholastic categories were abandoned, and

Edwin Arthur Burtt, *The Metaphysical Foundations of Modern Physical Science: A Historical and Critical Essay,* rev. ed., (New York: Humanities Press, 1951), pp. 5–7, 15–21, 25–26, 43–44, 58. Reprinted by permission of Winifred Burtt Brinster.

the modern metaphysical categories of space, time and force were embraced. Consequently, Newtonian metaphysics came to dominate philosophy, although it could not answer fundamental metaphysical questions.

. . . Let us try to fix in preliminary fashion, although as precisely as we may, the central metaphysical contrast between medieval and modern thought, in respect to their conception of man's relation to his natural environment. For the dominant trend in medieval thought, man occupied a more significant and determinative place in the universe than the realm of physical nature, while for the main current of modern thought, nature holds a more independent, more determinative, and more permanent place than man. It will be helpful to analyse this contrast more specifically. For the Middle Ages man was in every sense the centre of the universe. The whole world of nature was believed to be teleologically subordinate to him and his eternal destiny. Toward this conviction the two great movements which had become united in the medieval synthesis, Greek philosophy and Judeo-Christian theology, had irresistibly led. The prevailing world-view of the period was marked by a deep and persistent assurance that man, with his hopes and ideals, was the all-important, even controlling fact in the universe.

This view underlay medieval physics. The entire world of nature was held not only to exist for man's sake, but to be likewise immediately present and fully intelligible to his mind. Hence the categories in terms of which it was interpreted were not those of time, space, mass, energy, and the like; but substance, essence, matter, form, quality, quantity — categories developed in the attempt to throw into scientific form the facts and relations observed in man's unaided sense-experience of the world and the main uses which he made it serve. Man was believed to be active in his acquisition of knowledge — nature passive. When he observed a distant object, something proceeded from his eye to that object rather than from the object to his eye. And, of course, that which was real about objects was that which could be immediately perceived about them by human senses. Things that appeared different *were* different substances, such as ice, water, and steam. The famous puzzle of the water hot to one hand and cold to the other was a genuine difficulty to medieval physics, because for it heat and cold were distinct substances. How then could the same water possess both heat and cold? Light and heavy, being distinguished by the senses, were held to be distinct qualities, each as real as the other. Similarly on the teleological side: an explanation in terms of the relation to things of human purpose was accounted just as real as and often more important than an explanation in terms of efficient causality, which expressed their relations to each other. Rain fell because it nourished man's crops as truly as because it was expelled from the clouds. Analogies drawn from purposive activity were freely used. Light bodies, such as fire, tended upward to their proper place; heavy bodies, such as water or earth, tended downward to theirs. Quantitative differences were derived from these teleological distinctions. Inasmuch as a heavier body tends downward more strongly than a lighter, it will reach the earth more quickly when allowed to fall freely. Water in water was believed to have no weight, inasmuch as it was already in its proper place. But we need not multiply instances; these will sufficiently illustrate the many respects in which medieval science testified to its presupposition that man, with his means of knowledge and his needs, was the determinative fact in the world.

Furthermore, it was taken for granted that this terrestrial habitat of man was in the centre of the astronomical realm. With the exception of a few hardy but scattered thinkers, the legitimacy of selecting some other point of reference in astronomy than the earth, had never suggested itself to any one. The earth appeared a thing vast, solid, and quiet; the starry heavens seemed like a light, airy, and not too distant sphere moving easily about it; even the keenest scientific investigators of ancient times dared not suggest that the sun was a twentieth of its actual distance from the earth. What more natural than to hold that these regular, shining lights were made to circle round man's dwelling-place, existed in short for his enjoyment, instruction , and use? The whole universe was a small, finite place, and it was man's place. He occupied the centre; his good was the controlling end of the natural creation.

Finally, the visible universe itself was infinitely smaller than the realm of man. The medieval thinker never forgot that his philosophy was a religious philosophy, with a firm persuasion of man's immortal destiny. The Unmoved Mover of Aristotle and the personal Father of the Christian had become one. There was an eternal Reason and Love, at once Creator and End of the whole cosmic scheme, with whom man as a reasoning and loving being was essentially akin. In the religious experience was that kinship revealed, and the religious experience to the medieval philosopher was the crowning scientific fact. Reason had become married to mystic inwardness and entrancement; the crowning moment of the one, that transitory but inexpressibly ravishing vision of God, was likewise the moment in which the whole realm of man's knowledge gained final significance. The world of nature existed that it might be known and enjoyed by man. Man in turn existed that he might "know God and enjoy him forever." In this graciously vouchsafed kinship of man with an eternal Reason and Love, lay, for medieval philosophy, a guarantee that the whole natural world in its present form was but a moment in a great divine drama which reached over countless æons past and present and in which man's place was quite indestructible. . . .

. . . Just how did it come about that men began to think about the universe in terms of atoms of matter in space and time instead of the scholastic categories? Just when did teleological explanations, accounts in terms of use and the Good, become definitely abandoned in favour of the notion that true explanations, of man and his mind as well as of other things, must be in terms of their simplest parts? What was happening between the years 1500 and 1700 to accomplish this revolution? And then, what ultimate metaphysical implications were carried over into general philosophy in the course of the transformation? Who stated these implications in the form which gave them currency and conviction? How did they lead men to undertake such inquiries as that of modern epistemology? What effects did they have upon the intelligent modern man's ideas about his world?

When we begin to break up our puzzle into specific questions like these we realize that what we are proposing is a rather neglected type of historical inquiry, that is, an analysis of the philosophy of early modern science, and in particular of the metaphysics of Sir Isaac Newton. . . .

. . . It is the creative period of modern science, then, in the seventeenth century chiefly, to which we must turn for the main answer to our problem. As for pre-Newtonian science, it is one and the same movement with pre-Newtonian philosophy, both in England and on the continent; science was simply natural philosophy, and the influential figures of the period were both the greatest philosophers and the greatest scientists. It is largely due to Newton himself that a real distinction came to be made between the two; philosophy came to take science, in the main, for granted, and another way to put our central theme is, *did not the problems to which philosophers now devoted themselves arise directly out of that uncritical acceptance?* A brief summary of Newton's work will show that this is very possible.

Since his day, a two-fold importance has generally been ascribed to Newton. Popularly, he has profoundly affected the thinking of the average intelligent man by his outstanding scientific exploits, of which the most striking was his conquest of the heavens in the name of human science by identifying terrestrial gravitation with the centripetal movements of the celestial bodies. Great as is the name of Newton today, it is difficult for us to picture the adoration with which he was regarded all over Europe in the eighteenth century. It seemed to men, if we are to trust the voluminous literature of the time, that such achievements as the discovery of the laws of motion and the law of universal gravitation, represented an incomparable, uniquely important victory of mind, which it could fall to the lot of only one man throughout all time to realize—and Newton had been that man. Henry Pemberton, who edited the third edition of the *Principia* for Newton, and who wrote one of the numerous commentaries on it, declared that ". . . my admiration at the surprising inventions of this great man, carries me to conceive of him as a person, who not only must raise the glory of the country which gave him birth, but that he has even done honour to human nature, by having extended the greatest and most noble of our faculties, reason, to subjects which, till he attempted them, appeared to be wholly beyond the reach of our limited capacities." . . . Literary men like Pope found expression for the prevailing veneration of the great scientist in such a famous couplet as:

> "*Nature and Nature's laws lay hid in night;*
> *God said, 'Let Newton be,' and all was light.*" . . .

Such representative quotations disclose the creation, under Newton's leadership, of a new background in the minds of Europe's intelligentsia such that all problems must have been viewed afresh because they were seen against it.

A student of the history of physical science will assign to Newton a further importance which the average man can hardly appreciate. He will see in the English genius a leading figure in the invention of certain scientific tools necessary for fruitful further development such as the infinitesimal calculus. He will find in him the first clear statement of that union of the experimental and mathematical methods which has been exemplified in all subsequent discoveries of exact science. He will note the separation in Newton of positive scientific inquiries from questions of ultimate causation. Most important, perhaps, from the point of view of the exact scientist, Newton was the man who took vague terms like force and mass and gave them a precise meaning as quantitative continua, so that by their use the major phenomena of physics became amenable to mathematical treatment. It is because of these remarkable scientific performances that the history of mathematics and mechanics for a hundred years subsequent to Newton appears primarily as a period devoted to the assimilation of his work and the application of his laws to more varied types of phenomena. So far as objects were masses, moving in space and time under the impress of forces as he had defined them, their behaviour was now, as a result of his labours, fully explicable in terms of exact mathematics.

It may be, however, that Newton is an exceedingly important figure for still a third reason. He not only found a precise mathematical use for concepts like force, mass, inertia; he gave new meanings to the old terms space, time, and motion, which had hitherto been unimportant but were now becoming the fundamental categories of men's thinking. In his treatment of such ultimate concepts, together, with his doctrine of primary and secondary qualities, his notion of the nature of the physical universe and of its relation to human knowledge (in all of which he carried to a more influential position a movement already well advanced)—in a word, in his decisive portrayal of the ultimate postulates of the new science and its successful method as they appeared to him, Newton was constituting himself a philosopher rather than a scientist as we now distinguish them. He was presenting a metaphysical groundwork for the mathematical march of mind which in him had achieved its most notable victories. Imbedded directly and prominently in the *Principia*, Newton's most widely studied work, these metaphysical notions were carried wherever his scientific influence penetrated, and borrowed a possibly unjustified certainty from the clear demonstrability of the gravitational theorems to which they are appended as *Scholia*. Newton was unrivalled as a scientist—it may appear that he is not above criticism as a metaphysician. He tried scrupulously, at least in his experimental work, to avoid metaphysics. He disliked hypotheses, by which he meant explanatory propositions which were not immediately deduced from phenomena. At the same time, following his illustrious predecessors, he does give or assume definite answers to such fundamental questions as the nature of space, time, and matter; the relations of man with the objects of his knowledge; and it is just such answers that constitute metaphysics. . . .

. . . [E]ven had there been no religious scruples whatever against the Copernican astronomy, sensible men all over Europe, especially the most empirically minded, would have pronounced it a wild appeal to accept the premature fruits of an uncontrolled imagination, in preference to the solid inductions, built up gradually through the ages, of men's confirmed sense experience. In the strong stress on empiricism, so characteristic of present-day philosophy, it is well to remind ourselves of this fact. Contemporary empiricists, had they lived in the sixteenth century, would have been first to scoff out of court the new philosophy of the universe.

Why, in the face of such weighty facts, did Copernicus propound the new theory as a true account of the relations between the earth and the heavenly bodies? He must have been moved by strong reasons, and if we can locate them with precision we shall have discovered the cornerstone and the foundation structure of the philosophy of modern physical science. For to oppose to these profoundly serious objections he could plead only that *his conception threw the facts of astronomy into a simpler and more harmonious mathematical order.* It was simpler, since in place of some eighty epicycles of the Ptolemaic system, Copernicus was able to "save the phenomena" with only thirty-four, all those which had been required by the assumption that the earth remained at rest being now eliminated. It was more harmonious, in that the major part of the planetary phenomena could now fairly well be represented by a series of concentric circles around the sun, our moon being the only irregular intruder. But what was this increased simplicity and harmony against the solid philosophical objections just advanced? . . .

This was in fact the greatest point of conflict between the dominant Aristotelianism of the later Middle Ages and this somewhat submerged but still pervasive Platonism. The latter regarded a universal mathematics of nature as legitimate (though, to be sure, just how this was to be applied was not yet solved); the universe is fundamentally geometrical; its ultimate constituents are nothing but limited portions of space; as a whole it presents a simple, beautiful, geometrical harmony. On the other hand the orthodox Aristotelian school minimized the importance of mathematics. Quantity was only one of the ten predicaments and not the most important. Mathematics was assigned an intermediate dignity between metaphysics and physics. Nature was fundamentally qualitative as well as quantitative; the key to the highest knowledge must, therefore, be logic rather than mathematics. With the mathematical sciences allotted this subordinate place in his philosophy, it could not but appear ridiculous to an Aristotelian for any one to suggest seriously that his whole view of nature be set aside in the interest of a simpler and more harmonious geometrical astronomy. Whereas for a Platonist (especially as Platonism was understood at the time) it would appear a most natural, though still radical step, involving as it did a homogeneity of substance throughout the whole visible cosmos. However, Copernicus could take the step because, in addition to the motive factors already discussed, he had definitely placed himself in this dissenting Platonic movement. Already before he went to Italy in 1496 he had felt its appeal, and, while there, he found ample reinforcement for his daring leap in the energetic Neo-Platonic environment south of the Alps, and particularly in his long and fruitful intercourse with a bold and imaginative Pythagorean like Novara. It was no accident that he became familiar with the remains of the early Pythagoreans, who almost alone among the ancients had ventured to suggest a non-geocentric astronomy. His knowledge of Greek was first acquired while studying with Novara, perhaps with the explicit purpose of reading for himself the works of the Pythagorean astronomers. He had himself become convinced that the whole universe was made of numbers, hence whatever was mathematically true was really or astronomically true. Our earth was no exception—it, too, was essentially geometrical in nature—therefore the principle of relativity of mathematical values applied to man's domain just as to any other part of the astronomical realm. The transformation to the new world-view, for him, was nothing but a mathematical reduction, under the encouragement of the renewed Platonism of the day, of a complex geometrical labyrinth into a beautifully simple and harmonious system. . . .

The reason why there exists this vast and beautiful mathematical order in the universe is not further explicable for Kepler except by way of the religious aspect of his Neo-Platonism. He quotes with approval the famous saying of Plato, that God ever geometrizes; he created the world in accordance with numerical harmonies, and that is why he made the human mind such that it can only know by quantity. . . .

A. Rupert Hall

The Scientific Revolution 1500–1800: The Formation of the Modern Scientific Attitude, 1954

A. Rupert Hall, like Burtt, also emphasizes the relationship between science and philosophy, particularly in regard to epistemology and methodology. He argues that a scientist's approach to the natural world is grounded in the pre-suppositions he brings to his study of natural phenomena. Thus, the Greeks both described the physical world and also tried to explain it in terms of universal truths. According to Hall, seventeenth-century thinkers used different methodologies to explain nature. Bacon's empiricism was rooted in his rejection of prior speculative thought about nature, while Descartes emphasized rationalism and logic in his study of man and nature. Hall critiqued the Marxist approach to the history of science, by applauding the independence of "the finest minds" from determinative social and economic influences.

The Principles of Science in the Early Seventeenth Century

Conscious reflection on the relations between man and his natural environment can only be a product of an advanced state of civilization in which abstract thought flourishes. Greek philosophers seem to have been the first to discuss the problem, how can reason be most successfully applied to understanding the complex phenomena of material things?—and in so doing they introduced the generalizing of ideas that is essential to science and distinguishes it from the *ad hoc* solving of practical problems undertaken in man's struggle with nature. It is generally agreed that the foundations of scientific knowledge cannot be settled, or

A. Rupert Hall, *The Scientific Revolution, 1500–1800: The Formation of the Modern Scientific Attitude* (Boston: Beacon Press, 1954). Reprinted by permission of Longman Group UK.

even verified, by the normal processes of science itself. If such questions are asked as, what is the status of a scientific theory? or, what is the meaning of the word "explanation" in science? or, to what extent is science a logical structure? they cannot be answered without transcending the framework of science. The scientist must have some idea, which is essentially philosophical, of how he is going to set about acquiring an understanding of nature before he can apply himself to this task. He may in practice be entirely uninterested in philosophy, preferring to regard himself as a compiler of demonstrable facts; nevertheless, he cannot escape the implications of adopting a definite scientific method, which teaches him to record particular kinds of facts, by using certain recognized procedures. Thus the nature of science in different periods has been determined by the methods employed in collecting facts and reasoning about them, and by the prevailing approach to the study of natural phenomena. For example, when the mechanistic philosophy of the seventeenth century replaced the teleological outlook of earlier times the change in the character of scientific explanation was profound: it was no longer sufficient to ascribe the pattern of events to divine purpose or the necessary conditions for human existence.

Consequently, when comparing the scientific achievements of one epoch with those of another, it must be recognized that the aims and methods of scientific activity may themselves vary. The fundamental philosophy of science is neither fixed, nor static, nor inevitable. It cannot be claimed that any scientific method is correct, without considering the nature of the objects it seeks to achieve. Both may be subjected to criticism, for it may be asked whether scientists have the proper aims, or whether they are using fit methods; and, indeed, from the thirteenth to the seventeenth centuries there was continuous and effective criticism of science from each of these points of view. During the eighteenth and nineteenth centuries, however, there was a tendency for practising scientists to feel a confident complacency concerning their aims and methods, and to envelop themselves in an impenetrable detachment from any attempt to interpret their activities philosophically. They were scientists, devoted to a peculiarly rigorous pursuit of knowledge, not natural philosophers. They despised metaphysics and logic. Their limited outlook, and their often shallow pragmatism, would have been intolerable to the Greek founders of scientific method.

In essence, the Greek notion of scientific explanation (passing into the European tradition through the medieval dependence on the philosophy of antiquity) did not differ from that of modern science. When a phenomenon had been accurately described so that its characteristics were known, it was explained by relating it to the series of general or universal truths. The most important distinction between Hellenistic science (including that of the middle ages) and modern science is in the constitution of these universals, and the methods of recognizing them with certainty. For Platonists the universal truths were Ideas, the principal task of their philosophy—it cannot properly be called science—being the elucidation of the ideal world of perfect Forms of which the tangible world was a clumsy model framed in imperfect matter. Aristoteleans, on the other hand, denied the separability of Idea (or Form) and Matter (or Substance), but nevertheless were concerned with the processes by which Forms, the generalizations of their science, were detected in the materials provided by sense-perception. . . .

. . . Many passages in Bacon's writings indicate that he had a philosophic appreciation of the value of knowledge for its own sake, not merely for its utilitarian applications. The test by works, in Bacon's thought, assumed a particular importance not because works were the main end of science, but rather because they guaranteed the rectitude of the method used. A discovery or explanation which was barren of works could hold no positive merit not because it was useless to man, but because it lacked contact with reality and possibility of demonstration. Since Bacon's science was to deal with real things, its fruits must be real and perceptible.

Measured by these standards, Aristotelean science was a hollow structure, dealing with abstractions rather than real things, justified by no fertility in works. Bacon did not deny that there was truth in the content of orthodox science—he was quite as certain as Aristotle of the stability of the earth—but these truths were buried in a misleading and sterile philosophy. His remedy was to return to a consideration of the bare facts, and above all to increase vastly the range of facts available. Only when *all* the material upon a particular phenomenon, or natural process, had been collected, classified and tabulated could any general conclusions be drawn from it and generalizations be framed. The facts might be collected from experience, from reliable reports, from the lore of craftsmen, but above all from designed experiment. For Bacon clearly conceived of experiment not merely as a trial "to see what happens," but as a way of answering specific questions. The task of an investigator was to propose questions capable of an experimental answer, which could then be recorded as a new fact appertaining to the phenomenon under study. In this way the lists of "instances" were to be built up, as Bacon attempted himself to construct tables of instances of heat and motion. Other aids were then required in the intellectual process of finding order in the mass of fact compiled, for which also Bacon made suggestions. In the *New Atlantis* the work of the fact-gatherers is separated altogether from the work of the fact-interpreters, and this had been criticized as a defect in Bacon's system. Yet in practice in science it has often happened that a new generalization in theory has interpreted a mass of evidence assembled by a line of earlier experimental investigators.

Some comments on science have denied categorically that there is any such thing as a specific "scientific method," by saying, for example, that science is organized common sense. Bacon's method at least seems to suffer from excessive formalization and a top-heavy logical apparatus. Even in his own ventures into scientific research Bacon did not observe his complex rules very strictly, and hence the once popular notion that he invented and described the method of experimental science is no longer acceptable. Modern science was not consciously modelled upon Bacon's system. Mathematical reasoning especially, so freely and successfully exploited from the earliest stages of the scientific revolution, he never understood so that its essential rôle was hidden from him. It has also been said, with less justice, that the integration of theory and experiment typical of modern research was not allowed for in his system and that he did not foresee the importance of hypothesis in the conduct of an investigation. In fact Bacon did envisage the situation where reflection on the facts suggests several possible theories, and discussed the procedure to be adopted for the isolation of the correct one by falsification of the others. And certainly he understood the decisive nature of a "crucial experiment" in judging the merit of an idea taking shape in the investigator's mind. It should not be forgotten, too, that pure fact-collection (the first stage in Bacon's system) has been a most important fraction of all scientific work up to the present time. Even the routine verification of measurements, or the establishment of precise constants, has been productive of original discoveries. It is true that the main course of physical science in the seventeenth century ran in a very different direction, that in the new mechanics of Galileo the plodding fact-gathering imagined by Bacon had little significance; elsewhere in science, however, where the organization of ideas was less advanced and the material far more complex and subtle, the straightforward acquisition of accurate information was a more fruitful endeavour than premature efforts at conceptualization. This is most clearly true of the biological sciences; no Galileo could have defined the strategic ideas of geology or physiology which only emerged from the wider and deeper knowledge of facts obtained in the nineteenth century. Bacon's advice that solid facts, certified by experiment, should be collected and recorded was sound and practical; this task occupied chemistry and biology till towards the end of the next century. But in the long run the great generalizations in these fields did not follow from the kind of digestion and sublimation of fact that Bacon had described.

While Bacon's works gave a useful impetus to the growing interest in science, especially in England, his attempt to define the intellectual processes involved in the understanding of nature was limited and only partially helpful. Empiricism alone is an insufficient instrument in science. The history of the scientific revolution shows the fertility of the critical examination of concepts and theories, even when the modification of the simple account of the facts is insignificant (as with Galileo's new concepts of inertia and acceleration). Bacon's views were characterized by his approach to science, which was that of a philosopher rather than that of an experienced investigator. His own ventures in research are notoriously uninteresting and unproductive, for except in his leaning towards an atomistic materialism he was out of sympathy with the progressive ideas of the time, and remarkably indifferent to those developments which posterity has found most significant. . . .

Following the example of Galileo, the scientist may as it were work either upwards or downwards; he may seek for a more fundamental construct (like the law of inertia, or the laws of thermodynamics) or he may examine the applications of the construct to the details of a complex phenomenon (like the isochronism of the pendulum). In either case he may have to handle constructs which are not reducible to the ultimate physical realities, as was the case for instance with Newtonian mechanics where the law of gravitation had to be taken as descriptively correct, though gravity was not explicable in terms of matter and motion. For Galileo there was no anomaly in recognizing that certain constituents of the physical world had to be accepted as axiomatic; descriptive analysis can only advance gradually from the coarse to the refined, from the lower to the upper levels, each with its appropriate generalizations. In the period between Galileo and Newton, however, the validity of the purely descriptive generalization (which rests upon scepticism concerning the possibility of arriving at a final indubitable truth serving as the single origin of scientific thought) was challenged in the philosophy of Descartes, and rejected by the systematists who expounded Cartesian ideas. The chief difference between Galileo and Descartes lay in this, that while the former believed that a body of knowledge successful in organizing sense-perceptions (duly refined and analysed) and in framing generalizations based on them gave an adequate understanding of nature, the latter believed that there was no reliable test of the significance of sense-perceptions other than that which issues from a deeper metaphysical certainty. The mind, being extra-nature, was capable of doubting anything external to itself in nature.

As Descartes relates in the *Discourse on Method* (1637), after completing a thorough education, in which, "not contented with the sciences actually taught us, I had read all the books that had fallen into my hands, treating of such branches as are esteemed the most curious and rare," he found himself involved in many doubts and errors, persuading him that all his attempts at learning had taught him no more than the discovery of his own ignorance. In philosophy, despite all the efforts of the most distinguished intellects, everything was in dispute and therefore not beyond doubt, and as for the other sciences "inasmuch as these borrow their principles from philosophy," he reasoned that nothing solid could be built upon such insecure foundations.

In this perplexity, Descartes proposed to himself four "laws of reasoning" which he applied in the first place to the study of mathematics:

> In this way I believed that I could borrow all that was best both in geometrical analysis and in algebra, and correct all the defects of the one by the help of the other. And, in point of fact, the accurate observance of these few precepts gave me such ease in unravelling all the questions embraced in these two sciences, that in the two or three months I devoted to their examination, not only did I reach solutions of questions I had formerly deemed exceedingly difficult, but even as regards questions of solution of which I remained ignorant, I was enabled as it appeared to me, to determine the means whereby, and the extent to which, a solution was possible.

Mathematical ideas, then, could be understood with perfect clarity and mathematical demonstrations accepted with absolute confidence. These principles, to which Descartes held firm in all his scientific activities, ally him with Galileo in the attainment of the ideal of mathematization throughout science. Indeed, Descartes' most valuable contribution to the scientific revolution was the co-ordinate geometry described for the first time in the same volume as the *Method*. But his grasp of a starting point for the comprehension of *fact*, rather than the abstractions of mathematics, depended upon a form of psychical crisis from which he emerged possessed with the metaphysical force of the statement, *I think, therefore*

I am. . . . This led Descartes to inquire why he had found *Cogito, ergo sum* an infallible proposition, whence he convinced himself that all things clearly and distinctly perceived as true, are true, "only observing that there is some difficulty in rightly determining the objects which we distinctly perceive." Further, he declared that since the mind is aware of its own imperfection, there must be a being, God, which is perfect and that since perfection cannot deceive, those ideas which are clearly and distinctly perceived as true are so because they proceed from perfect and infinite Being. So much more certain are the fruits of reason, says Descartes, that we may be less assured of the existence of the physical universe itself, than of that of God, "neither our imagination nor our senses can give us assurance of anything unless our understanding intervene . . . whether awake or asleep, we ought never to allow ourselves to be persuaded of the truth of anything unless on the evidence of our reason."

After this denunciation of empiricism, this declaration that all knowledge of truth is implanted by God, this assertion that the task of the scientist is to frame propositions as clearly and distinctly true as those of geometry, what suggestions can be made for the deciphering of the enigma of nature? According to Descartes, it is necessary to follow exactly that procedure which Bacon had condemned in Aristotle, that is, to establish the prime generalizations that are "clearly and distinctly true." . . .

Why do men reject one kind of science in favour of another? Why in modern Europe alone did they move from the intermediate to the modern stage? The answer cannot be simple, or single. It requires psychological and philosophical insight, as well as a command of the historical facts, to which we have as yet scarcely attained, for the operation, the incidence, and the impact of the creative intellect are almost unknown. We cannot rely only upon appeal to experiment, observation, measurement, or any other over-simplification of the complex processes of science, to present us with a solution to this problem. Still less hopeful is the economic interpretation of the history of science, which seeks to tell us why men sought for control over natural forces, but cannot explain how they were able to acquire it. The economic motive may have made their attitude to Nature less disinterested, but cannot alone have changed its character. So, too, we recognize that precision in measurement has been of great importance, that experiment is the touchstone of hypothesis, that to the percipient observer the unexpected is always a fertile challenge. Yet many of the most dramatic challenges in the history of science have issued not from the unexpected, not from the spectrum that was oblong instead of round, not from the frog's leg that jerked instead of remaining still, but from the orthodox, the expected, the familiar pattern of experience and thought. What predisposed men to struggle for the moving earth, atomism, evolution, and so disturb the calm quiescence of their time when no awkward barrage of fact enforced their turbulence? For, contrary to the straightforward inductive view of science, it has often happened that men have looked for facts to demonstrate a theory, as Galileo, Boyle and Newton did, without science being any the worse for that. Perhaps the finest minds are capable of stretching far beyond the immediate warranty of facts.

If we admit so much, we may admit more. If modern science is not merely an elaborate digest of pointer-readings, then it is the more obvious that the scientific revolution involved more than the discovery of ways of making such readings and digesting them into a coherent synthesis. In the growth of modern science creative imagination, preferences, assumptions and preconceptions, ideas of the relations of God and Nature, arbitrary postulates, all played their parts. Here then is the crux; that we cannot write the full history of science save by reflecting the operations of original thought, which we do not understand; and that we cannot exclude from science, which is rational, the influence of factors which are irrational.

Alexandre Koyré

From the Closed World to the Infinite Universe, 1957

Alexandre Koyré belonged to a historiographic tradition that saw the seventeenth century as a period of general crisis and transformation in European thought and culture. He argues that the Scientific Revolution, begun by Copernicus and brought to culmination by Newton, was based on the mathematization of motion and a new understanding of basic philosophical and

Alexandre Koyré, *From the Closed World to the Infinite Universe* (New York: Harper & Brothers, 1957), pp. vii–ix, 1, 5, 6, 29, 30, 159–160, 161, 223, 224, 226, 227. © 1957 by Alexandre Koyré. Reprinted with permission of The Johns Hopkins University Press.

scientific principles. The "closed world" of the ancients and the Middle Ages was displaced by the "infinite universe" of Newtonian physics. In this selection, Koyré traces the role of Copernicus, who was unable to conceive of an infinitely large universe, and that of Newton, whose principles of absolute space and time reflect his religious belief in the ubiquity and omnipotence of God.

Preface

Time and again, when studying the history of scientific and philosophical thought in the sixteenth and the seventeenth centuries—they are, indeed, so closely interrelated and linked together that, separated, they become ununderstandable—I have been forced to recognize, as many others have before me, that during this period human, or at least European, minds underwent a deep revolution which changed the very framework and patterns of our thinking and of which modern science and modern philosophy are, at the same time, the root and the fruit.

This revolution or, as it has been called, this "crisis of European consciousness," has been described and explained in many different ways. Thus, whereas it is generally admitted that the development of the new cosmology, which replaced the geo- or even anthropocentric world of Greek and medieval astronomy by the heliocentric, and, later, by the centerless universe of modern astronomy, played a paramount role in this process, some historians, interested chiefly in the social implications of spiritual changes, have stressed the alleged conversion of the human mind from *theoria* to *praxis*, from the *scientia contemplativa* to the *scientia activa et operativa*, which transformed man from a spectator into an owner and master of nature; some others have stressed the replacement of the teleological and organismic pattern of thinking and explanation by the mechanical and causal pattern, leading, ultimately, to the "mechanisation of the world-view" so prominent in modern times, especially in the eighteenth century: still others have simply described the despair and confusion brought by the "new philosophy" into a world from which all coherence was gone and in which the skies no longer announced the glory of God.

As for myself, I have endeavored in my *Galilean Studies* to define the structural patterns of the old and the new world-views and to determine the changes brought forth by the revolution of the seventeenth century.

They seemed to me to be reducible to two fundamental and closely connected actions that I characterised as the destruction of the cosmos and the geometrization of space, that is, the substitution for the conception of the world as a finite and well-ordered whole, in which the spatial structure embodied a hierarchy of perfection and value, that of an indefinite or even infinite universe no longer united by natural subordination, but unified only by the identity of its ultimate and basic components and laws; and the replacement of the Aristotelian conception of space—a differentiated set of innerworldly places—by that of Euclidean geometry—an essentially infinite and homogenous extension—from now on considered as identical with the real space of the world. The spiritual change that I describe did not occur, of course, in a sudden mutation. Revolutions, too, need time for their accomplishment; revolutions, too, have a history. Thus the heavenly spheres that encompassed the world and held it together did not disappear at once in a mighty explosion; the world-bubble grew and swelled before bursting and merging with the space that surrounded it.

The path which led from the closed world of the ancients to the open one of the moderns was, as a matter of fact, not very long: barely a hundred years separate the *De revolutionibus orbium coelestium* of Copernicus (1543) from the *Principia philosophiae* of Descartes (1644); barely forty years these *Principia* from the *Philosophia naturalis principia mathematica* (1687). On the other hand, it was rather difficult, full of obstacles and dangerous road blocks. Or, to put it in simpler language, the problems involved in the infinitization of the universe are too deep, the implications of the solutions too far-reaching and too important to allow an unimpeded progress. Science, philosophy, even theology, are, all of them, legitimately interested in questions about the nature of space, structure of matter, patterns of action and, last but not least, about the nature, structure, and value of human thinking and of human science. Thus it is science, philosophy, and theology, represented as often as not by the very same men—Kepler and Newton, Descartes and Leibniz—that join and take part in the great debate that starts with Bruno and Kepler and ends— provisionally, to be sure—with Newton and Leibniz. . . .

Introduction

It is generally admitted that the seventeenth century underwent, and accomplished, a very radical spiritual revolution of which modern science is at the same time the root and the fruit. This revolution can be—and was—described in a number of different ways. Thus, for instance, some historians have seen its most characteristic feature in the secularization of consciousness, its turning away from transcendent goals to immanent aims, that is, in the replacement of the concern for the other world and the other life by preoccupation with this life and this world. Some others have seen it in the discovery, by man's consciousness, of its essential subjectivity and, therefore, in the substitution of the subjectivism of the moderns for the objectivism of mediaevals and ancients; still others, in the change of relationship between θεωρία and πράξις, the old ideal of the *vita contemplativa* yielding its place to that of the *vita activa*. Whereas mediaeval and ancient man aimed at the pure contemplation of nature and of being, the modern one wants domination and mastery.

These characterizations are by no means false, and they certainly point out some rather important aspects of the spiritual revolution—or crisis—of the seventeenth century, aspects that are exemplified and revealed to us, for example, by Montaigne, by Bacon, by Descartes, or by the general spread of skepticism and free thinking.

I. The Sky and the Heavens:
Nicholas of Cusa & Marcellus Palingenius

The conception of the infinity of the universe, like everything else or nearly everything else, originates, of course, with the Greeks; and it is certain that the speculations of the Greek thinkers about the infinity of space and the multiplicity of worlds have played an important part in the history we shall be dealing with. It seems to me, however, impossible to reduce the history of the infinitization of the universe to the rediscovery of the world-view of the Greek atomists which became better known through the newly discovered Lucretius or the newly translated Diogenes Laertius. We must not forget that the infinitist conceptions of the Greek atomists were rejected by the main trend, or trends, of Greek philosophical and scientific thought—the Epicurean tradition was not a scientific one—and that for this very reason, though never forgotten, they could not be accepted by the mediaevals.

We must not forget, moreover, that "influence" is not a simple, but on the contrary, a very complex, bilateral relation. We are not influenced by everything we read or learn. In one sense, and perhaps the deepest, we ourselves determine the influences we are submitting to; our intellectual ancestors are by no means given to, but are freely chosen by, us. At least to a large extent.

How could we explain otherwise that, in spite of their great popularity, neither Diogenes nor even Lucretius had, for more than a century, any influence on the fifteenth century's cosmological thinking? The first man to take Lucretian cosmology seriously was Giordano Bruno. Nicholas of Cusa—it is true that it is not certain whether at the time when he wrote his *Learned Ignorance* (1440) he knew the *De rerum natura*—does not seem to have paid much attention to it. Yet it was Nicholas of Cusa, the last great philosopher of the dying Middle Ages, who first rejected the mediaeval cosmos-conception and to whom, as often as not, is ascribed the merit, or the crime, of having asserted the infinity of the universe. . . .

I need not insist on the overwhelming scientific and philosophical importance of Copernican astronomy, which, by removing the earth from the center of the world and placing it among the planets, undermined the very foundations of the traditional cosmic world-order with its hierarchical structure and qualitative opposition of the celestial realm of immutable being to the terrestrial or sublunar region of change and decay. Compared to the deep criticism of its metaphysical basis by Nicholas of Cusa, the Copernican revolution may appear rather half-hearted and not very radical. It was, on the other hand, much more effective, at least in the long run; for, as we know, the immediate effect of the Copernican revolution was to spread skepticism and bewilderment of which the famous verses of John Donne give such a striking, though somewhat belated, expression, telling us that the

> . . . *new Philosophy calls all in doubt,*
> *The Element of fire is quite put out;*
> *The Sun is lost, and th'earth, and no mans wit*
> *Can well direct him where to looke for it.*
> *And freely men confesse that this world's spent,*
> *When in the Planets, and the Firmament*
> *They seeke so many new; then see that this*
> *Is crumbled out againe to his Atomies.*
> *'Tis all in peeces, all cohaerence gone;*
> *All just supply, and all Relation.*

To tell the truth, the world of Copernicus is by no means devoid of hierarchial features. Thus, if he asserts that it is not the skies which move, but the earth, it is not only because it seems irrational to move a tremendously big body instead of a relatively small one, "that which contains and locates and not that which is contained and located," but also because "the condition of *being at rest* is considered as nobler and more divine than that of *change* and *inconsistency*; the latter therefore, is more suited to the earth than to the universe." And it is on account of its supreme perfection and value—source of light and of life—that the place it occupies in the world is assigned to the sun: the central place which, following the Pythagorean tradition and thus reversing completely the Aristotelian and mediaeval scale, Copernicus believes to be the best and the most important one.

Thus, though the Copernican world is no more hierarchically structured (at least not fully; it has, so to say, two poles of perfection, the sun and the sphere of the fixed stars, with the planets in between), it is still a well-ordered world. Moreover, it is still a finite one. . . .

But not only philosophers shared, more or less, [the Cambridge Platonist] Henry More's conception of space: it was shared by Newton, and this, because of the unrivaled influence of Newton on the whole subsequent development, is, indeed, of overwhelming importance.

It may seem strange, at first glance, to link together Henry More and Isaac Newton. . . . And yet, this link is perfectly established. Moreover, as we shall see, More's explicit teaching will throw some light on the implicit premises of Newtonian thinking, a light all the more necessary as Isaac Newton, in contradistinction not only to Henry More but also to René Descartes, is neither a professional metaphysician like the former, nor, like the latter, at once a great philosopher and a great scientist: he is a professional scientist, and though science, at that time, had not yet accomplished its disastrous divorce from philosophy, and though physics was still not only designated, but also thought of, as "natural philosophy," it is nevertheless true that his primary interests are in the field of "science," and not of "philosophy." He deals, therefore, with metaphysics not *ex professo*, but only insofar as he needs it to establish the foundations of his intentionally empirical and allegedly positivistic mathematical investigation of nature. Thus the metaphysical pronouncements of Newton are not very numerous and, Newton being a very cautious and secretive person as well as a very careful writer, they are rather reticent and reserved. And yet they are sufficiently clear so as not to be misunderstood by his contemporaries.

Newton's physics, or, it would be better to say, Newton's natural philosophy, stands or falls with the concepts of absolute time and absolute space, the selfsame concepts for which Henry More fought his long-drawn-out and relentless battle against Descartes. Curiously enough, the Cartesian conception of the only relative, or relational, character of these and connected notions is branded by Newton as being "vulgar" and as based upon "prejudices."

Thus in the famous *scholium* which follows the *Definitions* that are placed at the very beginning of the *Principia*, Newton writes:

> *Hitherto I have laid down the definitions of such words as are less known, and explain the sense in which I would have them to be understood in the following discourse. I do not define time, space, place, and motion as being well known to all. Only I must observe that the vulgar conceive those quantities under no other notions but from the relations they bear to sensible objects. And thence arise certain prejudices, for the removing of which, it will be convenient to distinguish them into absolute and relative, true and apparent, mathematical and common.*

Absolute, true and mathematical time and space — for Newton these qualifications are equivalent and determine the nature both of the concepts in question and of the entities corresponding to them — are thus, in a manner of which we have already seen some examples, *opposed* to the merely common-sense time and space. As a matter of fact, they could just as well be called "intelligible" time and space in contradistinction to "sensible." Indeed, according to the "empiricist" Newton, "in philosophical disquisitions we ought to abstract from our senses and consider things themselves, distinct from what are only sensible measures of them." . . .

Time is not only not linked with motion — like Henry More before him, Newton takes up against Aristotle the Neoplatonic position — it is a reality in its own right:

> *Absolute, true and mathematical time, of itself and from its own nature, flows equably without regard to anything external,*

that is, it is *not*, as Descartes wants us to believe, something which pertains only to the external, material world and which would not exist if there were no such world, but something which has its *own nature* (a rather equivocal and dangerous assertion which Newton later had to correct by relating time, as well as space, to God), "and by another name is called duration." . . .

[Newton's] natural philosophy, leads necessarily not to the denial but to the affirmation of God's existence and of his action in the world. . . .

[H]e asserts not only the existence of absolute time and space but also their necessary connection with God. . . .

. . . Newton's pronouncements in the *General Scholium*, at least those concerning God's action in the world, are not very explicit. Thus, Newton does not tell us anything about the necessity of God's continuous concourse for the preservation of its structure; he seems even to admit that, once started, the motion of the heavenly bodies could continue forever; it is only at their beginning that God's direct intervention appears indispensable. On the other hand, the actual structure of the world (that is, of the solar system) is, of course, asserted to be the result of a conscious and intelligent choice. . . .

Newton's God is not merely a "philosophical" God, the impersonal and uninterested First Cause of the Aristotelians, or the—for Newton—utterly indifferent and world-absent God of Descartes. He is—or, in any case, Newton wants him to be—the Biblical God, the effective Master and Ruler of the world created by him. . . .

His duration reaches from eternity to eternity; his presence from infinity to infinity . . . the Newtonian God is, patently, not above time and space: His eternity is sempiternal duration, His omnipresence is infinite extension. This being so, it is clear why Newton insists:

> *He is not eternity and infinity, but eternal and infinite; he is not duration or space, but he endures and is present.*

And yet, like the God of Henry More and of Joseph Raphson, he not only "endures forever and is everywhere present"; but it is "by existing always and everywhere" that "he constitutes duration and space." . . .

> *He is omnipresent not virtually only, but also substantially; for virtue cannot subsist without substance. In him are all things contained and moved; yet neither affects the other: God suffers nothing from the motion of bodies; bodies find no resistance from the omnipresence of God. It is allowed by all that the Supreme God exists necessarily; and by the same necessity he exists always and everywhere.*

Thus "in Him we live, we move and we are," not metaphorically or metaphysically as St. Paul meant it, but in the most proper and literal meaning of these words.

We—that is, the world—are in God; in God's space, and in God's time. And it is because of this ubiquitous and sempiternal co-presence with things that God is able to exercise His dominion upon them; and it is this dominion or, more exactly, the effect of this dominion that reveals to us His otherwise unknowable and incomprehensible essence:

> *We know him only by his most wise and excellent contrivances of things, and final causes; we admire him for his perfections; but we reverence and adore him on account of his dominion: for we adore him as his servants; and a god without dominion; providence, and final causes, is nothing else but Fate and Nature. Blind metaphysical necessity, which is certainly the same always and everywhere, could produce no variety of things. All that diversity of natural things which we find suited to different times and places could arise from nothing but the ideas and will of a Being necessarily existing. . . .*

Richard S. Westfall

The Construction of Modern Science: Mechanisms and Mechanics, 1971

Whereas Koyré emphasized the mathematical tradition of natural philosophy in his work, and only later in his career considered the impact of mechanistic interpretations of nature, Richard S. Westfall considered the importance of both the mathematical and mechanical traditions. Trained as an engineer, he described the emergence of the mechanistic model of the universe in Descartes' philosophy, where the world of extension (matter) is devoid of any active principles, and causation is the result of the impact of one particle on another. In this selection, Westfall considers the thought of the French philosopher Pierre Gassendi, whose mechanistic universe was composed of

Richard S. Westfall, *The Construction of Modern Science: Mechanisms and Mechanics* (New York: Cambridge University Press, 1971), pp. 31–34, 38–41. Reprinted with the permission of Cambridge University Press.

atoms and a void. Westfall argues that the mathematical and mechanistic traditions of seventeenth century science were not harmonized until Newton.

In the famous Cartesian dualism, [Descartes] provided the reaction against Renaissance Naturalism with its metaphysical justification. All of reality, he argued, is composed of two substances. What we may call spirit is a substance characterized by the act of thinking; the material realm is a substance the essence of which is extension. *Res cogitans* and *res extensa*—Descartes defined them in a way to distinguish and separate them absolutely. To thinking substance one cannot attribute any property characteristic of matter—not extension, not place, not motion. Thinking, which includes the various modes which mental activity assumes, and thinking alone, is its property. From the point of view of natural science, the more important result of the dichotomy lay in the rigid exclusion of any and all psychic characteristics from material nature. Gilbert's magnetic soul of the world could have no place in Descartes' physical world. . . . [P]hysical nature is inert and devoid of sources of activity of its own. In Renaissance Naturalism, mind and matter, spirit and body were not considered as separate entities; the ultimate reality in every body was its active principle, which partook at least to some extent of the characteristics of mind or spirit. The Aristotelian principle of "form" had played an analogous role in a more subtle philosophy of nature. The effect of Cartesian dualism, in contrast, was to excise every trace of the psychic from material nature with surgical precision, leaving it a lifeless field knowing only the brute blows of inert chunks of matter. It was a conception of nature startling in its bleakness—but admirably contrived for the purposes of modern science. Only a few followed the full rigor of the Cartesian metaphysic, but virtually every scientist of importance in the second half of the century accepted as beyond question the dualism of body and spirit. The physical nature of modern science had been born.

Descartes was fully aware of his revolutionary role in regard to the received philosophic tradition. In his *Discours de la Méthode* (1637), he described his reaction to that tradition as his education had introduced him to it. He had entered upon his education filled with the promise that at its conclusion he would possess knowledge. Far from knowledge, alas, it left him with total doubt. Two thousand years of investigation and argument, he came to realize, had settled nothing. In philosophy, "one cannot imagine anything so strange and unbelievable but that it has been upheld by some philosopher." Descartes decided simply to sweep his mind clear of the past. By a process of systematic doubt, he would subject every idea to a rigorous examination, rejecting everything the least bit dubious until he should come upon a proposition, if such there were, that was impossible to doubt. On such a proposition as a rock of certainty, he could rebuild a structure of knowledge that shared the certainty of its foundation, a structure built anew from the very bottom by reason alone. With the perspective of hindsight, we can see that his repudiation of the past was far less complete than he thought. Nevertheless, his mechanical philosophy of nature was a sharp break with the prevailing conception as represented by Renaissance Naturalism, and scarcely less of a break with Aristotelianism; and in his sensation of making a fresh start he spoke for 17th century science as a whole.

As everyone knows, Descartes found the rock of certainty for which he was searching—that which could not be doubted—in the proposition, "*cogito ergo sum*" (I think, therefore I am). The *cogito* became the foundation of a new edifice of knowledge. From it, he reasoned to the existence of God, and then to the existence of the physical world. In the process of doubt, the existence of a world outside himself had been one of the first items to go; its existence had appeared to depend on the evidence of the senses, and the manifest propensity of the senses to err had called its existence into doubt. From the new foundation of certainty, he now felt able to demonstrate, as a conclusion also beyond doubt, that the physical world external to himself does exist. But to the conclusion he added a condition, perhaps the most important statement made in the 17th century for the work of the scientific revolution. Although the existence of the physical world can be proved by necessary arguments, there is no corresponding necessity that it be in any way similar to the world the senses depict. On the heap of sympathies, antipathies, and occult powers already pruned from the physical world were now thrown the real qualities of Aristotelian philosophy. A body appears red, Aristotle had said, because it has redness on its surface; a body appears hot because it contains the quality of heat. Qualities have real existence; they comprise one of the categories of being; by our senses we perceive reality directly. Not so, Descartes retorted. To imagine that redness or heat exist in bodies is to project our sensations onto the physical world, exactly as Renaissance Naturalism projected psychic processes onto the physical world. In fact, bodies comprise only particles of matter in motion, and all their apparent qualities (extension alone excluded) are merely sensations excited by bodies in motion impinging on the nerves. The familiar world of sensory experience turns out to be a mere illusion, like the occult powers of Renaissance Naturalism. The world is a machine, composed of inert bodies, moved by physical necessity, indifferent to the existence of thinking beings. Such was the basic proposition of the mechanical philosophy of nature.

In essays on *La dioptrique* (1637) and *Les météores* (1637), and in *Principia philosophiae* (1644), Descartes spelled out the details of his mechanical philosophy. One of its foundation stones was the principle of inertia. The mechanical philosophy insisted that all the phenomena of nature are produced by particles of matter in motion—that they must be so produced since physical reality contains only particles of matter in motion. What causes motion? Since matter is by definition inert stuff consciously pruned of active principles, it is obvious that matter cannot be the cause of its own motion. In the 17th century, everyone agreed that the origin of motion lay with God. In the beginning, He created matter and set it in motion. What keeps matter in motion? The very insistence with which the mechanical conception of nature repudiated active principles meant that its viability as a philosophy of nature depended on the principle of inertia. Nothing is required to keep matter in motion; motion is a state, and like every other state in which matter finds itself, it will continue as long as nothing external operates to change it. In impact, motion can be transferred from one body to another, but motion itself remains indestructible.

Descartes attempted to analyze impact in terms of the conservation of the total quantity of motion, a principle which approaches the conservation of momentum formulated later in the century. Since he held that a change in direction alone (without any change in speed) entails no change in the state of another body, the conclusions at which he arrived vary widely from those we accept. Nevertheless, Descartes' analysis of impact was the starting point of later efforts that bore more fruit. Meanwhile, his rules of impact provided the model of all dynamic action; in a mechanical universe shorn of active principles, bodies could act on one another by impact alone.

It was no accident that the men who constructed the two leading mechanical systems of nature, Descartes and Gassendi, also contributed significantly to the formulation of the concept of inertia. With Galileo, inertia was stated, in terms of circular motion corresponding to the diurnal rotation of the earth on its axis. Descartes and Gassendi were the first to insist that inertial motion must be rectilinear motion and that bodies that move in circles or curves must be constrained by some external cause. Such bodies, Descartes asserted, constantly exert a tendency to recede from the center around which they turn. Although he did not attempt to express a quantitative measure of the tendency, his demonstration that such a tendency to recede from the center exists was the first step in the analysis of the mechanical elements of circular motion. . . .

Earlier philosophies had seen nature in organic terms. Descartes turned the tables by picturing even organic phenomena as mechanisms. In his universe, man was unique—the one living being which was both soul and body. Even in the case of man, however, the soul was not considered to be the seat of life, and all organic functions were described in purely mechanistic terms. The heart became a tea kettle, its heat analogues to the heat of fermentation (in itself a mechanical process to Descartes), its action the boiling and expansion of the drops of blood which were forced into it from the veins and forced on by the pressure of vaporization. Other animals, lacking a rational soul, were nothing but complicated machines. If there were automata, Descartes asserted, "possessing the organs and outward form of a monkey or some other animal without reason, we should not have had any means of ascertaining that they were not of the same nature as those animals."

Many of Descartes' explanations of phenomena differ so widely from those we now believe to be correct that we are frequently tempted to scoff. We must attempt rather to understand what he was trying to do and how it fit into the work of the scientific revolution. The cornerstone of the entire edifice of his philosophy of nature was the assertion that physical reality is not in any way similar to the appearances of sensation. As Copernicus had rejected the commonsense view of an immovable earth, and Galileo the commonsense view of motion, so Descartes now generalized the reinterpretation of daily experience. He did not intend to conduct the sort of scientific investigation we are familiar with today. Rather his purpose was metaphysical—he proposed a new picture of the reality behind experience. However wild and incredible we find his explanations, we must remember that the whole course of modern science has been run, not by returning to the earlier philosophy of nature, but by following the path he chose.

Certainly the 17th century found the appeal of the mechanical philosophy of nature overwhelming. The mechanical philosophy did not mean solely the Cartesian philosophy, however, and among other mechanical approaches to nature, one at least stood as a viable and attractive alternative, Gassendi's atomism. Inevitably, the atomic philosophy of antiquity had reappeared in western Europe with the general recovery of ancient thought during the Renaissance. Galileo had felt its influence, and its mechanistic treatment of nature probably helped to shape Descartes' system. It remained, however, for a contemporary of Descartes, Pierre Gassendi (1592–1655), to espouse and expound atomism as an alternative mechanical philosophy. As a thinker, Gassendi was utterly unlike Descartes. Where Descartes saw himself as a systematic philosopher rebuilding the philosophic tradition on new principles of his own creation, Gassendi considered himself as a scholar drawing together the best elements that the tradition could offer. His principal work, *Syntagma Philosophicum* (1658), is an unreadable compilation of everything ever said on the topics discussed, a compilation further which intended to exhaust discussable topics. . . .

Being an atomist, Gassendi differed from Descartes on certain specific questions. Descartes argues that matter is infinitely divisible; Gassendi of course maintained that there are ultimate units which are never divided. The very word "atom" derives from the Greek word for indivisible. Descartes' universe was a plenum; Gassendi in contrast argued for the existence of voids, spaces empty of all matter. Both issues are important philosophic questions, but the disagreements of the two men pale beside their large areas of agreement. They asserted alike that physical nature is composed of qualitatively neutral matter, and that all the phenomena of nature are produced by particles of matter in motion.

Far more important for later science was another difference between Descartes and Gassendi which was logically connected with the question of the plenum. Descartes' insistence that nature is a plenum was the necessary consequence of his identification of matter with extension, and the identification of matter with extension in turn made possible the utilization of geometric reasoning in science. Because geometric space is equivalent to matter, natural science might hope to attain the same rigor in its demonstrations that geometry was agreed to have. Indeed his method, four rules to govern investigations, was little more than a restatement of the principles of geometric demonstration. Rebel against the prevailing tradition though he was, Descartes accepted an ideal of science that went back to Aristotle. It held that the name "science" applies, not to conjectures, not to probable explanations, but solely to necessary demonstrations rigorously deduced from necessary principles. If such a degree of certainty could not be attained in the details of causal explanations, where it was possible to imagine more than one satisfactory mechanism, at least the general principles were beyond doubt—the rigorous separation of the corporeal from the spiritual, and the consequent necessity of mechanical causation.

When Gassendi denied the equation of matter with extension, he denied as well the program of Cartesian science. Atoms are extended, but extension is not their essence. He was convinced indeed that knowledge of the essence of things is beyond the reach of finite man. Gassendi accepted a degree of skepticism as an inevitable ingredient of the human condition. God and God alone can know ultimate essences. Hence the ideal of science held by the dominant school of philosophy in the western tradition from Aristotle to the 17th century and reaffirmed by Descartes was labelled an illusion. Thoroughgoing skepticism was not Gassendi's conclusion, however; he offered instead a redefinition of science. Nature is not completely transparent to human reason; man can know her only externally, only as phenomena. It follows that the only science possible to man is the description of phenomena, a new ideal of science which found its earliest statement in Gassendi's logical writings. Implicit already in Galileo's description of the uniform acceleration of free fall whatever its cause, the ideal was stated formally by Gassendi as part of his denial of the traditional one. It was not an easy conception to grasp, and mechanical philosophers in the 17th century continued to imagine microscopic mechanisms to "cause" natural phenomena. In Isaac Newton, however, Gassendi found a follower, and in the work of Newton, his definition of science demonstrated what it could foster. It has become so deeply ingrained in the procedures of modern experimental science that we find it difficult today to comprehend the Cartesian (and Aristotelian) ideal of necessary demonstrations. . . .

[B]y insisting on particles and allowing differences solely in shape and motion, he [Gassendi] maintained allegiance to the basic principles of the mechanical philosophy of nature. Robert Boyle, a leading mechanical philosopher as well as chemist of the following generation, treated atomism and Cartesianism as two expressions of the same conception of nature. We owe the name, "mechanical philosophy," to Boyle. As he summed it up, the mechanical philosophy traces all natural phenomena to the "two catholic principles," matter and motion. He might have added that by "matter" the mechanical philosophy means qualitatively neutral stuff, shorn of every active principle and of every vestige of perception. Whatever the crudities of the 17th century's conception of nature, the rigid exclusion of the psychic from physical nature has remained as its permanent legacy.

Meanwhile, in the 17th century, the mechanical philosophy defined the framework in which nearly all creative scientific work was conducted. In its language questions were formulated; in its language answers were given. Since the mechanisms of 17th century thought were relatively crude, areas of science to which they were inappropriate were probably frustrated more than encouraged by its influence. . . .

Sprat's *History of the Royal Society*. The frontispiece of Sprat's *History of the Royal Society* emphasizes its Baconian experimental agenda as well as the Society's hope for royal patronage. (*The Granger Collection*)

PART

II Science and Religion

The discussion of the relationship between science and religion pre-dated modern scholars' discovery of the Scientific Revolution. Two influential nineteenth-century books argued that religion, especially Catholicism, was hostile to science. John William Draper's *History of the Conflict between Religion and Science* (1874) and Andrew Dickson White's *A History of the Warfare of Science with Theology in Christendom* (1896) were products of the antipathy liberals of the time felt for what they considered the deeply conservative and obstructionist policies of traditional religions, especially as expressed in the 1864 Vatican Syllabus of Errors—which condemned liberalism, rationalism, and faith in science.

For Draper and White, and others, the condemnation of Galileo by the Catholic Church in 1633 was emblematic of the essential and continuous opposition of science and religion. In the twentieth century, the martyrdom of Galileo has become a landmark of popular understanding of early modern and modern science, a landmark seemingly bolstered by religion's later condemnation of Darwinism.

Some scholars, however, have seen a more positive relationship between science and religion. The idea that science and religion could be harmonious and productive was perhaps most famously advocated by the sociologist Robert K. Merton, who in 1938 first published his doctoral thesis, *Science, Technology and Society in Seventeenth Century England.* Merton followed an earlier founder of sociology, Max Weber, who believed there was a direct correlation between Calvinism and capitalism. Merton believed that external social forces were of paramount importance in the development of science, and in the case of seventeenth-century England, the most important force was a broadly defined Puritanism. Merton reflected his disciplinary background; in the mid-twentieth century the social sciences were increasingly based on quantitative analysis. Merton, accordingly, statistically analyzed the religious allegiances of the members of the Royal Society to support his argument.

Pro-Protestant apologists could and did take heart from what has become known as "The Merton Thesis." Some Marxist historians also found much to admire in Merton's ideas. The chemist and historian S. F. Mason argued that Calvinist theology, as well as its social doctrines, provided support for the Scientific Revolution. Other historians have returned to the question of English science and identified other groups with it: Anglicans, royalists, or in the view of Barbara Shapiro, religious moderates. But most historians have taken the Merton thesis as a starting point for a more nuanced and complex analysis of the integration or opposition of science and religion. Few recent historians would argue for one universal prism or interpretive framework that explains science and religion. The historian John Hedley Brooke asserts that neither existed as unitary categories in the sixteenth and seventeenth century. As Robert S. Westman, who has studied the early reception of the Copernican theory, points out, there were many different religious reactions and accommodations to the new ideas. These reactions often reflected concerns that were not directly theological, for example, the traditional authority given to the different academic disciplines.

Westman's and Shapiro's analyses also point to another recent approach to the relationship between science and religion. Some historians, reflecting the ecumenism of the late twentieth century, have argued that theological categories and epistemologies have affected the content of science itself. The historian Amos Funkenstein, in *Theology and the Scientific Imagination* (1986), argued that a kind of secular theology characterized the sixteenth and seventeenth centuries, when "science, philosophy, and theology [were] seen as almost one and the same occupation." In her work Margaret J. Osler has seconded this view, arguing that a belief in voluntarist theology—the idea that God could do anything in the natural world, even if that meant overturning the laws of nature—penetrated the thought of many natural philosophers.

The problem of the relationship of science and religion continues to fascinate historians of science and religion. The relevance of this discussion to present-day history will no doubt only reemphasize the importance of this subject.

S. F. Mason

The Scientific Revolution and the Protestant Reformation

Calvin and Servetus in Relation to the New Astronomy and the Theory of the Circulation of the Blood

S. F. Mason taught at Oxford in the 1950s. He was influenced by Merton, and by Marxist historians like Edgar Zilsel, who emphasized the importance of economic factors on the development of science. However, Mason also felt that science and Protestantism, especially Calvinism, shared basic assumptions about how the universe worked. Both were anti-authoritarian: the Calvinists rejected Catholic theology and the proponents of the new science rejected Greek philosophy. Both also ascribed to an ethic of performing "good works," including the study of the natural world. And both exalted the power of an absolutely powerful God who maintained the order of the universe not through the mediation of angels, but who implemented His will

S. F. Mason, "The Scientific Revolution and the Protestant Reformation," *Annals of Science* 9 (1953): 64–87; 154–175. Reprinted by permission of Taylor & Francis, Ltd. <http:www.tandfco.uk/journals>

through the laws of nature. Mason, in addition, argues that the Calvinist doctrine of predestination prepared the way for the scientific idea of mechanical determinism. Mason concludes by arguing that both the Calvinists and Newton so abstracted God from a universe ruled by unchangeable law, He ultimately ceased to have a dynamic function in the natural world.

From the inception of the scientific revolution and the Protestant Reformation during the sixteenth century, it has been noted by various authors that there were some similarities between the new science and the new religion, and that Protestant beliefs have been more conducive than the Catholic faith to the promotion of scientific activity. The sixteenth-century medical writer, Richard Bostocke, held the view that the reform of religion had been indispensible to the reform of medicine, and that Copernicus and Paracelsus had restored the sciences just as Luther and Calvin had restored religion. . . .

During the following century, Thomas Sprat, who was himself an Anglican Churchman and a Fellow of the newly formed Royal Society, noted "the agreement that is between the present design of the Royal Society, and that of our Church in its beginning. They both may lay equal claim to the word Reformation; the one having compassed it in Religion, the other purposing it in Philosophy." A little more than a hundred years later, Joseph Priestley, the chemist and Unitarian minister, expressed the view that, in the degree to which the Pope patronized science and polite literature, he "was cherishing an enemy in disguise," for he had "reason to tremble even at an air pump, or an electrical machine." During the nineteenth century, when statistics came into vogue, Alphonse de Candolle, who came of a Huguenot family of scientists, pointed out that of the ninety-two foreign members elected to the Paris Academy of Sciences in the period 1666–1866, some seventy-one had been Protestant in their religion and sixteen had been Catholic, while the remaining five were either indeterminate or Jews. Correlating these figures with the respective religious populations of Europe outside of France, 107 million Catholics and 68 million Protestants, Candolle showed that more than six times as many Protestants as Catholics had become eminent enough in science to be elected to foreign membership of the Paris Academy of Sciences. Such a correlation left out of account the scientists of France, and so Candolle examined the religious affiliations of the foreign members of the Royal Society at two periods,

1829 and 1869, when there were more French scientists included than at other times. He found that at both periods there were about equal numbers of Catholic and Protestant foreign members of the Royal Society, yet outside of the United Kingdom there were 139 million Catholics and 44 million Protestants, figures which substantiated his view that Protestants tended to predominate over Catholics amongst the great scientists of Europe. Subsequent studies of the religious affiliations of scientists, which have been listed by R. K. Merton in his analysis of the connexions between Puritanism and science in seventeenth-century England, have confirmed and amplified the general burden of Candolle's findings, and more recent studies have extended the period covered by his correlation to the sixteenth and the twentieth centuries.

The occurrence of a preponderance of Protestants over Catholics among the important scientists of modern Europe may be ascribed to three main factors: first, a concordance between the early Protestant ethos and the scientific attitude; secondly, the use of science for the attainment of the religious aims of the later Calvinists, notably the English Puritans; and thirdly, a certain congruity between the more abstract elements of the Protestant theologies and the theories of modern science. The first factor seems to have been common to both of the main branches of the Reformation and to most of the significant developments composing the scientific revolution. In their early days, both the Swiss and the German Reformers taught that man should reject the guidance and the authority of the priests of the Catholic faith and should seek for spiritual truth in his own religious experience: he should interpret the Scriptures for himself. Similarly the early modern scientists turned away from the systems of the ancient philosophers and the medieval schoolmen to search for scientific truth in their own empirical and theoretical experiences: they interpreted Nature for themselves. Thomas Sprat, who belonged to the Calvinist tradition, well expressed such a consonance of aim between early modern science and Protestantism when he wrote that the Anglican Church and the Royal Society "may lay equal claim to the word Reformation; the one having compassed it in Religion, the other purposing it in Philosophy." . . . Early Lutheranism also seems to have been in accord with the scientific attitude, for the earliest technical study of the new Copernican theory of the world came from two scholars of the University of Wittenberg, which was the centre of the German Reformation, even though Luther himself, like Calvin, was opposed to the Copernican theory on the grounds that it conflicted with the literal word of the Scriptures. . . .

The second factor helping to account for the prominence of Protestants among the great scientists of modern Europe, the utilization of science for religious ends, appears to have become important amongst the Calvinists of the seventeenth century, notably the English Puritans, who stressed the religious duty of performing 'good works,' and who placed scientific activity amongst the good works beneficial to humanity. Neither Luther nor Calvin had laid much emphasis upon the religious importance of performing good works. Luther had taught that inner faith sufficed for man's salvation, though his outward actions and works should conform to his inner faith. Calvin taught that a certain number of elect persons were predestined to salvation, no one being able to know, however, whether he were saved or not, and that a man should behave as though he were saved even if he felt that he were lost. The later followers of Calvin felt an imperative need to know whether they were saved or whether they were lost, and the original doctrine was modified successively by the Scotch, Dutch, and English Calvinists, so that by the mid-seventeenth century it had become generally accepted by the Puritans that the continuous performance of good works indicated that a man was saved. Among the good works sanctioned by the Puritan ethic were scientific studies. The Puritan divine, John Cotton, writing in 1654, went so far as to declare that the study of Nature was a positive Christian duty. . . .

Such a point of view permeated the consciousness of the men composing the first generation of the Royal Society, among whom the Puritans were prominent. Robert Boyle, who was of this generation, in his last will and testament wished the Fellows of the Royal Society "a most happy success in their laudable attempts to discover the true nature of the works of God, and praying that they and all other searchers into physical truths may cordially refer their attainments to the glory of the Author of Nature and the benefit of mankind."

Of the two factors discussed hitherto with regard to the prevalence of Protestants among the important scientists of modern Europe, it was perhaps the second, which was marked among the later Calvinists, that had the greater weight. The anti-authoritarianism and empirical individualism common to the early Protestant and modern scientist gave at best a relation of congruity, while the later Calvinist promotion of good works gave a positive impulse to scientific activity. In this connexion it is of interest to note that after the days of Galileo and Kepler the main centres of scientific activity passed from Catholic Italy and Lutheran Germany to lands which had come specifically under the influence of Calvinism: England with her Puritans, Holland with her Calvinist Church, and France with her Huguenots, and her Calvinists within the creed, the Jansenists. After the foundation of the Royal Society of London and the Paris Academy of Sciences in the 1660's, the English and the French remained pre-eminent in the field of science for the next century and a half, and while the Dutch lost ground during the eighteenth century, the earlier homes of Calvinism, Scotland and Switzerland, became notable for their scientists in the same period. In Germany and Italy, however, it was not until the nineteenth century that scientists of the calibre of Galileo and Kepler appeared again.

While Protestant attitudes were in accord with, or were conducive to, the pursuit of scientific activities, neither Protestantism nor modern science consisted alone of a set of rules and values guiding human behaviour. Both developed bodies of theory, and the degree to which Protestant theologies have been congruent with the theories of science is a matter relevant to the problem of the influence of Protestantism upon modern science. Historians of the relations between science and religion, for the most part, have considered that Protestant theologies have had little or no influence, or at worst a discouraging effect, upon the development of science. . . .

The impulse which the religious ethos gave to scientific activity was perhaps the most important single element integrating science with religion in seventeenth-century England, but it cannot be said that the men of the time fully separated their natural philosophy from their theology. Moreover the medieval view of the world had been composed of a theology and a natural philosophy which were closely integrated, and its overthrow was accomplished simultaneously, though in a piece-meal fashion, on the one hand by the Protestant Reformers who criticized the theological aspects, and on the other by the scientists who criticized the cosmological features. In the development of the new sciences and the new theologies it is possible to discern that the criticisms of the Calvinists and of the astronomers proceeded along lines which bore some similarity one to the other, and that both prepared the way for a new mechanical-theological world view, which enjoyed considerable popularity during the late seventeenth and eighteenth centuries.

The *leit-motif* of the medieval view of the universe to which both the Protestant Reformers and the early modern scientists took exception was the concept of hierarchy. The concept was rooted in the idea that the universe was made up of a graded chain of beings, stretching down from the Deity in the empyrean Heaven at the periphery of the world, through the hierarchies of angelic beings inhabiting the celestial spheres, to the ranks of mankind, animals, plants, and minerals of the lowly terrestial sphere at the centre of the cosmic system. . . . According to the generally received theory of mechanics a body in motion required the constant action of a mover, and an important integration of ancient natural philosophy with early Christian theology had occurred through the identification of the movers of the heavenly bodies with the angelic beings mentioned in the Scriptures. . . .

It was against such a conception of a hierarchically ordered universe that the Protestant Reformers, particularly Calvin, and the early modern scientists rebelled. The pseudo-Dionysius the Areopagite, by means of his celestial hierarchy of angelic beings, had justified the setting up of the ecclesiastical hierarchy of Church government on earth, an organization which Calvin strongly opposed. . . .

Calvin affirmed that there was no "ground for subtle philosophical comparisons between the celestial and earthly hierarchy," and he averred that mankind could not know whether the angelic beings were ordered by rank or not. . . .

In formulating a positive point of view on these matters, Calvin tended to minimize the role of the angelic beings in the government of the universe, and to assign to the Deity a more absolute and direct control over His creatures. . . .

Not only did the Deity govern the universe directly, but also, according to Calvin, He had predetermined all events from the beginning:

> *"We hold," wrote Calvin, "that God is the disposer and ruler of all things—that from the remotest eternity according to His own wisdom, He decreed what He was to do, and now by His power executes what He has decreed. Hence we maintain that, by His Providence, not heaven and earth and inanimate creatures only, but also the counsels and wills of men are so governed as to move exactly in the course which He has destined."*

Thus the workings of the Calvinist universe were orderly, and were fully predeterminate. Miraculous happenings contravening the laws of Nature were no longer to be expected: "God alters no law of Nature," as it was put by John Preston, 1587–1628, the Puritan Master of Emmanuel College, Cambridge. The angelic beings lost their power, and ultimately their place in the cosmic scheme, and by the end of the seventeenth century they no longer played an important part in Calvinist theology. . . .

The removal of the angelic beings from the government of the universe in Calvinist theology was indeed a criticism of the idea that the universe was peopled by a graded scale of creatures, or rather it was a criticism of the concept of hierarchy which was the kernel of the idea in the medieval world-picture. The Deity no longer ruled the universe by delegating His authority to a hierarchy of spiritual beings, each with a degree of power which decreased as the scale was descended, but now He governed directly as an Absolute Power by means of decrees decided upon at the beginning. These decrees were nothing other than the laws of Nature, the theological doctrine of predestination thus preparing the way for the philosophy of mechanical determinism. Indeed it seems that both the term and the concept of 'laws of Nature' were first used consistently by the primary exponent of the mechanical philosophy, notably in the *Discourse on Method*, where Descartes spoke of the "laws established in Nature by God." The historian of the term, 'the laws of Nature,' has ascribed the usage of the phrase to the hypostatization into the cosmic realm of the earthly rule through statute law developed by the absolute monarchs of the sixteenth and seventeenth centuries. "It is not mere chance," wrote Zilsel, "that the Cartesian idea of God as the legislator of the universe developed only forty years after Jean Bodin's theory of sovreignty." Perhaps it is also not a matter of chance that, some forty years before Bodin, Calvin was working towards the conception of God as the law-giver of the universe, an Absolute Ruler who exercised His power directly, and not through the mediacy of subordinate beings.

Whilst the Calvinists in theology were moving away from the hierarchical conception of the government of the universe towards an absolutist theory of cosmic rule, the early modern scientists were effecting a not dissimilar transformation in natural philosophy. Copernicus, whose heliocentric system of the world was published in 1543, rejected, implicitly at least, the gradation of the elements, for he assigned to the earth that circularity of motion which hitherto had been the prerogative of celestial matter. Furthermore he invested the heavenly bodies with the property of gravitation, which previously had been considered to be peculiar to the earth, implying once more that the earth was similar to the other planets, and was not inferior. Again, according to his pupil, Rheticus, he rejected the hierarchical view that the higher celestial spheres influenced the motions of the lower. . . .

The most important single obstacle to the integration of the new natural philosophy with Calvinist theology was the early Protestant practice of interpreting the Scriptures literally. In England such a practice was criticized and lost its force when a coherent and organized scientific movement grew up in the 1640's, the Puritan clergyman, John Wilkins (1614–72), being a prominent figure in both developments. In 1638 Wilkins published his *Discovery of a New World*, a work attempting to prove that there was another world of animate and rational creatures on the moon. Here he had no texts from Scripture against him, indeed some were in his favour, but even these he rejected. Wilkins did not defend the Copernican theory in this work, but he endeavoured to establish the doctrines which had been derived from that theory, such as the notion that terrestial and celestial bodies were similar, or which had become ancillary to it, notably the doctrine of the plurality of worlds. Quoting the work of the astronomers, who had shown that comets move above the sphere of the moon, that there were spots on the face of the sun, and mountains, and apparently seas on the moon, Wilkins affirmed, "that the Heavens do not consist of any such Pure Matter, which can Priviledge them from the like Change and Corruption, as these Inferior Bodies are Liable unto." "Since the moon in particular resembled the earth," wrote Wilkins, "we may Guess in the General that there are some Inhabitants in that Plannet: for why else did Providence Furnish that place with all such Conveniences of Habitation?" A similar consequence followed, Wilkins noted, from the heliocentric theory of the world adopted by the Copernicans: "Now if our Earth were one of the Plannets (as it is according to them) then why may not another of the Plannets be an Earth?" Conversely, of course, if one of the planets were an earth, then the earth might be a planet.

Wilkins's next work, *A Discourse Concerning a New Plannet*, published in 1640, was a full defence of the Copernican theory. Much of the book, about half of it in fact, attempted to reconcile the Copernican theory with the Biblical texts which seemed to favour the idea of the diurnal motion of the heavenly bodies, or to oppose the theory of the motion of the earth. Here again Wilkins rejected the practice of interpreting the Scriptures literally, declaring that the Bible was not a philosophical treatise, but a work intended for the capacity of the popular mind. In bringing together his theology and the natural philosophy of the day, Wilkins applied Calvin's view that the angelic beings were largely superfluous in the government of the universe to the particular case of the motions of the heavenly bodies. "The imploying of Angels in these Motions of the World is both superfluous and very improbable," wrote Wilkins; moreover, "that opinion of Aquinas, Durand, Soncinas, with other School-men, seems to be without all reason; who make the Faculty, whereby the Angels move the Orbs, to be the very same with their Understandings and Will. . . . Since it were then a needless thing for Providence to have appointed Angels unto this business, which might have been done as well by the only Will of God." Wilkins's argument here exemplified his more general principle that Nature was essentially economical in her actions. It was "agreeable to the Wisdom of Providence," Wilkins felt, that Nature "does never use any tedious difficult means to perform that which may as well be accomplished by shorter and easier ways." Such a view, with its Calvinist flavour, was of considerable importance, serving as the root concept of the various 'minimum' principles, notably the principle of least action, which were developed, usually with theological justifications, by the scientists of the seventeenth and eighteenth centuries. While change took place by routes of minimum effort in nature, according to Wilkins, the world was peopled by a vast, if not a maximum, diversity of creatures. . . .

With Wilkins, and his colleagues, such as Boyle, and his pupils, such as Sprat, modern science and Calvinist theology reached a *modus vivendi* and some degree of integration. These men, and others with the same view, prepared the way for the physico-theological system of Newton, which encountered little religious opposition in England, as Wilkins and the men of his generation had met the brunt of the Anglican resistance to science. Both science and religion in mid-seventeenth century England adopted the Baconian aim of contributing to the "relief of man's estate," the former through the applications of science and the latter through the performance of good works, the one being identified with the other. In the realm of ideas, both modern science and Calvinist theology moved away from the hierarchical conception of cosmic rule, into which an element of the arbitrary had found its way, towards an absolutist theory of the government of the universe, in which events were to be subject to certain and irrevocable law. The conception that the entities of the natural world formed a scale of beings remained, for the most part, as a principle by which living creatures could be classified according to the degree of their 'perfection,' or later the complexity of their organization, but it was no longer a principle governing motion and action in Nature. For the natural philosophers and theologians of the mechanical school of thought, the Deity had provided the universe with only one kind of power governing physical events, that of mechanical force, which activated all material entities, irrespective of their status in the scale of beings, according to determinate laws. Prominent among them were laws prescribing that action, energy, or force, should be conserved, or should be minimal, in all motions, so that the world's unchanging perfection should be preserved. It was upon the tenet of the world's immutability that the alliance, or perhaps alliances, between Protestant theology and modern science ultimately broke down, for the development of the theories of evolution put an end to the view that the world had preserved its present form from all eternity. Science then seemed no longer compatible with Protestant theology, and, as A. D. White noted, "Strange as it may seem, the theological war against a scientific method in geology was waged more fiercely in Protestant countries than in Catholic."

The integration of natural philosophy with Calvinist theology during the seventeenth century had one curiously lasting influence upon modern science through the idea that there was a single, uniquely privileged, observer in the universe. In the development of the absolutist theory of the government of the universe, from Calvin to Newton, the Deity became less and less the direct Ruler of the universe and more and more the privileged spectator of cosmic events. Such an evolution was implicit in Calvin's view that the Deity had predetermined all happenings by means of irrevocable laws decided upon at the beginning, as divine participation in the day-to-day workings of the world were not necessary if those workings were governed by the laws of Nature. The implication was not discussed by Calvin, and he supposed that the Deity was both the primordial Legislator and the active and omnipotent Ruler of the universe. However, the English Puritans of the mid-seventeenth century developed the idea latent in Calvin's teachings that the Deity was bound by his own ordinances. . . .

In the systems of the natural philosophers the role of the Deity was changed similarly from that of the Ruler of the universe to that of the Observer of cosmic events. The implication present in Calvin's theology was inherent also in the Cartesian theory of cosmic absolutism, and Descartes, recognizing the difficulty, had presumed that the *concours ordinaire* of the Deity was necessary to the preservation of the universe from moment to moment. Newton, however, found but few defects in the machinery of the universe which required the continuous attention of the Cosmic Engineer, and it was not long before the Newtonian universe was shown to be entirely self-sustaining and self-repairing. But the Deity in the Newtonian system retained the prerogatives of the privileged observer.

Barbara Shapiro

Latitudinarianism and Science in Seventeenth-Century England, 1968

Merton's interpretation of science and theology in the late seventeenth century sparked a discussion among historians of science that still goes on. The members of the Royal Society have been analyzed, profiled, and sorted into all shades of political, social, and religious attitudes. Most recently, Margaret Jacob and James Jacob have emphasized the Anglican beliefs of English scientists and virtuosi (gentlemen amateurs interested in science); Lotte Mulligan has argued for their Anglican and royalist connections. Barbara Shapiro's contribution to this literature has focused on the religious moderation or Latitudinarianism of members of the Royal Society like John Wilkins and Joseph Glanvill, who held a shared approach to nature and God, emphasizing the uncertainty of human knowledge and the consequent necessity for humility and lack of dogmatism in science and religion.

Merton's nearly all-inclusive definition [of Puritanism] makes precise historical analysis nearly impossible because it fails to distinguish between the significant religious groups in seventeenth-century England. To hold that there is a close correlation between Puritanism and science, while including nearly the whole spectrum of English thought under the Puritan rubric, is simply to say that a correlation exists between Englishness and English science. This is true but not very helpful. If the object is to show the influence of Puritanism, viewed as a unique religious and social ethic, on science, it would seem necessary to arrive at a definition of Puritanism that reflects the actual historical division on religious questions in England.

Furthermore the alleged Puritan contribution to rationalism, empiricism and utilitarianism is open to question. It is unlikely that these

Barbara Shapiro, "Latitudinarianism and Science in Seventeenth-Century England," *Past and Present* No. 40 (July, 1968), 16–44. This article first appeared in Past and Present, No. 40 (1968), and is reprinted here by permission of the Past and Present Society.

elements were fundamental to the Puritan movement, and in fact they seem to have entered Puritanism at a rather late stage in its development. Indeed proponents of the Puritanism and science hypothesis often seem to succumb to the temptation of ascribing characteristics to Puritanism which it acquired during a later period or even as a result of its acceptance of science. . . .

More important, the whole process of dividing Englishmen into Puritans and Anglicans, and equating Anglicanism with Laudianism, obscures the fact that there was a broad middle category of divines, scholars, and politicians who wanted mild reforms in the church and sought moderate means of accomplishing them. Some of this group were men who were Puritans in the sense of falling within the stream of thought "associated with men like Perkins, Bownde, Preston, Sibbes, Thomas Taylor, William Gouge, Thomas Goodwin, Richard Baxter. Others were Anglicans in the sense of maintaining their basic allegiance to the traditional forms of organization and ceremony in the Church of England. In short it is possible to speak of moderate Anglicans and moderate Puritans. . . .

One of the most striking patterns that emerges from an examination of the thought of sixteenth- and seventeenth-century English and continental scientists, whatever their particular religious commitments, is a quite universal suspicion of religious disputes accompanied by a pronounced desire for religious compromise and unity. Copernicus, for example, strove for an accommodation between Roman Catholics and Lutherans. Galileo and Kepler were unconcerned with or hostile to dogmatic theology. . . .

English scientists appear to have shared the view of their continental colleagues. Although Francis Bacon, the outstanding spokesman of English science, has been claimed for the Puritans, there is not much profit in so labelling this intensely secular mind. He was as unsympathetic to the quibblings of the theologians of his own time as to those of the scholastics, and his advocacy of a moderate policy toward the Puritans may be attributed to his distaste for persecution rather than to Puritan sympathies. Bacon, like the majority of later scientists, made it clear that "controversies of religion" could only "hinder the advancement of science." . . .

When the Commonwealth government considered changing the statutes of the colleges and university, it made no moves or even gestures towards emphasizing science in the university. If, as has been so prominently argued, the Puritans were the great champions of new science against traditional learning, it is strange that they failed to take advantage of this sterling opportunity really to reform the university, and indeed expended most of their efforts on enforcing obedience to the old curriculum. The visitors were basically concerned with a religious reformation. They wanted to eliminate the "corruptions" of the past not to alter traditional education. In fact it even appears that "the new philosophy was interdicted in some colleges" by Presbyterians, who feared that it would lead to innovations in religion and that intellectual liberty would inspire religious speculation as well.

Part of the case for Puritan encouragement of science at Oxford, of course, rests on the simple logic we have encountered before in a larger arena: the university was Puritan, the university did science, *ergo*. . . . Actually the religious complexion of the university was not as uniform as one might expect. Those willing to accept the Covenant and Engagement were permitted to remain. For example, Gerald Langbaine, an Anglican, continued as Provost of Queen's. Puritan forms of religious observance certainly dominated, but Anglican services were held covertly at the home of Dr. Thomas Willis, one of the Wadham scientific circle, and were attended by Matthew and Christopher Wren, also members of the group.

Thus if one were not so anxious to impose the Puritan-science hypothesis on the actual historical data, it would become apparent, I think, that from at least the early seventeenth century there was a steadily increasing appreciation of the sciences at Oxford. This movement reached its height during the 1650s not because of Puritanism but because a group of men with widely differing political and religious beliefs found themselves in a situation conducive to scientific work. This situation was created by the Puritans only in the negative sense that many of these men sought refuge at Oxford precisely because the religious and political conflicts associated with Puritanism had made their positions elsewhere untenable.

It is not difficult to see why scientific activities attracted so many during this period of religious and political upheaval. Science provided a respite, a non-controversial topic of conversation, where men might have "the satisfaction of breathing a freer air, and of conversing in quiet one with another, without being engaged in the passions and madness of that dismal Age." . . .

In other ways too the political and religious upheaval proved to be a stimulus to the Oxford scientific group. Science provided an outlet for creative energies which could no longer be employed in normal channels. Many men were forced out of their professions and into a position of enforced leisure. . . . A good part of the scientific activity of the war and post-war periods, both among stay-at-homes and exiles seems to have had its roots in a desire to escape from the turmoil of religious fanaticism and the upsets of revolution.

The closer we look at those involved in the Oxford group, and later the Royal Society, the further we are led away from Puritanism as a unifying factor. Very few of these men were actually Puritans. The most striking thing about their religious views and the progress of their careers is their ability to make peace with whatever government was in power, their toleration of disparate views, their repudiation of all forms of dogmatic religion and their tendency to move in the direction of latitudinarianism and natural religion.

The acceptance of *de facto* situations by so many of the scientists was frequently not the result of vacillation or expediency but of a particular religious outlook, best designated by the term latitudinarianism. One of the prominent features of this faith was its concept of church government. The latitudinarian rejected both the Presbyterian view that forms of church government and discipline were to be found in Scripture and the toleration of many religious groups desired by the Independents. The civil government had both the power and authority to establish forms of church government and public prayer. The individual's duty was to submit to the establishment unless the imposed forms were obviously anti-Christian. While the national church was to enjoy a religious monopoly, it was not to demand uniformity of belief or ceremony, since only a few basic tenets were necessary to insure salvation for the individual and peace within the church. . . .

Furthermore, the latitudinarian did not possess one of the prime qualities of the staunch Puritan — confidence that his views were correct. Latitudinarians frequently noted that men were naturally prone to error and that impartiality was a rare quality. Differences of opinion on religious issues were inevitable and insoluble. Therefore hostility stemming from divergent views was intellectually indefensible and socially destructive. While these misgivings did not lead to scepticism, they do suggest why the latitudinarian lacked the fervour and zeal associated with Puritanism. Both scientists and latitudinarians suspected any allegiance based on claims of unchallengeable authority.

Thus the keynote is moderation, "A thing most reasonable and fitting . . . because of the fallibility of human judgment." It was necessary [according to Joseph Glanvill] to

> *Study the moderate pacific ways, . . . and run not into extremes; both truth, and love are in the middle; . . . when we travel in uncertain roads, 'tis safest to choose the middle. In this, though we should miss a lesser truth, . . . we shall meet with charity. . . . He that is extreme in his principles, must needs be narrow in his affections: whereas he that stands on the middle path, may extend the arms of his charity to those of both sides.*

For the scientists of latitudinarian persuasion the impartial search for religious truth, not the final position reached, was the true mark of piety. . . . Still another element in latitudinarian thought which separates its proponents from most Puritans is a greater emphasis on the moral aspects of religion. Doctrinal questions were pushed into the background in order to focus on the moral elements of Christianity and the fundamentals of religion. . . .

In John Locke we again see the combination of liberal religion and scientific interest. Locke, like so many virtuosi members of the Royal Society, not only numbered Boyle, Tillotson, Barrow, Cudsworth and Patrick among his intimate friends, but adopted the rational theology typical of the group and supported the comprehension schemes which they promoted.

Among politicians of the Restoration seeking a more liberal religious settlement an unusual number were interested in science and became active members of the Royal Society. . . .

In still another area too we can see the connection of latitudinarianism and science, for both were advocates of a plain and more simplified style of discourse. . . .

This preoccupation with style did not reflect simply the pursuit of clarity for clarity's sake. Here again the scientist and the religious moderate are linked by their concentration on avoiding methodologies or modes of discourse that would encourage intemperate claims and inhibit the tentative, step-by-step investigation that they saw as the central vehicle for successful scientific and religious investigation. A clear, unpretentious style of discourse might contribute to clearer and less dogmatic philosophic and theological stances among the discoursers.

Thomas Sprat's official apologia for the Royal Society made perfectly plain the open alliance between liberal religion and scientific inquiry, insisting that the quality of the humble Christian and the scientific experimenter were the same. He argued it was "requisite" that the scientists "be well practis'd in all modest, humble, friendly Vertues; should be willing to be taught, and to give way to the Judgment of others." Able philosophers could never be produced by "high earnest, insulting Wits," who could "neither bear partnership or opposition." Wilkins and Glanvill too noted the parallel between the moderate Christian and the scientific experimenter, particularly emphasizing consciousness of one's own and others fallibility as the mark of the true Christian and the true scientist.

Many scientists, however, saw more than correspondence between the attitudes of science and religion. Glanvill insisted that scientific inquiry itself provided a remedy for religious dissensions. It "dispose[d] mens Spirits to more calmness and Modesty, Charity and Prudence in the Differences of Religion, and even silence disputes there." . . .

The alliance between latitudinarianism and science, however, went far deeper than a common core of practitioners and a mutual distaste for dogmatism. For the two movements also shared a common theory of knowledge, and members of both became the principal proponents of a rationalized religion and natural theology. In their respective areas both scientists and theologians sought a *via media* between scepticism and dogmatism. On the scientific side this search resulted in an emphasis on hypothesis and a science without overt metaphysics. In spiritual matters it led to an emphasis on broad fundamentals and the eschewing of any detailed, orthodox theology claiming infallibility.

It was Sebastian Castellio writing nearly a century earlier, who first attempted to deal with theological problems in the way later adopted by Wilkins and his circle of latitudinarian and scientific associates. Castellio suggested that while there was no way of eliminating all doubts concerning the validity of religious knowledge, it was possible to arrive at a type of assurance about basic truths that would suffice. . . .

. . . Wilkins and Glanvill . . . were concerned with both religious and scientific methodology, so that it would be unrealistic rigidly to separate religious and scientific movements and suppose a one-way flow of ideas from the former to the latter. Wilkins's treatment of the problem of certainty, and of epistemology more generally, was an attempt to find a means of establishing a sufficient level of certainty in both the religious and scientific areas to avoid the pitfalls of dogmatism and claimed infallibility on the one hand and outright scepticism on the other. . . .

Thus the theory of certainty permitted both the latitudinarians and scientists who espoused it to direct attention away from traditional theological disputes, for most of these disputes were over matters that fell into a very low category of certainty, and in fact were usually to be placed only in the realm of probability and opinion. Overconfidence and dogmatism on such doubtful matters as the forms of church government and ceremony simply led to persecution over truths which might or might not be true and could not in any event be established with a sufficient level of certainty to justify coercive policies. The inevitable limitations on human certainty that were so clearly operative and significant in science were equally decisive in religion. . . .

The scientists were not only reluctant to accept traditional authorities but hesitant to create new ones. Overconfident assertions constrained investigation by presenting hypotheses as unquestionable truths. One of the basic qualities of the scientific attitude was humility before an ever increasing body of facts and willingness to give way to the judgements of others. Their humility was coupled with the intense feeling that freedom to differ and investigate was the most important tool of the scientist. This was not the stance of the zealous Puritan or the zealous Anglican but of the religious moderates who were rejecting dogmatism and the principle of authority in the sphere of religion. . . .

The virtuosi's lack of sympathy for those who thought they possessed the unquestionable truth in any but the most general and fundamental questions of religion, more than any other quality, separates them from the Puritans of both the pre- or post-Restoration periods. In fact, their approach to religion, with its emphasis on reason, was probably more congenial to Anglicans than Puritans who placed immense confidence in the infallibility of their authorities and dogmatic methods. . . . The scientists were essentially Erasmian. Not only did they emphasize the unity between piety and learning and focus on practical morality , but they were unsympathetic with the bickerings over dogma and ceremony that they felt resulted in the neglect of true piety. . . .

Thus it is not surprising that so many scientists espoused the new latitudinarian currents of the Restoration. For the co-operative and tentative attitudes of the scientists were easily translated into the sphere of religious discourse and resulted in a reduction of the temperature of religious debate. Perhaps even more significant, however, were the mutually reinforcing elements of latitude, moderation, and modest, tentative rationality that the spokesmen of the Royal Society advocated in both the religious and scientific spheres. Not only was science a haven from religious dogmatism and conflict, but the methods of science, if instilled in the public mind, could contribute to improvement in the religious climate. The virtuosi hoped that eventually science and a moderate, latitudinarian, natural religion might serve as the two pillars supporting an intellectual life in which the calm, friendly and practical pursuit of truth and goodness could replace abstract debate and ideologically motivated civil strife.

There is then an intimate connection between religion and science in seventeenth-century England, but it is hardly a simple cause-and-effect relation between Puritanism and scientific innovation. The innovators were largely drawn from the ranks of the religious moderates, and the great impetus to science in the Wilkins period at Oxford seems to have been largely a function of the purposeful establishment of a scientific haven from the dogmatic religious conflict associated with the Puritans. Indeed in the last analysis the new science and a new latitudinarian theology became inextricably interconnected in an effort to provide a substitute for the perilous certainties of the Puritan divines.

Robert S. Westman

The Copernicans and the Churches, 1986

Robert S. Westman's analysis of the reception of the Scientific Revolution begins in an earlier period than the analyses of Merton and Shapiro, and in a different place. Many historians, particularly those who see opposition between science and any form of religion, have uncritically accepted the view that both Luther and Calvin rejected Copernicanism out of hand. Westman instead has examined the attitudes of a group of early Lutheran theologians at the University of Wittenberg. He demonstrates that Philipp

Robert S. Westman, "The Copernicans and the Churches," David C. Lindberg and Ronald L. Numbers, eds., *God and Nature: Historical Essays on the Encounter between Christianity and Science* (Berkeley and Los Angeles: University of California Press, 1986). Copyright © 1986 The Regents of the University of California. Reprinted by permission.

Melanchthon, Luther's second-in command, embraced the idea that astronomical theories should represent physical reality; the Ptolemaic version of geocentrism had employed mathematical constructs like epicycles and equants in order to predict planetary motions without suggesting these devices actually existed. Nevertheless, Melanchthon rejected the Copernican theory on Biblical grounds and because he thought the traditional hierarchy of the disciplines relegated mathematics to a lower rank of certainty than mathematics. Likewise, the Jesuit Christopher Clavius felt Aristotelian physics trumped mathematical astronomy when it came to ascertaining truths about the physical universe, but he still wanted to mediate a realist compromise between physics and astronomy.

In 1543, on his deathbed, Nicolaus Copernicus received the published results of his life's main work, a book magisterially entitled *De Revolutionibus Orbium Coelestium Libri Sex (Six Books on the Revolutions of the Celestial Orbs)*, which urged the principal thesis that the earth is a planet revolving about a motionless central sun. In 1616, seventy-three years after its author's death, the book was placed on the Catholic Index of Prohibited Books with instructions that it not be read "until corrected." Sixteen years later—and, by then, ninety years after Copernicus first set forth his views—Galileo Galilei (1564–1642) was condemned by a tribunal of the Inquisition for "teaching, holding, and defending" the Copernican theory. These facts are well known, but the dramatic events that befell Galileo in the period 1616–1632 have tended to overshadow the relations between pre-Galilean Copernicans and the Christian churches and to suggest, sometimes by implication, that the Galileo affair was the consummation of a longstanding conflict between science and Christianity.

In this chapter we shall focus our attention on the long period between the appearance of *De Revolutionibus* and the decree of 1616. It will be helpful if we can suspend polar categories customarily used to describe the events of this period, such as Copernican versus anti-Copernican, Protestant versus Catholic, the individual versus the church. The central issue is better expressed as a conflict over the standards to be applied to the interpretation of texts, for this was a problem common to astronomers, natural philosophers, and theologians of whatever confessional stripe. In the case of the Bible, should its words and sentences in all instances be taken to *mean* literally what they say and, for that reason, to describe actual events and physical truths? Is the subject matter of the biblical text *always* conveyed by the literal or historical meaning of its words? Where does the ultimate authority reside to decide on the mode of interpretation appropriate to a given passage? In the case of an astronomical text, should its diagrams be taken to refer literally to actual paths of bodies in space? Given two different interpretations of the same celestial event, where does the authority reside to decide on the particular mode of interpretation that would render one hypothesis preferable to another? When the subject matters of two different *kinds of text* (e.g., astronomical and biblical or astronomical and physical) coincide, which standards of meaning and truth should govern their assessment? And finally, how did different accounts of the God-Nature relationship affect appraisal of the Copernican theory? Questions of this sort define the issue faced by sixteenth- and early seventeenth-century Copernicans. . . .

Copernicus, like all great innovators, straddled the old world into which he was born and the new one that he created. On the one hand he was a conservative reformer who sought to reconcile natural philosophy and mathematical astronomy by proclaiming the absolute principle that all motions are uniform and circular, with all spheres turning uniformly about their own centers. But, far more radically, Copernicus argued for the earth's status as a planet by appealing to arguments from the *mathematical part* of astronomy. In so doing he shifted the weight of evidence for the earth's planetary status to the lower discipline of geometry, thereby violating the traditional hierarchy of the disciplines. If anything can be called revolutionary in Copernicus's work, it was this mode of argument—this manner of challenging the central proposition of Aristotelian physics.

Pre-Galilean Copernicans were . . . faced with several serious problems. First, their central premise had the status of an assumed, unproven, and (to most people) absurd proposition. Second, whatever probability it possessed was drawn primarily from consequences in a lower discipline (geometry). Third, even granting the legitimacy of arguing for equivalent predictive accuracy with Ptolemy, the practical derivation of Copernicus's numerical parameters was highly problematic. Fourth, the Copernican system flagrantly contradicted a fundamental dictum of a higher discipline, physics—namely, that a simple body can have only one motion proper to it—for the earth both orbited the sun and rotated on its axis. And finally, it appeared to conflict with the interpretations of another higher discipline, biblical theology—in particular, the literal exegesis of certain passages in the Old Testament. . . .

[W]e must distinguish between the Protestant Reformers and men who happened to be Protestants and were also well versed in the reading of astronomical texts. The Reformers Luther and Calvin were learned men who knew enough astronomy to understand its basic principles; but neither had ever practiced the subject. It used to be thought that Luther played an important role in condemning Copernicus's theory when, in the course of one of his *Tischreden* or *Table Talks*, he said: "That fool wants to turn the whole art of astronomy upside down." But the statement itself is vague on details and, in any event, was uttered in 1539, sometime before the publication of either Rheticus's *Narratio Prima* or Copernicus's *De Revolutionibus*. As for Calvin, there is no positive evidence that he had ever heard of Copernicus or his theory; if he knew of the new doctrine, he did not deem it of sufficient importance for public comment. In short, there are no known opinions by these two leading Protestant Reformers that significantly influenced the reception of the Copernican system.

There was, however, a third Reformer, a close associate of Luther's and the educational arm of the Reformation in Germany, Philipp Melanchthon (1497–1560), known as *Praeceptor Germaniae*. A charismatic man, beloved teacher, and talented humanist, Melanchthon was also a brilliant administrator with a gift for finding compromise positions. In the face of serious disturbances from the Peasants' Revolt of 1524–1525 and plunging enrollments all over Germany, Melanchthon instituted far-reaching reforms that led to the rewriting of the constitutions of the leading German Protestant universities (Wittenberg, Tübingen, Leipzig, Frankfurt, Greifswald, Rostock, and Heidelberg), profoundly influencing the spirit of education at several newly founded institutions (Marburg, Königsberg, Jena, and Helmstedt). Most important of all, Melanchthon believed that mathematics (and thus astronomy) deserved a special place in the curriculum because through study of the heavens we come to appreciate the order and beauty of the divine creation. Furthermore, mathematics was an excellent subject for instilling mental discipline in students. Such views alone would not predispose one toward a particular cosmology, but they did help to give greater respectability to the astronomical enterprise. Thus, a powerful tradition of mathematical astronomy developed at Wittenberg from the late 1530s and spread throughout the German and Scandinavian universities. At Wittenberg itself, three astronomers in the humanistic circle gathered around Melanchthon were preeminent: Erasmus Reinhold (1511–1553), his pupil Rheticus, and their joint pupil and the future son-in-law of Melanchthon, Caspar Peucer (1525–1603). Melanchthon was the *pater* of this small *familia scholarium*. Many of the major elements in the subsequent interpretation of Copernicus's theory in the sixteenth century would be prefigured in this group at Wittenberg.

The "Wittenberg Interpretation," as we will call it, was a reflection of the views of the Melanchthon circle. Melanchthon himself was initially hostile to the Copernican theory but subsequently shifted his position, perhaps under the influence of Reinhold. Melanchthon rejected the earth's motion because it conflicted with a literal reading of certain biblical passages and with the Aristotelian doctrine of simple motion. But Copernicus's conservative reform—his effort to bring the calculating mechanisms of mathematical astronomy into agreement with the physical assumption of spheres uniformly revolving about their diametral axes—was warmly accepted. Reinhold's personal copy of *De Revolutionibus*, which still survives today, is testimony; it has written carefully across the title page the following formulation: "The Astronomical Axiom: Celestial motion is both uniform and circular or composed of uniform and circular motions." As it stands, this proposition simply ignores physical claims for the earth's motion, but commits itself to an equantless astronomy. It is, we might say today, a "research program," one which Copernicus tried to make compatible with the assumption that the earth is a planet. But the Wittenbergers, with the noticeable exception of Rheticus, refused to follow Copernicus in upsetting the traditional hierarchy of the disciplines. Instead, Reinhold and his extensive group of disciplines accepted Melanchthon's physical and scriptural objections to the Copernican theory. In the prevalent mood of reform, Copernicus was perceived not as a revolutionary but as a modern reformer (like Melanchthon), returning to an ancient, pristine wisdom before Ptolemy. . . .

The Jesuits

The Society of Jesus, founded at about the time the Council of Trent began and *De Revolutionibus* was published, was the real sword of the Counter-Reformation. Worldly and militant, the Jesuits eagerly engaged the Protestants in polemics and ingratiated themselves with the royal courts as privileged advisers. Even more impressively, they challenged the Melanchthonian hegemony by founding their own colleges all over Europe. Systematically dividing the Continent into regions, they rapidly established dozens of colleges in the 1550s and 1560s within each area from the Iberian Peninsula to the Provinces of the Netherlands, from the German principalities east to the Hapsburg lands. The flagship of these colleges was the Collegio Romano in Rome. Its professors were among the best in the Society and were the leaders in establishing curricular policy for the college system. Perhaps because of this position of leadership, the Collegio Romano was also a site of controversy among its most important lecturers. Not only was wrangling prevalent within disciplines, but serious debates also occurred between the philosophers and mathematicians. In the 1580s, debates over educational policy came to a head with the promulgation of the *Ratio Studiorum*. A primary author of this document, Christopher Clavius (1537–1612), succeeded in elevating the status of mathematics to an unprecedented level of academic responsibility, arguing for its pedagogical indispensability to philosophy and the other disciplines.

Clavius, an outstanding astronomer and mathematician, disagreed particularly with those philosophers who had no practical experience as astronomers, yet insisted on questioning the physical reality of the mechanisms posited by Ptolemaists like Clavius. The debate then turned on the degree of certitude to which astronomy could aspire in constructing true explanations. In his authoritative textbook, which became the standard of the Jesuits, Clavius argued that astronomy, like physics, was concerned with true causes. . . . Clavius introduced the case of the Copernican theory, which successfully uses epicycles and eccentrics to save the phenomena. Are we thereby left with another skeptical dilemma, unable now to choose between Copernicus and Ptolemy? In such a case of (what we would perhaps call) inter-theoretic conflict, Clavius argues, one respects the traditional disciplinary hierarchy and turns to natural philosophy and theology for assistance in discovering true causes. The point is an interesting one because it reveals the limits to Clavius's assertion of the primacy of mathematics over the other disciplines. His deeper aim was to bring *concordance* between Ptolemaic astronomy and natural philosophy. Copernicus's mathematical harmonies were not alone sufficient to induce Clavius to seek out a fundamentally new kind of physics.

Clavius's authority was enormous. The astronomical text in which he stated his views was used throughout the Jesuit colleges. It is thus no surprise that when Jesuit theologians considered Diego de Zuñiga's Copernican reading of Job 9:6, they turned to Clavius for guidance. . . .

Although the Jesuit theologians took a dim view of what we might call Zuñiga's "commentatorial Copernicanism"—encoded as it was in a biblical commentary—it is important to stress again the moderately progressive spirit of Clavius's astronomy. Clavius's textbooks underwent constant emendation in order to include references to new issues. . . . Clavius included a brief reference to Galileo's telescopic discoveries, which, he said, would need to be accommodated to a new system of the world. That this was not intended as support for the Copernican system is certain; yet Clavius was also too cautious to give public support to the new cosmology of Tycho Brahe, although he had been aware of it at least since 1600. Only after Clavius's death in 1612 would his students at the Collegio Romano make Tycho's geoheliocentric cosmology their own.

Conclusion

The official Catholic response to Copernicus's theory on 5 March 1616 masks the very complex history that we have constructed—the diversity of Copernican discourses, the variety of disciplinary and exegetical strategies employed by Protestants and Catholics, and finally the struggle *within the church itself* between reformers and traditionalists. The decree published by the Congregation of the Index ordering that Copernicus's *De Revolutionibus* and Zuñiga's *Commentary on Job* be "suspended until corrected" represented a local victory for the conservative Tridentine faction of the church, for the maintenance of traditional hierarchical authority in the universities and within the Jesuit Order. . . .

Margaret J. Osler

Baptizing Epicurean Atomism: Pierre Gassendi on the Immortality of the Soul, 1985

Margaret Osler brings the sensibilities of intellectualist historiography to her study of the thought of the French Catholic priest Pierre Gassendi, the first natural philosopher to embrace the ancient atomistic system of Democritus and Epicurus. For Osler, a student of Westfall's, ideas have weight. She believes that the ideas of religion were of paramount importance in determining the new metaphysics of the mechanical universe. Thus, Gassendi, in his effort to rid atomism of its atheistic connotations and make it acceptable to Christians, used every philosophical tradition at his disposal in developing an orthodox, but mechanistic, concept of the human immortal soul.

During the early decades of the seventeenth century, European intellectuals interested in the new science were actively concerned with formulating a philosophy of nature to replace the traditional Aristotelianism, which had suffered major setbacks in the wake of the Copernican revolution, the skeptical crisis following the Protestant Reformation, and the revival by the humanists of various alternative philosophies of nature. The main contenders in this search for foundations for the new science were the mechanical philosophy of René Descartes and Pierre Gassendi, the animistic philosophies associated with the hermetic tradition, and the chemical philosophy espoused by the followers of Paracelsus. Although the mechanical philosophy ultimately emerged triumphant,

Margaret J. Osler "Baptizing Epicurean Atomism: Pierre Gassendi on the Immortality of the Soul," Margaret J. Osler and Paul Lawrence Farber, eds., *Religion, Science, and Worldview: Essays in Honor of Richard S. Westfall* (Cambridge: Cambridge University Press, 1985). Reprinted with the permission of Cambridge University Press.

the outcome was not certain during the 1630s and 1640s. Many of the points of contention dividing these philosophies of nature were theological. To a seventeenth-century Christian of reasonably orthodox belief, each of the views was theologically problematic. The mechanical philosophy was perceived by some as leading to materialism and atheism. The chemical and Hermetic view that matter possesses its own internal sources of activity also seemed to threaten God's role in nature. Theology was a central concern to seventeenth-century thinkers, and any proposal to provide new metaphysical foundations for science had to be shown to be theologically acceptable. It is in this context that we must understand Gassendi's profound concern with the immortality of the human soul.

The entire corpus of Gassendi's writing, particularly his major work, the *Syntagma Philosophicum,* can best be understood as an attempt to restore and Christianize Epicurean atomism. The Epicurean philosophy was traditionally considered to be materialistic and atheistic. Gassendi sought to expunge the atheistic components of Epicureanism and to retain the atomism as a philosophy of nature underpinning the new science. One of the Epicurean doctrines most offensive to orthodox Christians was his claim that the human soul is corporeal and mortal. In order for Gassendi to propose Epicurean atomism as a viable philosophy of nature, he had to modify the Epicurean philosophy to incorporate the Christian position on the immortality of the soul.

The aim of this chapter is to elucidate Gassendi's views on the immorality of the soul and to attempt, as far as possible, to trace his views to their sources in the writings of Epicurus, Lucretius, Aristotle, and Thomas Aquinas. I claim, as a working hypothesis, that Gassendi took as much as he could from the atomists without violating the tenets of Christian belief, and supplemented their views with ideas drawn from Aristotle and the Scholastics in order to preserve the Christian doctrine of the immortality of the soul. The result is eclectic and not always consistent, but it gives us insight into the theological and ideological struggles the mechanical philosophy faced at its inception.

Pierre Gassendi (1592–1655) is most frequently remembered for reintroducing the philosophy of Epicurus into the mainstream of European thought. Gassendi's version of Epicurean atomism and his adaptation of Epicurean hedonism exerted a major influence on seventeenth-century developments in science and political philosophy. Before European intellectuals could embrace the philosophy of Epicurus, however, his views had to be purged of the accusations of atheism that had followed them since antiquity. Gassendi, a Catholic priest, assumed the task of baptizing Epicurus by identifying the objectionable elements in his philosophy of nature and modifying them accordingly. For example, he denied the Epicurean doctrines of the eternity of the world, the infinitude of atoms, and the existence of the *clinamen,* of swerve, which Epicurus had introduced in order to account for the impact among atoms in an infinite universe; he also took great pains to emphasize God's providential relationship with the creation.

One of the most troublesome aspects of Epicureanism was his denial of the immortality of the soul. Epicurus had considered the soul, like everything else in the cosmos, to be composed of atoms and the void. Epicurus's Roman disciple, Lucretius, had argued for the corporeality of the soul on two grounds: The soul has the power to move the body, which is material; and "our mind suffers along with the body, and is distressed by the blow of bodily weapons." For Lucretius, these facts proved that the nature of the mind is corporeal and that the soul is mortal. ". . . when the body has perished, you must needs confess that the soul too has passed away, rent asunder in the whole body."

The Epicurean theory of the soul is not compatible with orthodox Christian belief, which includes as articles of faith the survival of the soul after death, divine punishment and reward in the afterlife, the resurrection of Christ, and the possibility of human resurrection at the time of the second coming. Gassendi understood that the nature of the soul was a serious problem for a Christian rendition of atomism, and he devoted many pages of his monumental *Syntagma Philosophicum* to a consideration of this issue. Significantly, the final book of the "Physics" (Part II of the tripartite *Syntagma Philosophicum*) is entitled "On the Immortality of Souls" and deals comprehensively with this issue.

Gassendi discussed the soul systematically. He took as his starting point the nature of the soul in general. Then he considered the souls of animals, their nature and function, and the human soul, and he concluded by attempting to demonstrate the immortality of the human soul. His arguments and analysis are eclectic, drawing on the views of Epicurus, Aristotle, and Thomas Aquinas, among others. He culled what he could use from each of these thinkers. His concern with refuting the heterodoxical portion of the Epicurean position is clear. He devoted an entire chapter to a point-by-point refutation of Epicurus's objections to the immortality of the soul.

. . . At the outset, Gassendi adopted the distinction between *anima* and *animus*, which he drew directly from Lucretius. "The *anima* is that by which we are nourished and by which we feel; and the *animus* is that by which we reason." Gassendi agreed with Lucretius that the *anima*, or sentient soul, is present throughout the body; he disagreed with Lucretius on the locus of the *animus*, or rational soul, placing it in the head rather than the chest. Gassendi also disagreed with the ancient atomists, who had maintained the corporeality of the soul. Epicurus had said that the soul is corporeal because there is nothing incorporeal except the void. Thus, if the soul were not corporeal, it could neither do anything nor suffer anything bodily. Gassendi's rebuttal of the Epicurean argument draws on the voluntarist theology that provides the conceptual background for his approach to natural philosophy. He stated that "the actions of God are not necessary"; even if nothing incorporeal can be imagined except the void, it does not follow that God's creative act is restricted by the limitations of human imagination.

The human soul consists of two parts, the rational soul or *animus*, and the irrational, sentient, vegetative soul, or *anima*. Gassendi began his discussion of the soul with a long account of the souls of animals. Because humans differ from animals by uniquely possessing rational souls, the souls of animals correspond to the irrational parts of the human soul. The soul of animals is "something which can be said to live in the body of the animal while it is alive, leaving it at death. Clearly, life is its presence in the body of the animal, and death is its absence." Because of the fact that it is in the various parts of the body while the animal is alive, "the soul seems to be something very fine." Denying that it is a form or merely a symmetrical disposition of matter, as various Peripatetics had maintained, Gassendi claimed that

> the soul seems to be a very tenuous substance, just like the flower of matter [florem materiae] with a special disposition, condition, and symmetry holding among the crasser mass of the parts of the body. . . .

Besides the fact that vital heat is a sign of life, evidence for the claim that the soul of animals is like a little flame can be found in the fact that "just as a snuffed out candle is repeatedly rekindled . . . so a suffocated and strangled animal, not yet dead, having been led from the water or heavy smoke or released from the halter, can repeatedly be brought to inhale the air" and can thus be revived. Like a flame, the soul is in constant motion, not only when the animal is awake, but also in sleep, a fact confirmed by the existence of dreams. It is "the principle of vegetation, sensation, and every other vital action."

The soul of animals and the animal part of the human soul presented no problem for Gassendi, the mechanical philosopher. Like every other version of the mechanical philosophy, he held as a fundamental tenet that all the phenomena of nature must be explained in terms of matter and motion. For Gassendi the facts of biology and perception presented no special problem, as they could be readily explained (or so he thought) in terms of the motion of atoms. His insistence on the special tenuousness, subtlety, and mobility of the atoms comprising the animal soul signals the difficulty that these phenomena present to any attempt at materialistic reduction. Gassendi, however, was content to state simply that they were so reducible. His claim that the rational soul, in contrast to the animal soul, is incorporeal establishes the boundaries of his mechanization of the world. . . .

After rehearsing the various theories about the nature of the human soul put forward by ancient and medieval philosophers and theologians, Gassendi declared that

> the human soul is composed of two parts: . . . the irrational, embracing the vegetative and sensitive, is corporeal, originates from the parents, and is like a medium or fastening [nexus] joining reason to the body; and . . . reason, or the mind, which is incorporeal, was created by God, and is infused and unified as the true form of the body. . . .

Gassendi argued for the double composition of the human soul on several grounds. In an interesting aside, he noted that if one were to hold the position that the soul develops along with the body, as the Epicureans maintained, then one would not "commit homicide according to either civil or canon law [by procuring] an abortion in the first day after conception." To the seventeenth-century Catholic priest, this view was patently absurd. . . .

. . . Throughout his discussion, Gassendi's terminology is anything but consistent. Although he spoke in terms of the three souls described by Aristotle in *De Anima*, he also used the Epicurean distinction between *anima* and *animus*. I think he can be understood as amalgamating the two conceptualizations: The functions of the *anima* correspond to those of Aristotle's vegetative and sensitive souls, whereas the functions of the *animus* correspond to those of Aristotle's rational soul. Gassendi differed from Epicurus in denying the materiality and mortality of the *animus* or rational soul.

. . . His argument is directed at establishing that the rational soul is incorporeal. He began by considering the faculties of the mind or rational soul, namely, intellect and will. The intellect is the primary faculty, according to Gassendi, since the will is rooted in the intellect. His discussion, therefore, focuses on the actions and objects of the intellect. . . .

Having established to his satisfaction that the "rational soul or human mind" is incorporeal, Gassendi proceeded to argue that "it has God as its author by whom it was brought into being or who created it from nothing." The passage from nothing into something is infinite; execution of this transformation requires more than the finite force which belongs to natural things, "but an infinite [force], which is God alone, so that the rational soul, which is an incorporeal substance, can only know God as author." . . .

Truly there is nothing which does not proclaim that there "was an acting infinite force in the great maker of all, who alone depends on nothing else, who is not limited by the action of any force. . . ." It is no reproach to physics to resort to the author of nature, especially in the case of the rational soul which, "since it is immaterial and unless [it is created from nothing], cannot be created by any other cause than God." Since the soul was created by God, like all other things in the world, "it is within the order of things which God constituted in nature and protects by his providence. . . ." In this sense, the soul is nothing extraordinary or beyond the natural order, "since wherever and whenever a man is born [God] creates a rational soul which he infuses into his body." Unlike the material components of mechanical nature, which are all composed of atoms and the void and are produced by second causes, the rational soul of each person is individually and directly created by God. . . .

Having begun with a statement of faith, Gassendi immediately undertook to argue for the immortality of the soul on what he called physical grounds. He stated his argument succinctly: "the rational soul is immaterial; therefore it is immortal." The reason why, according to Gassendi, an immaterial thing is also immortal or incorruptible is that, "lacking matter, it also lacks mass and parts into which it can be divided and analysed. Indeed, what is of this kind neither has in itself nor fears from another . . . dissolution." . . .

Gassendi concluded his painstaking discussion of the immortality of the soul by stating that the reasons presented for establishing it are not known with the certainty of mathematical evidence. Although they cannot replace "the Sacred Faith, as if it needs the light of reason," nevertheless, they can support the truths of faith by overcoming some of the obstructions in its path.

Lack of mathematical certainty did not deprive Gassendi's arguments for the immortality of the soul of any sound foundation at all. On the contrary, it gave them the same epistemological status as all the rest of empirical knowledge: high probability. Arguing that the lack of certainty, which followed from the skeptical arguments, does not entail lack of any knowledge at all, Gassendi advocated a probabilistic account of scientific knowledge, a "mitigated scepticism" to use Popkin's phrase, which was sufficient for the needs of life in this world. The fact that Gassendi thought that articles of faith, such as the immortality of the soul, do not require rational proof, reveals the influence of fideism on his thought. In this respect, Gassendi's philosophical and theological views can be understood in the context of the debates about skepticism, faith, and reason that followed the Reformation and the revival of the ancient skeptical philosophers in the sixteenth and seventeenth centuries.

Gassendi's concern with the immortality of the soul must be understood in the context of his desire to restore Epicurean atomism as a viable philosophy of nature. To do so, it was necessary for him to rid it of the stigma of atheism. To the seventeenth-century Christian natural philosopher, one of the most objectionable aspects of Epicureanism was its claim that the human soul is material and mortal. Eclectic as he was, Gassendi utilized as much of the Epicurean philosophy as he could, in this case retaining the distinction between *animus* and *anima*. Rejecting the portions he found objectionable, he superimposed bits of Aristotelianism and Scholasticism onto Epicurean foundations in order to render his atomism theologically acceptable. Gassendi's arguments were not always consistent and clear, and his writing is tediously prolix. But his ultimate goal—to restore a theologically sound atomistic philosophy of nature—was always in clear view. . . .

Galileo Galilei, 1564–1642. This portrait of the Italian astronomer and physicist emphasizes his role as philosopher and mathematician to the Grand Duke of Tuscany. (© *Corbis*)

PART

III Science and Society

Robert K. Merton's examination of the effect of Puritanism on science reflected another important historiographic tradition in the history of science. The idea that science could be affected by factors outside its own inner developing logic has always been an explanatory strategy in examining the Scientific Revolution. Historians who emphasize the influence of social, economic, political, or cultural factors often deal with the same group of thinkers treated by the intellectualists discussed in Part I—Copernicus, Galileo, Newton, and the other "geniuses" of the period—but see their accomplishments as the result of forces and attitudes that were not "scientific."

Thus, Marxist historians advocated an interpretation of the development of scientific thought that expressly connected the rise of science to the rise of early capitalism in the sixteenth and seventeenth centuries. Because Marxists believed that all political and social features of society reflected who controlled the means of production, it made sense to argue that scientists were reflecting the needs and imperatives of the emerging bourgeoisie. This interpretation was presented initially in 1931 at a meeting of the Second International Congress of the History of Technology in London. Soviet representatives emphasized the importance of technology in the history of

75

science, and Professor Boris Hessen argued that Newton's *Principia* was the result of early English commercial and industrial capitalism.

Although Hessen's account has been largely discounted as an ideological misreading of history, another Marxist historian, Edgar Zilsel, has been taken more seriously. He was more moderate in his claims, but he continued to argue that science was ultimately the product of intellectuals driven by the needs of early capitalism to expand the insights into nature already gained by craftsmen.

As we have seen above, such an interpretation of the Scientific Revolution scandalized historians who saw science as the ultimate triumph of freethinking. They were both supported and undermined in this point of view by one of the most important thinkers of the late twentieth century. Thomas S. Kuhn's *The Copernican Revolution* (1957) made the idea of revolution in science widely known, and his *Structure of Scientific Revolutions* (1970) developed a theory of revolution in science as a profound and sudden alteration of the way one sees the world, a paradigm shift—a term that has since invaded popular culture. Originally a physicist, Kuhn was deeply indebted to the intellectualist tradition, but his analysis also incorporated aspects of the externalist approach. Paradigm shifts happen not only because of objective scientific advance, but also because of psychological and social factors. "To astronomers," Kuhn wrote, "the initial choice between Copernicus' system and Ptolemy's could only be a matter of taste, and matters of taste are the most difficult of all to define or debate."

Kuhn developed a philosophy of science that seemed to discount linear progress in science. Most members of the scientific community, he argued, do "normal science," explicating the insights of their theoretical masters. It is to the work of normal scientists that Steven Shapin and Simon Schaffer turn in their influential *Leviathan and the Air-Pump* (1985). Shapin and Schaffer are sociologists of science, and their work revitalized the contextual approach to the history of science. They wanted to understand how experimentation became the only legitimate way to produce scientific knowledge. To do so, they examined the social practices and linguistic strategies of Robert Boyle and other members of the Royal Society. Shapin and Schaffer represent two major trends in the historiography of the Scientific Revolution: the desire to historicize the past, to understand the Scientific Revolution in seventeenth-century terms, and to do close studies of more localized subjects. They reflect a general "post-structuralist" attitude in modern historians, who see facts themselves as socially conditioned and not a reflection of any objective reality.

Shapin and Schaffer examined the quasi-public space of the laboratory. Mario Biagioli turned to a time when scientific academies were just beginning to emerge in late Renaissance Italy. His study of the court world that Galileo occupied brought a new dimension to this canonical figure. Instead of viewing Galileo heroically as the victim of the Catholic Church, Biagioli borrowed the concept of self-fashioning from English literary scholars, who view the formation of identity in the Renaissance as a self-constructed attempt to master a social space. The context of Galileo's rise and fall was the court of an absolute prince, who controlled access to status, honor, and advancement through patronage. Although, other scholars, including Westfall, had examined the role of patronage in the emergence of the new science, Biagioli made patronage central to his analysis. His approach returned the historiography of the Scientific Revolution to the study of the individual, but the individual not as genius but as social actor in a complex social and political environment.

Edgar Zilsel

The Origins of William Gilbert's Scientific Method, 1941

The Austrian historian Edgar Zilsel felt that economic factors were determinative in the history of science. In his study of William Gilbert's discovery of magnetism, Zilsel argued that it was the craftsmen of the sixteenth and seventeenth centuries who taught humanistic scholars how to experiment. Scholars turned to the technological advances made by craftsmen that had

Edgar Zilsel, "The Origins of William Gilbert's Scientific Method," *Journal of the History of Ideas*, 2, No. 1 (January 1941): 1–32. © Journal of the History of Ideas, Inc. Reprinted with permission of The Johns Hopkins University Press.

arisen because of the emerging needs of capitalism. Like other historians included in this volume such as Burtt and Westman, Zilsel re-examined the hierarchy of disciplines, but he was interested in the difference between manual labor and learned thought, rather than the importance accorded to different intellectual practices. Thus, not the liberal arts but the formerly despised mechanical arts gave rise to modern objective science.

. . . We have traced numerous authors to whom Gilbert was not indebted for his scientific method. . . . The origins of his experimental technique and his scientific criticism are almost as enigmatic as they were before we started collecting his quotations. But we may have proceeded incorrectly. It was wrong, in fact, to look for his intellectual predecessors among scholars and philosophers. One has but to turn over the leaves of *De Magnete* in order to realize that he was interested in unscholar-like people and non-scholastic subjects too. . . . The very first printed book on experimental physics deals so extensively with practical problems, that in some respects it is nearer to a technological than to a physical work of our time. And this give the clue to the solution of our problem. . . .

[Gilbert] realizes that in navigation simply built instruments are necessary which can be handled in spite of the rolling of the ship, and he invents and draws nomograms because he feels complicated calculations and "the exercises of mathematical genius" to be out of place on shipboard. On the method of preparing, magnetizing, and balancing the needle of the compass he gives a few practical hints. He discusses at length the various types of compasses that are used by the sailors of the various European nations. This chapter, however, is based on statements of Robert Norman without mentioning his name.

Norman's influence on Gilbert's investigation is so important that it must be discussed in greater detail. Gilbert himself does not emphasize it at all, but rather hides it. In the first chapter, . . . Gilbert goes on: "Others invented and made public magnetic instruments and expedient methods of observation, necessary to navigators and long-distance travellers, *e.g.*, William Borough in his booklet on the Declination of the Compass, William Barlow in his Supplement, and Robert Norman in his New Attractive." He adds that Norman, "an expert mariner and ingenious artificer," discovered the dip of the needle. A second time also Norman is quoted with approval. There Gilbert explains that the adjusting of the magnetic needle with the meridian is not effected by attraction but by some "disposing and turning faculty" of the earth, and adds that this was stressed by Norman. . . .

. . . This remarkable man who, twenty-five years before Galileo's first publication, speaks of the "incredible delight" of experimental discovery, was a craftsman. At the end of the first edition of his booklet a kind of advertisement was printed, stating that the instruments described "are made by Robert Norman and may be had at his home in Ratclif." When the seamen of the sixteenth century went to sea, they laid the foundation-stone of the British Empire and when they retired and made compasses, of modern experimental science. . . .

Robert Norman is of great importance for our problem. Except for the Latin erudition, the quotations and polemics, and the metaphysical philosophy of nature, he has everything that is peculiar to Gilbert. Norman as well as Gilbert proceeds by experiment and, "not regarding the words but the matter," bases his statements on experience rather than on books. Moreover, the measuring-instruments and the details of the experimental technique, the most exact experiments, and many single empirical statements of *De Magnete* are already contained in his booklet. It is true that the compass-maker Norman is a craftsman and Gilbert a scholar; but Norman already feels "incredible delight" at his discoveries and is interested in knowledge for its own sake: neither his experiment on the ponderability of magnetism nor his dilemma concerning "point respective" or "point attractive" has any practical bearing. In things that are farther away from his occupation he is a little less critical than his followers of higher birth; he modestly believes in the story of Paracelsus which is vehemently criticized by Gilbert. On the other hand he is more religious than Gilbert: where Gilbert takes to Neoplatonic theories of universal animation, he retreats to God's impenetrable providence and avoids further explanation. Socially this is the difference between the highly educated scholar of the late Renaissance and the retired mariner. As to scientific value, however, Norman's attitude does not compare at all unfavorably with Gilbert's. Far reaching theories are lacking in his book; but is Gilbert's metaphysics of "distinguished spherical form" that brings about magnetism a useful scientific explanation? The modern scientist may miss it in Norman's paper as little as he does Gilbert's quarrelsome polemics and erudite quotations. By the absence of all these Renaissance paraphernalia the experimenting compass-maker is even nearer than Gilbert to the sober objectivity of modern natural science. Or, if we may put it the other way round: modern science and the modern mind in general are nearer to the experimenting manual workers of early capitalism, in which they had their origin, than to Renaissance humanism, which still influences even Gilbert.

III

The last paragraphs have answered our main question. Gilbert's experimental method and his independent attitude towards authorities were derived, not from ancient and contemporary learned literature, but on the one hand from the miners and foundrymen, on the other from the navigators and instrument-makers of the period. . . .

Altogether, the impression of Gilbert's originality is considerably impaired, when he is confronted with his sources and especially with Norman. In spite of that, Norman is virtually unknown today, whereas Gilbert is counted among the pioneers of natural science. But this proves to be less unjust when the rise of science is viewed as a sociological process. Unfortunately we can only give a sketchy and simplified exposition of that view here and, of necessity, must omit a part of the evidence bearing on the point.

From antiquity until about 1600 a sharp dividing-line existed between liberal and mechanical arts, i.e., in the final analysis, between arts needing heads and tongues only and others needing the use of hands also. The former were considered as worthy of well-bred men, the latter were left to lower-class people. Thus the contempt for manual labor tended to exclude experiment (and dissection) from respectable science. The prejudice against manual labor, however, did not prevent the experiments of the alchemists. Alchemy is not an occupation as carpentering, or forging; it is made respectable by the charm of both magic and gold, and even well-bred people may practise it as a hobby. But no respectable scholar who was proud of his position as a representative of the liberal arts even thought of using the methods of the mechanical arts. The case of those craftsmen who aspired to a higher social level is different; they—e.g. the Italian artists of the fifteenth century—discussed the social qualifications of manual work again and again, and stressed that they were connected with mathematics, i.e., with science.

The social background and the professional conditions of the scholars of the fifteenth and sixteenth centuries can not be discussed here. Nearly all of them had academic degrees and were consequently more or less linked to the universities, or they were humanists. Though several humanists had obtained academic chairs, generally speaking the universities of the period were still dominated by the spirit of Scholasticism. Both the university-scholars and the humanistic literati were accustomed to deal with natural phenomena chiefly in so far as they had been treated before by the authorities of Scholasticism and humanism respectively. On the other hand, since the decay of the guilds and their traditionalism real observation of natural phenomena, and even some experimentation, were to be found among skilled manual workers. Very little, however, is known of their intellectual interests. Since they got no education but the practical one in the workshops of their masters, their observations and experiments must have proceeded rather unmethodically.

With the advancement of early capitalistic society two major intellectual developments occurred: on the one hand, by virtue of technological inventions, geographical discoveries, and economic changes, the contrast between present times and the past became so obvious, that in the second half of the sixteenth century rebellion against both Scholasticism and humanism began among the scholars themselves. Representatives of the learned upper ranks, such as Telesio, Patrizzi, Bruno, and Campanella, vehemently attacked Aristotle and the belief in "words," felt enthusiastic about nature and physical experience, but did not experiment. Merely speculative metaphysics was, as it were, the older brother rather than the father of modern experimental science.

On the other hand, among the ranks of manual laborers a few groups of superior craftsmen formed connections with respectable scholars. During the fifteenth century Italian painters, sculptors and architects had slowly separated from whitewashers, stone-dressers and masons. As the division of labor was still only slightly developed, the same artist usually worked in several fields of art, and often in engineering too. The technical problems of their occupations led them more and more to experimentation. Many of them made contacts with humanistic literati. . . . Another group of superior manual workers were the surgeons, who practised dissection and made contacts on the one hand with artists interested in anatomy, and on the other with medical doctors. Others were the navigators, who formed connections with mathematicians, astronomers, and cosmographers and published treatises on navigation; and, finally, the makers of nautical and of musical instruments. These superior craftsmen were the predecessors of modern experimental science, though they were not regarded as respectable scientists by contemporary public opinion. . . . One has only to recall the humble apologies in Norman's preface to realize the barrier between craftsmen-literature and scholar-literature at the end of the sixteenth century. Experimental science could not have come into existence before this barrier was demolished.

But a few learned authors, very few, comparatively, already showed an understanding of mechanical arts before 1600. The German physician George Agricola published Latin treatises on mining and metallurgy (1544 and 1556); the chaplain at the royal court of Madrid, Peter Martyr, wrote two Latin books on the great geographical discoveries of the period (1511 and 1530); the learned secretary of the Senate of Venice, Ramusio, did the same in Italian (1550); a few Portuguese and Spanish cosmographers, such as Nuñes and Pedro de Medina, wrote mostly vernacular books on navigation. But especially in England, and in the period of Gilbert, similar studies increased. The Oxford B.A. Richard Hakluyt (1552–1616) edited Peter Martyr and published his own widely read books on the great English voyages and discoveries; the prebendary of Winchester, William Barlowe, wrote an English treatise on navigation (1597). The East India Company engaged the Cambridge graduate William Wright as a lecturer on navigation to their master-mariners. Wright and two more mathematicians, the Oxford graduates Thomas Harriot and Robert Hues, published Latin and English books in the same field (1588, 1594, 1599).

All these half-technical, half-learned activities show that some branches of the mechanical arts had become so important economically that they began to engage and to interest a few scholars. But they dealt with metallurgy and mostly with navigation rather than with experiments. The first academically trained scholar who dared to adopt the experimental method from the superior craftsmen and to communicate the results in a book not to helmsmen and mechanics but to the learned public was William Gilbert, who was a personal friend of most of these English authors. This is Gilbert's achievement in history. It might have been as difficult for the physician in ordinary to Queen Elizabeth to overcome the prejudice against manual labor as it was for the craftsman Norman to raise and answer his theoretical problems—though the two achievements are of a rather different kind. By his understanding of the scientific importance of experiment Gilbert made it—or helped to make it—respectable among the ranks of the educated. A few years later two other scholars likewise followed the method of the superior craftsmen: Francis Bacon, who ranked the great inventors and navigators above the scholars of his period, and Galileo, who started from military engineering. . . .

Thomas S. Kuhn

The Copernican Revolution: Planetary Astronomy in the History of Western Thought, 1957

Many of the themes in Thomas S. Kuhn's discussion of the Copernican Revolution are familiar from earlier selections in this volume. Kuhn emphasizes Copernicus's conservatism in most parts of his astronomic system, which retained many elements of Aristotelian natural philosophy. But he argues that Copernicus was truly a man of the Renaissance, whose preconceptions were upset by new discoveries and new ideas. In particular, Copernicus was influenced by Neoplatonism and the value that this philosophy gave to harmony, simplicity, and order. Later converts to heliocentrism began where Copernicus stopped. The Scientific Revolution is a matter of conversion, an ability to focus on one aspect of a problem in order to see the world in a totally new way.

A scientist's willingness to use a conceptual scheme in explanations is an index of his commitment to the scheme, a token of his belief that his model is the only valid one. Such commitment or belief is always rash, because economy and cosmological satisfaction cannot guarantee truth, whatever "truth" may mean. The history of science is cluttered with the relics of conceptual schemes that were once fervently believed and that have since been replaced by incompatible theories. There is no way of proving that a conceptual scheme is final. But, rash or not, this commitment to a conceptual scheme is a common phenomenon in the sciences, and it seems an indispensable one, because it endows conceptual schemes with one new and all-important function. Conceptual

Thomas S. Kuhn: *The Copernican Revolution: Planetary Astronomy in the Development of Western Thought* (Cambridge: Harvard University Press, 1957), pp. 9, 122, 123, 132, 153, 154, 171, 180–183, 192–193. Reprinted by permission of the publisher. Copyright © 1957 by the President and Fellows of Harvard College, Copyright © renewed 1985 by Thomas S. Kuhn.

schemes are comprehensive; their consequences are not limited to what is already known. Therefore, an astronomer committed to, say, the two-sphere universe will expect nature to show the additional, but as yet unobserved, properties that the conceptual scheme predicts. For him the theory will transcend the known, becoming first and foremost a powerful tool for predicting and exploring the unknown. It will affect the future of science as well as its past. . . .

. . . The centuries of scholasticism are the centuries in which the tradition of ancient science and philosophy was simultaneously reconstituted, assimilated, and tested for adequacy. As weak spots were discovered, they immediately became foci for the first effective research in the modern world. The great new scientific theories of the sixteenth and seventeenth centuries all originate from rents torn by scholastic criticism in the fabric of Aristotelian thought. Most of those theories also embody key concepts created by scholastic science. And more important even than these is the attitude that modern scientists inherited from their medieval predecessors: an unbounded faith in the power of human reason to solve the problems of nature. As the late Professor Whitehead remarked, "Faith in the possibility of science, generated antecedently to the development of modern scientific theory, in an unconscious derivative from medieval theology." . . .

To Europeans of Copernicus' generation planetary astronomy was . . . almost a new field, and it was practiced in an intellectual and social environment quite different from any in which astronomy had been practiced before. In part that difference arose from the theological accretions to the astronomical tradition that we have examined in the work of Aquinas and Dante. Even more essential changes were produced by the logical and cosmological criticism of men like Buridan and Oresme. But these were medieval contributions, and Copernicus did not live during the Middle Ages. His lifetime, 1473–1543, occupied the central decades of the Renaissance and Reformation, and novelties characteristic of this later age were also effective in inaugurating and shaping his work.

Since stereotypes are most readily discarded during periods of general ferment, the turbulence of Europe during the Renaissance and Reformation itself facilitated Copernicus' astronomical innovation. Change in one field decreases the hold of stereotypes in others. Radical innovations in science have repeatedly occurred during periods of national or international convulsion, and Copernicus' lifetime was such a period. . . .

Copernicus began his cosmological and astronomical researches very nearly where Aristotle and Ptolemy had stopped. In that sense he is the immediate heir of the ancient scientific tradition. But his inheritance took almost two milleniums to reach him. In the interim the very process of rediscovery, the medieval integration of science and theology, the centuries of scholastic criticism, and the new currents of Renaissance life and thought, all had combined to change men's attitude toward the scientific heritage that they learned in school. . . .

[Previously] we have Copernicus' theory of motion, a conceptual scheme that he designed to permit his transposing the earth and sun without tearing apart an essentially Aristotelian universe in the process. According to Copernicus' physics all matter, celestial and terrestrial aggregates naturally into spheres, and the spheres then rotate of their own nature. A bit of matter separated from its natural position will continue to rotate with its sphere, simultaneously returning to its natural place by a rectilinear motion. It is a singularly incongruous theory, . . . and, in all but its most incongruous portions, it is a relatively unoriginal one. Copernicus may possibly have reinvented it for himself, but most of the essential elements in both his criticism of Aristotle and his theory of motion can be found in earlier scholastic writers. . . .

Failure to provide an adequate physical basis for the earth's motion does not discredit Copernicus. He did not conceive or accept the earth's motion for reasons drawn from physics. The physical and cosmological problem treated so crudely in the First Book are of his making, but they are not really his problems; he might have avoided them altogether if he could. But the inadequacies of Copernicus' physics do illustrate the way in which the consequences of his astronomical innovation transcend the astronomical problem from which the innovation was derived, and they do show how little the author of the innovation was himself able to assimilate the Revolution born from his work. The moving earth is an anomaly in a classical Aristotelian universe, but the universe of the *De Revolutionibus* is classical in every respect that Copernicus can make seem compatible with the motion of the earth. As he says himself, the motion of the sun has simply been transferred to the earth. The sun is not yet a star but the unique central body about which the universe is constructed; it inherits the old functions of the earth and some new ones besides. As we shall soon discover, Copernicus' universe is still finite, and concentric nesting spheres still move all planets, even though they can no longer be driven by the outer sphere, which is now at rest. All motions must be compounded of circles; moving the earth does not even enable Copernicus to dispense with epicycles. The Copernican Revolution, as we know it, is scarcely to be found in the *De Revolutionibus* and that is the second essential incongruity of the text. . . .

The Harmony of the Copernican System

Judged on purely practical grounds, Copernicus' new planetary system was a failure; it was neither more accurate nor significantly simpler than its Ptolemaic predecessors. But historically the new system was a great success; the *De Revolutionibus* did convince a few of Copernicus' successors that sun-centered astronomy held the key to the problem of the planets, and these men finally provided the simple and accurate solution that Copernicus had sought. We shall examine their work in the next chapter, but first we must try to discover why they became Copernicans—in the absence of increased economy or precision, what reasons were there for transposing the earth and the sun? The answer to this question is not easily disentangled from the technical details that fill the *De Revolutionibus*, because, as Copernicus himself recognized, the real appeal of sun-centered astronomy was aesthetic rather than pragmatic. To astronomers the initial choice between Copernicus' system and Ptolemy's could only be a matter of taste, and matters of taste are the most difficult of all of define or debate. Yet, as the Copernican Revolution itself indicates, matters of taste are not negligible. The ear equipped to discern geometric harmony could detect a new neatness and coherence in the sun-centered astronomy of Copernicus, and if that neatness and coherence had not been recognized, there might have been no Revolution.

We have already examined one of the aesthetic advantages of Copernicus' system. It explains the principal *qualitative* features of the planetary motions without using epicycles. Retrograde motion, in particular, is transformed to a natural and immediate consequence of the geometry of sun-centered orbits. But only astronomers who valued qualitative neatness far more than quantitative accuracy (and there were a few—Galileo among them) could consider this a convincing argument in the face of the complex system of epicycles and eccentrics elaborated in the *De Revolutionibus*. Fortunately there were other, less ephemeral, arguments for the new system. For example, it gives a simpler and far more natural account than Ptolemy's of the motions of the inferior planets. . . .

Throughout this crucially important tenth chapter Copernicus' emphasis is upon the "admirable symmetry" and the "clear bond of harmony in the motion and magnitude of the Spheres" that a sun-centered geometry imparts to the appearances of the heavens. If the sun is the center, then an inferior planet cannot possibly appear far from the sun; if the sun is the center, then a superior planet must be in opposition to the sun when it is closest to the earth; and so on and on. It is through arguments like these that Copernicus seeks to persuade his contemporaries of the validity of his new approach. Each argument cites an aspect of the appearances that can be explained by *either* the Ptolemaic *or* the Copernican system, and each then proceeds to point out how much more harmonious, coherent, and natural the Copernican explanation is. There are a great many such arguments. The sum of the evidence drawn from harmony is nothing if not impressive.

But it may well be nothing. "Harmony" seems a strange basis on which to argue for the earth's motion, particularly since the harmony is so obscured by the complex multitude of circles that make up the full Copernican system. Copernicus' arguments are not pragmatic. They appeal, if at all, not to the utilitarian sense of the practicing astronomer but to his aesthetic sense and to that alone. They had no appeal to laymen, who, even when they understood the arguments, were unwilling to substitute minor celestial harmonies for major terrestrial discord. They did not necessarily appeal to astronomers, for the harmonies to which Copernicus' arguments pointed did not enable the astronomer to perform his job better. New harmonies did not increase accuracy or simplicity. Therefore they could and did appeal primarily to that limited and perhaps irrational subgroup of mathematical astronomers whose Neoplatonic ear for mathematical harmonies could not be obstructed by page after page of complex mathematics leading finally to numerical predictions scarcely better than those they had known before. Fortunately, as we shall discover in the next chapter, there were a few such astronomers. Their work is also an essential ingredient of the Copernican Revolution.

Revolution by Degrees

Because he was the first fully to develop an astronomical system based upon the motion of the earth, Copernicus is frequently called the first modern astronomer. But, as the text of the *De Revolutionibus* indicates, an equally persuasive case might be made for calling him the last great

Ptolemaic astronomer. Ptolemaic astronomy meant far more than astronomy predicated on a stationary earth, and it is only with respect to the position and motion of the earth that Copernicus broke with the Ptolemaic tradition. The cosmological frame in which his astronomy was embedded, his physics, terrestrial and celestial, and even the mathematical devices that he employed to make his system give adequate predictions are all in the tradition established by ancient and medieval scientists.

Though historians have occasionally grown livid arguing whether Copernicus is really the last of the ancient or the first of the modern astronomers, the debate is in principle absurd. Copernicus is neither an ancient nor a modern but rather a Renaissance astronomer in whose work the two traditions merge. . . .

For Copernicus' sixteenth- and seventeenth-century followers, the primary importance of the *De Revolutionibus* derived from its single novel concept, the planetary earth, and from the novel astronomical consequences, the new harmonies, which Copernicus had derived from that concept. To them Copernicanism meant the three-fold motion of the earth and, initially, that alone. The traditional conceptions with which Copernicus had clothed his innovation were not to his followers essential elements of his work, simply because, as traditional elements, they were not Copernicus' contribution to science. It was not because of its traditional elements that people quarreled about the *De Revolutionibus*.

That is why the *De Revolutionibus* could be the starting point for a new astronomical and cosmological tradition as well as the culmination of an old one. Those whom Copernicus converted to the concept of a moving earth began their research from the point at which Copernicus had stopped. Their starting point was the earth's motion, which was all they necessarily took from Copernicus, and the problems to which they devoted themselves were not the problems of the old astronomy, which had occupied Copernicus, but the problems of the new sun-centered astronomy, which they discovered in the *De Revolutionibus*. Copernicus presented them with a set of problems that neither he nor his predecessors had had to face. In the pursuit of those problems the Copernican Revolution was completed, and a new astronomical tradition, deriving from the *De Revolutionibus*, was founded. Modern astronomy looks back to the *De Revolutionibus* as Copernicus had looked back to Hipparchus and Ptolemy.

Major upheavals in the fundamental concepts of science occur by degrees. The work of a single individual may play a preëminent role in such a conceptual revolution, but if it does, it achieves preëminence either because, like the *De Revolutionibus*, it initiates revolution by a small innovation which presents science with new problems, or because, like Newton's *Principia*, it terminates revolution by integrating concepts derived from many sources. The extent of the innovation that any individual can produce is necessarily limited, for each individual must employ in his research the tools that he acquires from a traditional education, and he cannot in his own lifetime replace them all. It seems therefore that many of the elements in the *De Revolutionibus* which, in the earlier parts of this chapter, we pointed to as incongruities are not really incongruities at all. The *De Revolutionibus* seems incongruous only to those who expect to find the entire Copernican Revolution in the work which gives that revolution its name, and such an expectation derives from a misunderstanding of the way in which new patterns of scientific thought are produced. The limitations of the *De Revolutionibus* might better be regarded as essential and typical characteristics of any revolution-making work.

Most of the apparent incongruities in the *De Revolutionibus* reflect the personality of its author, and Copernicus' personality seems entirely appropriate to his seminal role in the development of astronomy. Copernicus was a dedicated specialist. He belonged to the revived Hellenistic tradition of mathematical astronomy which emphasized the mathematical problem of the planets at the expense of cosmology. For his Hellenistic predecessors the physical incongruity of an epicycle had not been an important drawback of the Ptolemaic system, and Copernicus displayed a similar indifference to cosmological detail when he failed to note the incongruities of a moving earth in an otherwise traditional universe. For him, mathematical and celestial detail came first; he wore blinders that kept his gaze focused upon the mathematical harmonies of the heavens. To anyone who did not share his specialty Copernicus' view of the universe was narrow and his sense of values distorted.

But an excessive concern with the heavens and a distorted sense of values may be essential characteristics of the man who inaugurated the revolution in astronomy and cosmology. The blinders that restricted Copernicus' gaze to the heavens may have been functional. They made him so perturbed by discrepancies of a few degrees in astronomical prediction that in an attempt to resolve them he could embrace a cosmological heresy, the earth's motion. They gave him an eye so absorbed with geometrical harmony that he could adhere to his heresy for its harmony alone, even when it had failed to solve the problem that had led him to it. And they helped him evade the nonastronomical consequences of his innovation, consequences that led men of less restricted vision to reject his innovation as absurd.

Above all, Copernicus' dedication to the celestial motions is responsible for the painstaking detail with which he explored the mathematical consequences of the earth's motion and fitted those consequences to an existing knowledge of the heavens. That detailed technical study is Copernicus' real contribution. . . .

. . . Copernicanism was potentially destructive of an entire fabric of thought. . . . More than a picture of the universe and more than a few lines of Scripture were at stake. The drama of Christian life and the morality that had been made dependent upon it would not readily adapt to a universe in which the earth was just one of a number of planets. Cosmology, morality, and theology had long been interwoven in the traditional fabric of Christian thought described by Dante at the beginning of the fourteenth century. The vigor and venom displayed at the height of the Copernican controversy, three centuries later, testifies to the strength and vitality of the tradition.

When it was taken seriously, Copernicus' proposal raised many gigantic problems for the believing Christian. If, for example, the earth were merely one of six planets, how were the stories of the Fall and of the Salvation, with their immense bearing on Christian life, to be preserved? If there were other bodies essentially like the earth, God's goodness would surely necessitate that they, too, be inhabited. But if there were men on other planets, how could they be descendants of Adam and Eve, and how could they have inherited the original sin, which explains man's otherwise incomprehensible travail on an earth made for him by a good and omnipotent deity? Again, how could men on other planets know of the Saviour who opened to them the possibility of eternal life? Or, if the earth is a planet and therefore a celestial body located away from the center of the universe, what becomes of man's intermediate but focal position between the devils and the angels? If the earth, as a planet, participates in the nature of celestial bodies, it can not be a sink of iniquity from which man will long to escape to the divine purity of the heavens. Nor can the heavens be a suitable abode for God if they participate in the evils and imperfection so clearly visible on a planetary earth. Worst of all, if the universe is infinite, as many of the later Copernicans thought, where can God's Throne be located? In an infinite universe, how is man to find God or God man?

These questions have answers. But the answers were not easily achieved; they were not inconsequential; and they helped to alter the religious experience of the common man. Copernicanism required a transformation in man's view of his relation to God and of the bases of his morality. Such a transformation could not be worked out overnight, and it was scarcely even begun while the evidence for Copernicanism remained as indecisive as it had been in the *De Revolutionibus*. Until that transformation was achieved, sensitive observers might well find traditional values incompatible with the new cosmology, and the frequency with which the charge of atheism was hurled at the Copernicans is evidence of the threat to the established order posed to many observers by the concept of a planetary earth. . . .

Steven Shapin and Simon Schaffer

Leviathan and the Air-Pump: Hobbes, Boyle, and the Experimental Life, 1985

In this selection, Shapin and Schaffer discuss what was at stake when the English natural philosopher Robert Boyle disputed with the mechanical and political philosopher Thomas Hobbes. Shapin and Schaffer argue that the crux of the dispute about the status of knowledge generated by experimenting with the air-pump was social control. Boyle thought experimentation, when witnessed by reliable observers, could produce certitude in the sciences.

Steven Shapin and Simon Schaffer, *Leviathan and the Air-Pump: Hobbes, Boyle, and the Experimental Life* (Princeton: Princeton University Press, 1985). © 1986 Princeton University Press, 1989 paperback edition. Reprinted by permission of Princeton University Press.

Hobbes felt that such claims opened the way for chaos in science and the state, because knowledge could only be the product of deductive reasoning from first principles. Shapin and Schaffer conclude that epistemological disputes are essentially about social order, not the acquisition of knowledge.

I: Understanding Experiment

. . . Our subject is experiment. We want to understand the nature and status of experimental practices and their intellectual products. These are the questions to which we seek answers: What is an experiment? How is an experiment performed? What are the means by which experiments can be said to produce matters of fact, and what is the relationship between experimental facts and explanatory constructs? How is a successful experiment identified, and how is success distinguished from experimental failure? Behind this series of particular questions lie more general ones: *Why* does one do experiments in order to arrive at scientific truth? Is experiment a privileged means of arriving at consensually agreed knowledge of nature, or are other means possible? What recommends the experimental way in science over alternatives to it?

We want our answers to be historical in character. To that end, we will deal with the historical circumstances in which experiment as a systematic means of generating natural knowledge arose, in which experimental practices became institutionalized, and in which experimentally produced matters of fact were made into the foundations of what counted as proper scientific knowledge. We start, therefore, with that great paradigm of experimental procedure: Robert Boyle's researches in pneumatics and his employment of the air-pump in that enterprise.

Boyle's air-pump experiments have a canonical character in science texts, in science pedagogy, and in the academic discipline of the history of science. Of all subjects in the history of science it might be thought that this would be the one which least new could be said. It is an oft-told tale and, in the main, a well-told tale. Indeed, there are many aspects of Boyle's experimental work and the setting in which it occurred that have been sufficiently documented and about which we shall have little novel to say: our debt to previous historical writing is too extensive to acknowledge adequately. It is entirely appropriate that an excellent account of Boyle's pneumatic experiments of the 1660s constitutes the first of the celebrated series of *Harvard Case Histories in Experimental Science*. This thirty-five-year-old study admirably establishes our point of departure: it shows that Boyle's air-pump experiments were designed to provide (and have since provided) a heuristic model of how authentic scientific knowledge should be secured.

Interestingly, the Harvard history has itself acquired a canonical status: through its justified place in the teaching of history of science it has provided a concrete exemplar of how to do research in the discipline, what sorts of historical questions are pertinent to ask, what kinds of historical materials are relevant to the inquiry, what sorts are not germane, and what the general form of historical narrative and explanation ought to be. Yet it is now time to move on from the methods, assumptions, and the historical programme embedded in the Harvard case history and other studies like it. We want to look again at the air-pump experiments, to put additional questions to these materials and to rephrase traditional questions. We did not initiate our project with a view to criticizing existing accounts of Boyle's experimental work. In fact, at the outset we were doubtful that we could add much to the work of distinguished Boyle scholars of the past. Yet, as our analysis proceeded, we became increasingly convinced that the questions we wished to have answered had not been systematically posed by previous writers. Why not?

A solution might reside in the distinction between "member's accounts" and "stranger's accounts." Being a member of the culture one seeks to understand has enormous advantages. Indeed, it is difficult to see how one could understand a culture to which one was a complete stranger. Nevertheless, unreflective membership also carries with it serious disadvantages to the search for understanding, and the chief of these might be called "the self-evident method." One reason why historians have not systematically and searchingly pressed the questions we want to ask about experimental practices is that they have, to a great extent, been producing accounts coloured by the member's self-evident method. In this method the presuppositions of our own culture's routine practices are not regarded as problematic and in need of explanation. Ordinarily, our culture's beliefs and practices are referred to the unambiguous facts of nature or to universal and impersonal criteria of how people just do things (or do them when behaving "rationally"). . . . In the case of experimental culture, the self-evident method is particularly noticeable in historians' accounts; and it is easy to see why this should be the case, for historians are in wide agreement in identifying Boyle as a founder of the experimental world in which scientists now live and operate. Thus, historians start with the assumption that they (and modern scientists) share a culture with Robert Boyle, and treat their subject accordingly: the historian and the seventeenth-century experimentalist are both members. The historical career of experimental culture can be enlisted in support of this assumption. Boyle's programme triumphed over alternatives and objections, and his own country it did so very rapidly, largely aided and abetted by the vigorously partisan publicity of the Royal Society of London. The success of the experimental programme is commonly treated as its own explanation. Even so, the usual way in which the self-evident method presents itself in historical practice is more subtle—not as a set of explicit claims about the rise, acceptance, and institutionalization of experiment, but as a disposition not to see the point of putting certain questions about the nature of experiment and its status in our overall intellectual map.

The member's account, and its associated self-evident method, have great instinctive appeal; the social forces that protect and sustain them are powerful. The member who poses awkward questions about "what everybody knows" in the shared culture runs a real risk of being dealt with as a troublemaker or an idiot. Indeed, there are few more reliable ways of being expelled from a culture than continuing seriously to query its taken-for-granted intellectual framework. Playing the stranger is therefore a difficult business; yet this is precisely what we need to do with respect to the culture of experiment. We need to *play* the stranger, not to *be* the stranger. A genuine stranger is simply ignorant. We wish to adopt a calculated and an informed suspension of our taken-for-granted perceptions of experimental practice and its products. By playing the stranger we hope to move away from self-evidence. . . . If we pretend to be a stranger to experimental culture, we can seek to appropriate one great advantage the stranger has over the member in explaining the beliefs and practices of a specific culture: the stranger is in a position to *know* that there are alternatives to those beliefs and practices. The awareness of alternatives and the pertinence of the explanatory project go together. . . .

[W]e shall be adopting something close to a "member's account" of Hobbes's anti-experimentalism. That is to say, we want to put ourselves in a position where objections to the experimental programme seem plausible, sensible, and rational. Following Gellner, we shall be offering a "charitable interpretation" of Hobbes's point of view. Our purpose is not to take Hobbes's side, nor even to resuscitate his scientific reputation (though this, in our opinion, has been seriously undervalued). Our goal is to break down the aura of self-evidence surrounding the experimental way of producing knowledge, and "charitable interpretation" of the opposition to experimentalism is a valuable means of accomplishing this. Of course, our ambition is not to rewrite the clear judgment of history: Hobbes's views found little support in the English natural philosophical community. Yet we want to show that there was nothing self-evident or inevitable about the series of historical judgments in that context which yielded a natural philosophical consensus in favour of the experimental programme. Given other circumstances bearing upon that philosophical community, Hobbes's views might well have found a different reception. They were not widely credited or believed — but they were *believable*; they were not counted to be correct — but there was nothing inherent in them that prevented a different evaluation. (True, there were points at which Hobbes's criticisms were less than well-informed, just as there were aspects of Boyle's position that might be regarded as ill-informed and even sloppy. If the historian *wanted* to evaluate the actors by the standards of present-day scientific procedure, he would find both Hobbes and Boyle vulnerable.) On the other hand, our treatment of Boyle's experimentalism will stress the fundamental roles of convention, of practical agreement, and of labor in the creation and positive evaluation of experimental knowledge. We shall try to identify those features of the historical setting that bore upon intellectuals' decisions that these conventions were appropriate, that such agreement was necessary, and that the labor involved in experimental knowledge-production was worthwhile and to be preferred over alternatives.

Far from avoiding questions of "truth," "objectivity," and "proper method," we will be confronting such matters centrally. But we will make liberal, but informal, use of Wittgenstein's notions of a "language-game" and a "form of life." We mean to approach scientific method as integrated into *patterns of activity*. Just as for Wittgenstein "the term 'language-*game*' is meant to bring into prominence the fact that the *speaking* of language is part of an activity or of a form of life," so we shall treat controversies over scientific method as disputes over different patterns of doing things and of organizing men to practical ends. We shall suggest that solutions to the problem of knowledge are embedded within practical solutions to the problem of social order, and that different practical solutions to the problem of social order encapsulate contrasting practical solutions to the problem of knowledge. *That* is what the Hobbes-Boyle controversies were about.

It will not escape our readers' notice that this book is an exercise in the sociology of scientific knowledge. One can either debate the possibility of the sociology of knowledge, or one can get on with the job of doing the thing. We have chosen the latter option. It follows from our decision that we shall be making relatively few references to the theoretical literature in the sociology of knowledge that has been a major and continuing source of inspiration to our project. Nevertheless, we trust that our practical historical procedures will bear sufficient witness to our obligations in that quarter. . . .

II: Seeing and Believing: The Experimental Production of Pneumatic Facts

. . . Robert Boyle maintained that proper natural philosophical knowledge should be generated through experiment and that the foundations of such knowledge were to be constituted by experimentally produced matters of fact. Thomas Hobbes disagreed. In Hobbes's view Boyle's procedures could never yield the degree of certainty requisite in any enterprise worthy of being called philosophical. This book is about that dispute and about the issues that were seen to depend upon its resolution.

Hobbes's position has the historical appeal of the exotic. How was it possible for any rational man to deny the value of experiment and the foundational status of the matter of fact? By contrast, Boyle's programme appears to exude the banality of the self-evident. How could any rational man think otherwise? In this chapter we intend to address the problem of self-evidence by dissecting and displaying the mechanisms by which Boyle's experimental procedures were held to produce knowledge and, in particular, the variety of knowledge called "matters of fact." We will show that the experimental production of matters of fact involved an immense amount of labour, that it rested upon the acceptance of certain social and discursive conventions, and that it depended upon the production and protection of a special form of social organization. . . . The acceptance or rejection of that [experimental] programme amounted to the acceptance or rejection of the form of life that Boyle and his colleagues proposed. Once this point is made, neither the acceptance of the experimental programme nor the epistemological status of the matter of fact ought to appear self-evident.

In the conventions of the intellectual world we now inhabit there is no item of knowledge so solid as a matter of fact. . . .

Robert Boyle sought to secure assent by way of the experimentally generated matter of fact. Facts were certain; other items of knowledge much less so. Boyle was therefore one of the most important actors in the seventeenth-century English movement towards a probabilistic and fallibilistic conception of man's natural knowledge. . . .

Witnessing Science

We have begun to develop the idea that experimental knowledge production rested upon a set of *conventions* for generating matters of fact and for handling their explications. Taking the matter of fact as foundational to the experimental form of life, let us proceed to analyze and display how the conventions of generating the fact actually worked. In Boyle's view the capacity of experiments to yield matters of fact depended not only upon their actual performance but essentially upon the assurance of the relevant community that they had been so performed. He therefore made a vital distinction between actual experiments and what are now termed "thought experiments." If knowledge was to be empirically based, as Boyle and other English experimentalists insisted it should, then its experimental foundations had to be *witnessed*. Experimental performances and their products had to be attested by the testimony of eye witnesses. Many phenomena, and particularly those alleged by the alchemists, were difficult to accept by those adhering to the corpuscular and mechanical philosophies. In these cases Boyle averred "that they that have seen them can much more reasonably believe them, than they that have not." The problem with eye witnessing as a criterion for assurance was one of *discipline*. How did one police the reports of witnesses so as to avoid radical individualism? Was one obliged to credit a report on the testimony of any witness whatsoever?

Boyle insisted that witnessing was to be a collective act. In natural philosophy, as in criminal law, the reliability of testimony depended upon its multiplicity. . . .

. . . The multiplication of witness was an indication that testimony referred to a true state of affairs in nature. Multiple witnessing was accounted an active licence rather than just a descriptive licence. Did it not force the conclusion that such and such an action was done (a specific trial), and that subsequent action (offering assent) was warranted?

In experimental practice one way of securing the multiplication of witnesses was to perform experiments in a social space. The experimental "laboratory" was contrasted to the alchemist's closet precisely in that the former was said to be a public and the latter a private space. . . .

. . . The credibility of witnesses followed the taken-for-granted conventions of that setting for assessing individuals' reliability and trustworthiness: Oxford professors were accounted more reliable witnesses than Oxfordshire peasants. The natural philosopher had no option but to rely for a substantial part of his knowledge on the testimony of witnesses; and, in assessing that testimony, he (no less than judge or jury) had to determine their credibility. . . .

. . . What, then, was the status of factual knowledge in Hobbes's scheme? Interestingly, *Leviathan* radically downgraded the standing of factual knowledge, distinguished it from "science" and "philosophy" and assimilated it to the experiences of individuals. To Hobbes, knowledge of fact, "as when we see a fact doing, or remember it done," was "nothing else, but sense and memory." The "nothing else" derived from Hobbes's theory of sensory impression. These impressions were caused by the motions of matter impinging on man's sensory organs, and carried on to the brain and heart. Therefore, our sense that such impressions correspond to the external objects themselves was, to Hobbes, but "seeming, or fancy." The same impressions could be obtained dreaming or waking, by the motions of matter in a real external object or by rubbing the eye. Thus, in Hobbes's view, factual knowledge, based on sensory impressions, did not have an epistemologically privileged position. It did not matter how one proposed socially to process such factual knowledge, the limitations remained. Factual knowledge, it was true, had a valuable role to play in constituting our overall knowledge, but it was not of the sort to secure certainty and universal assent. Indeed, Hobbes wished to call the body of factual knowledge by a different name, to distinguish it from "philosophy" or "science." The "register of the *knowledge of fact*" Hobbes called "history," "natural history" being the catalogue of "such facts, or effects of nature, as have no dependence of man's *will.*" Thus the fundamental distinction Hobbes made between factual knowledge (or history) and philosophy involved the exercise of man's agency. Man had no control over the effects of nature, but he did over settling definitions and agreeing notions of intelligible cause. Philosophy and science were constituted by the knowledge of consequences and causes, and, again, the model was provided by geometry: "As when we know, that, if the figure shown be a circle, then any straight line through the centre shall divide it into two equal parts." "And this," Hobbes said, "is the knowledge required in a philosopher."

We have shown that for Boyle and the early Royal Society there were two major threats to the social forms of experimental philosophy: the private judgment of "secretists" and enthusiasts and the tyranny of "modern dogmatists." For Hobbes in 1651 and later, only private judgment counted as a potentially fatal threat to good philosophy and to good order. If the aim was certain knowledge and irrevocable assent, then the way towards it could not traverse anything as private and unreachable as individual states of belief. Knowledge, science and philosophy were set on one side; belief and opinion on the other. The former were certain, hard and indisputable; the latter were provisional, variable and inherently contentious. . . .

The Ends of Philosophy

Boyle aimed to achieve peace and to terminate scandal in natural philosophy by securing a space within which a specified kind of dissent was manageable and safe. In the experimental form of life it was legitimate for philosophers to disagree about the causes of natural effects: causal knowledge was removed from the domain of the certain or even the morally certain. For Hobbes there was no philosophical space within which dissent was safe or permissible. Dissent over physical causes was a sign that one had not begun to do philosophy or that the enterprise in question was not philosophy. Philosophy was defined as a constitutively causal enterprise; causal knowledge was one of its starting points. Philosophy was "such knowledge of effects or appearances, as we acquire by true ratiocination from the knowledge we have first of their causes or generation: And again, of such causes or generations as may be from knowing first their effects." In the next chapter we shall discuss the unequal status of these two methods, but, for the present, it is enough to note that any programme which attempted to erect a procedural boundary between speech of matters of fact and speech of their physical causes was not, on this basis, philosophical. The aim of philosophy was the highest degree of certainty that could be obtained. Philosophy was contrasted to other intellectual enterprises precisely on the grounds of the degree of certainty one could expect of each. Authentic natural philosophy, founded upon proper method, was new, no older than the revolution made by Galileo, Harvey, and not least by Hobbes himself. . . .

It is vital that we understand what our ends are when we do philosophy. The production of certainty would terminate disputes and secure total assent. . . .

"Ingenuity," Dogmatism, and the Experimental Community

The point to be made is not that Hobbes "despised" experiment, nor that he argued that experiments ought not to be performed, nor even that experiments had no significant place in a properly constituted philosophy of nature. What Hobbes was claiming, however, was that the systematic doing of experiments was not to be equated with philosophy: going on in the way Boyle recommended for experimentalists was not the same thing as philosophical practice. It was not the case that one could ground philosophy in experimentally generated matters of fact. This experimental way and the philosophical way were fundamentally different: they differed in their capacity to secure assent among intellectuals and peace in the polity. The distinctions that Hobbes wanted to make involved four considerations that were regarded as intimately related in mid-seventeenth-century schemes: the status of the philosopher's role, his social and moral character, the thought process involved in doing intellectual work, and the nature of the knowledge that was the outcome of this work. By claiming that adopting an experimental form of life changed proper physicists into "quacks," Hobbes was saying something highly derogatory about the experimentalist's role, character, and practice. Machine-minders were not, in Hobbes's view, to be accounted philosophers. Philosophers should not be identified with mechanical tricksters who produced "various spectacles of an amusing nature."

The modes of thought associated with the philosopher and the mechanic were different. In the *Dialogus physicus* Hobbes insisted upon that contrast: "Ingenuity is one thing and method [*ars*] is another. Here method is needed." The repeated juxtaposition in Hobbes's critiques of method or philosophy, on the one hand, and ingenuity, on the other, is significant. It is plausible that Hobbes was making a substantive point about the experimental mentality by way of etymological punning. The Latin *ingenium* denotes "natural ability, cleverness, inventiveness." In Latin *ingenio* also means a kind of mill, and, from this root, are derived the Old French *engin* and the Middle English *gin*. Thus Hobbes's identification of ingenuity with, as it were, "engine philosophy" is precisely right for the evaluation he wanted to be placed upon the experimental programme and its products: it relied upon the intellectual processes of artificers and mechanics and, therefore, it yielded an inferior grade of knowledge. . . .

Hobbes and Boyle had two things in common in this connection: first, they both gauged the worth of knowledge by taking into consideration the moral constitution and known probity of its producers. This was taken for granted in mid-seventeenth-century calculations, and the problem of assessing testimony made these calculations important, as we have discussed in chapter 2. Second, both Hobbes and Boyle reckoned that the philosopher should be seen as *noble*. Yet their characterizations of the philosopher's role and practice were diametrically opposed. Whose version of the philosopher was, indeed, noble? We have seen that Boyle and his colleagues liked to describe the experimental philosopher as "humble," "modest," an "under-builder," and a "drudge," while specifying that this was a noble character. Boyle and his associates in the Royal Society wanted, for specified purposes, to use the language of the craftsman and to put on the guise of the humble artisan. Hobbes was trying to insinuate that, through their celebration of ingenuity, the Greshamites *really were* making philosophy ignoble. This could have been a seriously damaging imputation in early Restoration society. . . .

Mario Biagioli

Galileo, Courtier: The Practice of Science in the Culture of Absolutism, 1993

Like Zilsel, Biagioli begins his study with a discussion of disciplinary hierarchies, but instead of linking Galileo with military engineers, he returns to the traditional ordering of the disciplines of mathematics and philosophy. Biagioli argues that Galileo wanted to be accepted as a philosopher rather than as a

Selections from Mario Biagioli, *Galileo, Courtier: The Practice of Science in the Culture of Absolutism* (Chicago: University of Chicago Press, 1993). Copyright © 1993 by The University of Chicago. Reprinted by permission.

mathematician, and that such acceptance could happen only in the princely court. The patronage of a great prince would secure not only the social success of the scientist, but also the legitimization of his ideas. Biagioli rejects Merton and Kuhn, noting that much so-called scientific activity began before the consolidation of scientific communities and their commitment to "paradigmatic" science.

The relationship between patronage, court culture, and Galileo's career is not just a matter of the history or sociology of scientific professions. Copernicus and some of his followers faced a crucial obstacle when they tried to legitimize their work as not only a *mathematical* computational model but also a *physical* representation of the cosmos. The received hierarchy among the liberal arts was such an obstacle. According to this hierarchy (one that was justified by scholastic views on the differences between the disciplines and their methodologies), mathematics was subordinated to philosophy and theology. The mathematicians were not expected (or supposed) to deal with the physical dimensions of natural phenomena, which (together with the causes of change and motion) were considered to be the philosopher's domain. Consequently, the philosophers perceived Copernicus not just as putting forward a new planetary theory, but as "invading" their own disciplinary and professional domain. In general, this invasion was unacceptable to them and, having higher disciplinary status than the mathematicians, the philosophers had resources to control such an invasion. The usual tactic (one that worked quite well in institutions that accepted this disciplinary hierarchy) was to delegitimize the mathematicians' claims by presenting them as coming from a lower discipline.

The so-called Copernican revolution was two revolutions in one. The acceptance of dramatic cosmological changes required drastic modifications in the organization of the disciplines that studied the cosmos. As we know, this process was a very long one. The legitimation of Copernican astronomy implied a restructuring of the hierarchies among the liberal arts which, in turn, involved an increase in the mathematician's social status. Such changes did not simply result from the strength of the new theories but from an institutional migration as well. Although the traditional disciplinary hierarchy was quite entrenched in the university, it was not so at court. There, one's status was determined by the prince's favor rather than by the discipline one belonged to.

The court, then, was a social space in which mathematicians could gain higher social status and credibility, thereby offsetting the disciplinary gap traditionally existing between them and the philosophers. This increased socio-disciplinary status would in turn contribute to the legitimation of the new worldview they were proposing. If we look at the so-called scientific revolution from the point of view of its sites of activity we may notice (at least on the Continent) a trajectory that leads from the university, to the court, and, eventually, to the scientific academy. To a large extent, Galileo's career exemplifies this trajectory of social and cognitive legitimation. After being a university mathematician, he became a natural philosopher at a court and then a member of what is often considered the first scientific academy—the Accademia dei Lincei. This pattern of institutional migration (one that mathematicians shared with the visual artists and, to some extent, the writers) is another of the ongoing themes of *Galileo, Courtier*. . . .

More recent historians, broadly influenced by Mertonian sociology of science and the Kuhnian notion of "paradigm" and related categories such as "scientific community" and "professionalization," have seen the development of scientific societies (and the related establishment of scientific communities) toward the end of the scientific revolution as marking the beginning of "paradigmatic" science. Although I find the distinction between paradigmatic and pre-paradigmatic less heuristically crippling than the one between modern rationality and whatever preceded it, it is still problematic in that it represents much of earlier science in terms of what it is *not*. Science before 1660 *lacked* a well-structured social system, real scientific institutions, organized professions, and forms of professional communication. In short, early science, in this view, was still represented as the "other" of modern science; what had changed were only the parameters by which it was constructed as such.

In such a view a historian would find it difficult to use "paradigm" to link scientific change to the structure and dynamics of the social system of science simply because there is no real social system of science to speak of. Also, one would tend *not* to perceive patronage as the social system of early modern science because such a perception would go against the fundamental assumption that scientific paradigms are supposed to be connected to well-structured scientific *communities*. . . .

A finely articulated notion of patronage may allow for a better integration of the social and conceptual dimensions of early modern science. The first step of this project involves the rejection of the notion of patronage as a mere set of rational strategies and relations through which a scientist makes a career (acquires money, power, and free time to do research). By perceiving patronage only in terms of its economic dimensions, we may end up believing clients to be rational individuals fully committed to some sort of research program in favor of which they try to manipulate the patronage system. However, "ends" and "means" are not categories that exist outside of the processes of self-fashioning that shape them. Consequently, it is by linking patronage to the social process of self-fashioning of the clients and patrons (rather than simply to their economic subsistence) that we can relate cultural production and social context. Rather than looking for paradigms, we may focus on the study of the client's identity in all its sociocultural dimensions, as well as on a scrutiny of the processes through which such an identity is shaped.

In fact, the process of identity formation need not take place in well-circumscribed professional groups such as scientific communities or institutions. The sociological and conceptual dimensions of modern science that the historiography informed by Kuhn or Merton attributes to the professional identity one develops by being socialized into a scientific community or social group must be sought for in the process of self-fashioning that early modern scientists underwent by entering into patronage relationships and networks. I am not claiming that patronage is the early analogue of scientific community. I am suggesting that patronage is the key to understanding processes of identity and status formation that are the keys to understanding *both* the scientists' cognitive attitudes *and* career strategies. . . .

Having been connected only marginally to the court networks of power during his youth, and possessing mostly un-courtly skills such as mathematics, Galileo would become a top court client only after his astronomical discoveries of 1609–10. . . . Before 1610, there was a major gap between Galileo's own perception of his worth and his actual value on the courtly market. Probably, that gap could have been bridged only by adhering to (and training the tastes of) a future grand duke. . . . His career following his discovery of the four satellites of Jupiter which he called "Medicean Stars" was not the fruit of chance but of an earlier systematic weaving of patronage relationships according to typical patterns and tactics. Without those carefully forged relationships, the Medicean Stars would not have projected him into prominence. . . .

Writing early in 1609 to a Florentine courtier, Galileo expressed his desire to obtain a court position. He claimed that his interest in such a position was not related to the *amount,* but to the *type* of work he would have to face at court:

> Regarding the everyday duties, I shun only that type of prostitution consisting of having to expose my labor to the arbitrary prices set by every customer. Instead, I will never look down on serving a prince or a great lord or those who may depend on him, but, to the contrary, I will always desire such a position.

Galileo understood that a patronage relationship with a great patron brought "purity" (i.e., high status) because it was "monogamous," exclusive, and paid through a regular stipend. To serve many low patrons and be paid piecemeal was a sort of prostitution (*servitù meretricia*). By developing an exclusive and full-time relationship with a great patron one participated in "nobility"—a high status that could be transferred from one's social identity to one's discipline or activity. And, as mentioned earlier, high social status was instrumental in securing the epistemological status of a discipline and method like Galileo's, whose legitimacy was undermined by the existing disciplinary hierarchy.

Finally, by going up in the social ladder through connections to an increasingly *smaller* number of patrons of *higher* power, a successful client like Galileo built a pyramid of clients below him. Patronage requests addressed to Galileo took a sudden jump around 1610. It would be wrong to assign that jump to Galileo's popularity as a discoverer. Discoverers get power from their discoveries only through the institutions that legitimize them. Galileo's power as a courtly star in Florence was much higher than that he had or could have had as a university professor of the Republic of Venice. While in Padua, Galileo received a few requests for patronage, but he seems not to have fulfilled any of them. After 1610 he was able to place a range of mathematicians and philosophers (Castelli, Cavalieri, Aggiunti, and Papazzoni) as professors at the universities of Pisa, Rome, and Bologna. A more complex reading of patronage dynamics shows that Galileo was seeking much more than free time at the Medici court.

Marvelous Conjunctures and Providential Deaths

Recurrent features of clients' lives in early modern Europe were the discontinuities and disruptions produced by the termination of patronage relationships, usually as a result of the patron's death. The trajectories of early modern clients were not smooth curves but tortuous and discontinuous paths punctuated by patronage crises. The careers of Commandino, Leibniz, Dee, Kepler, Tycho, and Galileo exemplify these dynamics.

Biographies of Galileo present the turning points of his career as related to discoveries and controversies like the Medicean Stars, the "Letter to the Grand Duchess," the dispute on comets and the *Assayer*, the trial of 1633, and the last dispute with the philosopher Liceti. Another pattern emerges when we compare the chronology of these turning points and those of his patronage relations.

The first phase of Galileo's career was much indebted to Guidobaldo del Monte, the patron/broker through whom Galileo gained the university positions at Pisa in 1589 and at Padua in 1591. Actually, this segment of Galileo's career was an indirect result of the accession of Ferdinand I de' Medici following the death of his older brother, Francesco I in 1587. At the time of Francesco's death, Ferdinand was a cardinal, and he maintained that title until the end of 1588 because there was no other member of the Medici family who could take over the post. . . .

. . . In 1609, Ferdinand's death turned Galileo's young princely student Cosimo into a grand duke, just a few months before Galileo's astronomical discoveries. Neither Francesco nor Ferdinand had been direct patrons of Galileo. Grand Duchess Cristina and Belisario Vinta were the main brokers through whom Galileo maintained Medici patronage. Yet it was the deaths of the two Medici grand dukes that proved crucially beneficial for his career.

We find another remarkable instance of synchronization between Galileo's scientific production and continuing patronage crises: the death of Pope Gregory XV and the election of Maffeo Barberini to the pontificate as Urban VIII precisely when Galileo's *Assayer* (then dedicated to Urban) was in press. Pope Gregory's was the third providential death in Galileo's career. As with Cosimo II thirteen years before, a new patron (one Galileo had been cultivating for a number of years, as he had Cosimo) suddenly reaches an important status and is willing to support Galileo's provocative views in order to develop a necessarily new image for himself. In terms of patronage, the *Sidereus nuncius* was to Cosimo II's reign what the *Assayer* was to Urban VIII's. Galileo was quite right in calling this remarkable synchronization "a marvelous conjuncture" (*una mirabil congiuntura*).

There is no perverse pleasure on my part in stressing the "providentiality" of these deaths for Galileo's career. As we will see, deaths of great patrons—especially of monarchs like popes, who were not members of a hereditary dynasty—were perceived by contemporaries as major patronage crises. Careers were suddenly made and destroyed on those occasions. As shown by Virginio Cesarini and Giovanni Ciampoli (two clients of Urban VIII and supporters of Galileo), who found themselves suddenly lifted to the top of the Roman court, brand-new cadres would come to power with a new pope. In a true pilgrimage toward the center of power, non-Romans too would try to exploit the new patronage system by traveling to Rome to pay homage to the pope. Galileo himself was a participant in the patronage pilgrimage of 1623–24. Alluding to the comets that had appeared a few years before Urban's election, the Florentine poet Jacopo Soldani compared the clients' pilgrimage to the trip undertaken by the Three Magi to pay homage to the baby Jesus. The gift which Galileo presented to the new pope was the *Assayer*. . . .

The chronological synchronization of Galileo's publications and the crisis of his patronage relationships indicates more than a series of remarkable coincidences. Although patronage was not a fully predictable process, it was far from being chaotic. It had its logic, etiquette, and periodical crises tuned to generational cycles that could be expected and intelligently bet upon. Successful careers were those of clients who extended their patronage networks and tuned their cultural production to patronage cycles so as to turn the play of chance into "marvelous conjunctures."

Gift-Exchange as the Logic of Patronage

Galileo's correspondence shows that gifts and other economically nonquantifiable services and privileges were the medium through which patronage relationships were articulated and maintained. Even when much cash entered the scene—as with Galileo's remarkable thousand-scudi stipend at the Medici court—we should not view it only in our capitalistic perspective and reduce the significance of a thousand-scudi salary to its buying power alone. Its symbolic dimension was also important: income was both a sign and a material cause of status.

Galileo did not formally negotiate his stipend. All his efforts were aimed at securing Medici patronage in some stable fashion, and when his wishes eventually materialized, he simply told Vinta how much he made at Padua and left the final figure to the generosity of the grand duke. Galileo's stipend was a result of both Galileo's value and of the grand duke's *noblesse oblige*. . . .

Framing Galileo's Trail

Very few events in the history of science have received more attention than Galileo's trial of 1633. However, while much literature has focused on the trial's conceptual (theological, cosmological, methodological) dimensions and on the specific personal interactions between Galileo and his friends and foes, it is only in the recent work of Westfall that the role patronage might have played in the events of 1633 has been finally addressed.

Given the major gaps in the available documentary evidence, what I propose here cannot be a comprehensive narrative about "what really happened" but only a possible alternative interpretative framework based on the analysis of patronage and courtly dynamics presented earlier. In particular, I will argue that Galileo's career was propelled and then undone by the same patronage dynamics. I will try to show that the dynamics that led to Galileo's troubles were typical of a princely court: they resembled what was known as "the fall of the favorite." . . .

The uncertainty of favor was the most powerful tool the prince had to maintain control of the court. Therefore the fall of the favorite was a mechanism that worked both for the prince and for the upward-moving courtiers. The fall of the courtier did not harm the prince. Paradoxically, the prince's power was increased or maintained both by a courtier's becoming the favorite and by his subsequent falling in disgrace. By being successful, the courtier enhanced the prince's image. If he failed, his fall would also help the preservation of the prince's power by allowing him to display it mercilessly and remind the other courtiers of what could happen to them if they misbehaved. . . .

The Trial and the Structural Constraints of Court Patronage

This refocusing of the trial of Galileo through the lens of the downfall of the favorite has provided a possible framework in which to contextualize the various claims, accusations, and moves that characterized that intricate process. Although cosmological, theological, and juridical arguments were the issues being debated or deployed in the trial, the logic that weaved them together was not that of Aristotle's *Posterior Analytics*, but that of the power image of the absolute prince. In other words, we should not confuse the trigger with the process it sets in motion. At the

Roman court, somebody could fall after being accused of having held an opinion contrary to the scriptures or of having revised too heavily a Latin letter written by the pope. At the court of Elizabeth I, a favorite could fall after being accused of having seduced a maid of honor. Although these cases are evidently quite different, they share something in that they all were rooted in the economy of the prince's power image. While a wide range of different events or arguments could trigger somebody's fall at court, the dynamics of the downfall itself displayed much less variability.

It is precisely the economy of the prince's power in its relation with courtly culture and patronage that has been analyzed in this book. While in the earlier chapters I have shown how these dynamics made possible Galileo's self-fashioning as a "new philosopher," this conclusion has suggested how they may have framed his downfall as well. Galileo's career was structured—from beginning to end—by the patronage and culture of a baroque court. . . .

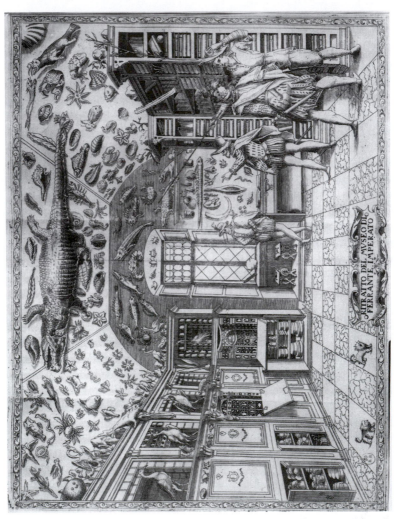

Collection of Naturalia, Ferrante Imperato. The many specimens of exotic animals and objects gathered in this private museum were supposed to evoke wonder from the viewers. (*Private Collection/Bridgeman Art Library*)

Outside the Tradition

The historians featured in the last two chapters believed there were aspects of the Scientific Revolution that had been overlooked by a purely intellectual account of the achievements of great men. In the last few decades, historians have broadened the definition of who or what constitutes the essence of the change in natural philosophy in the sixteenth and seventeenth century. Recent historians of science possess a healthy suspicion of universal categories and absolute statements. They are wary of traditional frameworks that have limited the exploration of various aspects of early modern science. They seek to understand the past through increasingly specialized studies of subjects that were ignored or discounted in the traditional historiography of the Scientific Revolution.

Recent historians have sought to expand the theoretical and disciplinary boundaries of the developing ideas about the natural world. Perhaps the most important early effort to introduce categories excluded from other accounts of the Scientific Revolution was that of Frances Yates. In her 1964 study, *Giordano Bruno and the Hermetic Tradition,* she argued that magical and mystical ideas contributed to the development of scientific thought in the sixteenth and seventeenth century. Bruno, who was burned at the stake by the

Inquisition in 1600, was not only an advocate of Copernicanism, but also a kind of magus, who subscribed to an occult tradition of knowledge, Hermeticism. Yates argued that this tradition, which earlier historians had viewed as antithetical or at least tangential to the growth of rational science, was actually one of the reasons for its development.

Paula Findlen and William Eamon have also widened the boundaries of what constituted the natural philosophical community of the sixteenth and seventeenth centuries. Findlen's discussion of collecting and collectors in Italy during this period identifies a field of activity and a site of knowledge that have often been neglected by traditional historians of science: natural history and the museum. Like Biagioli, Findlen views the collecting of the strange and unusual objects displayed in museums as a social function intended to bolster the status of the collector, who sought control over the many new aspects of the natural world discovered in early modern times. Findlen is part of a recent historiographical tradition that has attempted to integrate material culture into the analysis of the past. The new science, as Francis Bacon would have acknowledged, was not just about ideas but also about things. The sixteenth-century collectors of objects tried to integrate an expanded Aristotelianism with the new discoveries; they represented a bridge between or even a union of elements that earlier historians of science had separated: old and new, occult and scientific, professional and amateur.

Eamon also investigates an arena that earlier historians have ignored, and comes to conclusions similar to Findlen's. Eamon examines the tradition of the "Book of Secrets" in the Middle Ages and the sixteenth and seventeenth centuries. His analysis reflects a new interest in the history of the book, which began with the work of the historian Elizabeth Eisenstein, who argued that the dissemination and critical scrutiny of books made possible by printing ultimately resulted in the dissection of old systems and the development of new ones. Eamon amends Eisenstein's thesis and argues that the many published books of secrets allowed those interested in the new Baconian sciences—chemistry, magnetism, electricity and metallurgy—to utilize the craft and technical knowledge these manuals contained. Eamon returns to the Marxist tradition, arguing that there was a direct link between the work of craftsmen and the experimental tradition of the new science. Distinctions between old and new, amateur and professional, artisan and scientist, once again seem anachronistic, if not just plain wrong.

The idea of the cross-fertilization of ideas, concepts, activities, and people is part of what is called the new cultural history, and is reflected in Sara Schechner Genuth's study of the history of comet theory in medieval and early modern thought. Following the lead of historians of culture such as Robert Darnton and Carlo Ginzburg, Genuth argues that elite and popular culture—the culture of the learned and the culture of the people—were mutually interactive, and it is incorrect to exempt scientists from the influence of popular ideas. Even Isaac Newton, the paradigmatic genius of the Scientific Revolution, integrated aspects of popular culture into his work, whether self-consciously or not.

There has been a renaissance of Newton studies in the recent work of historians of the Scientific Revolution. They present a Newton that earlier historians of science would barely have recognized: alchemist, student of Biblical chronology, theologian. He is a symbol of the discipline's current ferment, in which the insights of other fields threaten to dissolve the coherence of the Scientific Revolution itself. A deeper historicism allows canonical thinkers to be analyzed in ways more appropriate to their actual time, and other figures to be admitted into the arena of historical study. The result is a much richer tapestry of early modern science, one that incorporates threads earlier historiographic traditions would not have recognized or allowed.

William Eamon

Science and the Secrets of Nature: Books of Secrets in Medieval and Early Modern Culture, 1994

In this selection, William Eamon describes the "Book of Secrets" tradition. By the sixteenth century, these books were "how-to" manuals, describing the correct techniques for manipulating the occult forces of nature. As such, they were experimental in emphasis, promising to give the reader control and power over the natural world. The books continued to be popular into the seventeenth century, read by not only the barely literate but also by intellectuals. Eamon argues that the concept of experimentation advocated in these books ultimately informed the development of Baconian science: they were the link between the secret techniques of craftsmen and the ideal of scientific communication advocated by Bacon.

Introduction: Printing, Popular Culture, and the Scientific Revolution

When the English physician and virtuoso Sir Thomas Browne sat down to catalog "vulgar errors" in his *Pseudodoxia Epidemica* of 1646, he warned against, among others, authors who "pretend to write of secrets, to deliver Antipathies, Sympathies, and the occult abstrusities of things." An avowed Baconian, Browne was convinced that science would not advance until men's minds were rid of the errors and prejudices that had blocked the progress of knowledge. Browne's repudiation of the "books of secrets" signifies an important break with a tradition of remarkable durability. Although for him the books of secrets were sources of popular errors,

William Eamon, *Science and the Secrets of Nature: Books of Secrets in Medieval and Early Modern Culture* (Princeton: Princeton University Press, 1994). © 1994 Princeton University Press, 1996 paperback edition. Reprinted by permission of Princeton University Press.

the authors he warned against had not always written for the people. Indeed, implicit in the tradition he condemned was the notion that to reveal secrets to the vulgar was to cast pearls before swine. Yet ironically, for a century and a half prior to Browne's writing, Europe had been inundated with scores of treatises that professed to reveal the "secrets of nature" to anyone who could read. Browne singled out two of the most famous of these books of secrets as being particularly objectionable: Alessio Piemontese's *Secreti*, which had already been published in more than seventy editions since its appearance in 1555, and Giambattista Della Porta's *Magia naturalis*, which, though written in Latin primarily for a learned audience, went through almost twenty editions. A campaign against such suspect authors, "not greedily to be swallowed," seemed to Browne both necessary and appropriate.

In repudiating the books of secrets, Browne cast into the rubbish heap of obsolete science a body of literature that for centuries had fascinated, informed, and repelled readers. Alessio and Della Porta were but the apogee of a literary tradition, going back at least to Hellenistic times, of writings purporting to reveal secrets jealously guarded by famous sages and experimenters, or locked up in the bosom of nature itself. These writings exist in countless medieval manuscripts and in printed books of almost every European language. . . .

Why did these writings so capture the medieval imagination, and why did their popularity and authority persist for so long? One reason is that they were linked with a literary tradition of works that promised to reveal the esoteric teachings of revered authorities like Aristotle and Albertus Magnus. Such teachings appealed forcefully to the medieval mind, which was inclined to believe that everything knowable was contained in ancient sources. But they also appealed to Renaissance thinkers, who searched for a *prisca theologica*, an original wisdom rooted in revelation, as an alternative to what they regarded as a bankrupt scholastic tradition. Moreover, the books of secrets promised to give readers access to "secrets of nature" that might be exploited for material gain or used for the betterment of humanity. Underlying these works was the assumption that nature was a repository of occult forces that might be manipulated, not by the magus's cunning, but merely by the use of correct techniques. The utilitarian character of the books of secrets gave concrete substance to this claim. Unlike the recondite treatises on the philosophical foundations of magic, which barely touched base with the real world, the books of secrets were grounded upon a down-to-earth, experimental outlook: they did not affirm underlying principles but taught "how to." Hence they seemed to hold forth a real and accessible promise of power.

Thus the books of secrets were not, perhaps, what the term itself might conjure up in the imagination. Modern readers expecting to encounter some mysterious, arcane wisdom are bound to find these works disappointing. What they revealed were recipes, formulas, and "experiments" associated with one of the crafts or with medicine: for example, instructions for making quenching waters to harden iron and steel, recipes for mixing dyes and pigments, "empirical" remedies, cooking recipes, and practical alchemical formulas such as a jeweler or tinsmith might use. To the modern reader, they more closely resemble how-to books than magic books. Doubtless, many were used as all-purpose household handbooks.

Yet the connotation attached to "secrets" and to books of secrets in the medieval and early modern periods was not as neutral as this characterization might suggest. The books of secrets were not regarded with the same detachment we would have for, say, a cookbook or chemical formulary, the closet modern equivalent of such a work. We do not take very seriously the claim of the cookbook that professes to reveal "all the secrets of the culinary art," or the how-to book that promises to unveil the "secrets of woodworking." Such books may be useful, but few users will imagine they are going to learn more than how to make a tolerable meal or a sturdy piece of furniture. In the medieval and early modern eras, such claims carried much more weight than they do today. It seemed to many readers of the books of secrets that there was much more to be learned from a recipe than merely "how to"—even though in the long run that may have been what they actually learned. Linguistic shifts often signify changes in worldviews: a word's change of meaning may be a clue that the world is also changing. By the eighteenth century, such "secrets" were techniques and nothing more. In the sixteenth century, however, the term was still densely packed with its ancient and medieval connotations: the association with esoteric wisdom, the domain of occult or forbidden knowledge, the artisan's cunning, the moral injunctions to protect secrets from the *vulgus*, and the political power that attended knowledge of secrets. The Scientific Revolution exposed and neutralized nature's "secrets." . . .

. . . The books of secrets published scores of artisanal recipes from a broad range of crafts, from metallurgy and "practical alchemy" to dyeing textiles and preparing drugs. One of my purposes is to demonstrate that these works played an instrumental role in disseminating craft information to the virtuosi. However, I also want to make a stronger claim about the significance of the books of secrets for the Scientific Revolution. I hope to show that these works were not merely passive vehicles for the transmission of "raw data" to natural philosophers, but were bearers of attitudes and values that proved instrumental in shaping scientific culture in the early modern era. In particular, I shall argue that the books of secrets articulated a novel concept of experimentation. With their roots in a largely oral and practical tradition, the books of secrets enable us to rummage through the prehistory, so to speak, of the Baconian sciences. In the Middle Ages, the type of experiments Bacon advocated doing (according to a prescribed method involving the collaborative effort of many scientific workers) were still "secrets." That is, they were the "private experiments" of individual practitioners, the sort of events that occurred frequently within the craft tradition but were communicated orally (if communicated at all) and rarely published. Bacon urged that experience be made to "learn her letters"—in other words, that experiments be recorded and communicated to other experimenters. Only when "experience has been taught to read and write," he thought, could scientific progress be hoped for. The books of secrets were examples of such "literate experience," for the recipe distills the arduous trial-and-error experience of practitioners and collapses it into a formula for making. Finally, I want to emphasize and, I hope, to clarify the important distinction between the medieval notion of an "experiment" (or a "secret")— a fortuitous, unexpected, and essentially private experience—and the Baconian concept of experimentation, a scientific program involving the communication of experimental findings to a community of scientists, and the collaborative testing of them. I hope to show that the books of secrets were the "missing link" between medieval "secrets" and Baconian experiments. . . .

It has often been said that to succeed, a revolution must win the hearts and minds of the people. That statement may also be applied to the Scientific Revolution. To succeed, it had to create a cosmology and an epistemology that were consistent with the secularistic attitudes that emerged, especially among the urban middle class, in early modern culture. The "new philosophy" of the seventeenth century was ideally suited to this purpose. By overruling the action of supernatural forces in the universe, the mechanistic cosmology ratified the boundary between the sacred and the profane. The mechanical philosophy also validated the "maker's knowledge" (*verum factum*) model of scientific explanation, the maxim of reasoning according to which to know something means knowing how to make it. In the new philosophy, the capacity to reproduce nature's effects became a sort of touchstone upon which claims to knowledge would have to be tested. In radical contrast to the scholastic view of knowledge, the new philosophy made how-to knowledge a criterion of truth. From this vantage point, we may begin to see the social and economic history of the Scientific Revolution in a new light. Why did the limited "mechanical know-how" model of natural knowledge win out over the unitary, comprehensive view of knowledge that characterized scholastic natural philosophy? One answer is that "maker's knowledge" mattered more to the emergent middle class than did knowledge based on abstract principles. It was more consistent with bourgeois values. Unpacking the "secrets of nature" may help us make sense of why the Scientific Revolution occurred during the period of early capitalism. . . .

. . . I will argue that in the sixteenth-century books of secrets, a new concept of the scientific enterprise emerged: that of science as a *venatio*, or a great hunt after the secrets of nature. This concept of science was essentially a popular image promoted by the "professors of secrets" as a means of selling their books. It was, in other words, a consequence of the transformation of "secrets" and "experiments" into commodities. Nevertheless the conception of science as a *venatio* entailed a new definition of the function of experiments in science. This new conception of experimentation emerged independently of the academic tradition. In due course, it was appropriated by the virtuosi as part of a program for the advancement of science and was implemented in the research program of the Royal Society of London. I do not mean to suggest that the Scientific Revolution was a "revolution from below." But I do believe that any discussion of the "foundations" of the Scientific Revolution must consider a much broader base for it than historians of science have so far attempted. . . .

New Worlds of Secrets

. . . What is significant about these examples is that all were premised on the idea of scientific inquiry conceived as the discovery of *new* things rather than as attempts to demonstrate the known. The theme of novelty appears repeatedly in the scientific literature of the early modern period. Lynn Thorndike observed that words such as *novus* and "unheard-of" recur in the titles of hundreds of scientific books of the seventeenth century. The *Ne plus ultra* inscribed on the ancient pillars of Hercules became a favorite device to illustrate the tyranny of ancient philosophy over creative thought. The growing awareness that superstitious reverence for antiquity hampered progress in learning magnified the importance of new discoveries and the value of novelty for its own sake.

One of the most important events contributing to Europe's heightened consciousness of novelty was the discovery of the New World—or rather, of new worlds, since the geographical explorations of the era brought back accounts of discoveries made in Asia and Africa as well as in America. . . .

The New World explorer provided natural philosophers with a heroic self-image. . . .

In the new philosophies, the concept of occult qualities was not an ending point but a beginning of inquiry. However, the new philosophers maintained that the opaqueness of nature prevented reason from plumbing its depths. . . . But if occult qualities were in principle knowable, as the new philosophers claimed, by what means might they be known? If reason and the unaided senses were incapable of unlocking the door to "nature's workshop," where was the key to that locked door to be found?

Seventeenth-century natural philosophers were in general agreement that they could gain access to nature's secrets only by adopting a twofold strategy that consisted of right method combined with instruments to aid the senses. . . .

Instead of expecting nature to "follow us into our Chambers, and there in idlenesse communicate her secrets unto us," the new philosophers insisted that nature had to be interrogated by methodical inquiry and "anatomized" by experiment. In the 1680s, Robert Hooke (1635–1703), the Royal Society of London's curator of experiments, formulated a detailed set of research principles to guide the society's virtuosi. Hooke's *General Scheme, or Idea of the Present State of Natural Philosophy* embodies many of the ideals characterizing the new experimental philosophy of the seventeenth century. In spite of numerous improvements over Scholasticism, Hooke asserted, natural philosophy was still defective and in need of reform. In attempting to account for these defects, Hooke noted that humans gain information about nature solely by sensations. The senses, however, are deficient because they give us information only about nature's exterior. "Man is not indued with an intuitive Faculty, to see farther into the Nature of things at first, than the Superficies and out-sides, and so must go a long way about before he can be able to behold the Internal Nature of things." Hooke maintained that logic was useful for some purposes, but "as to the Inquiry into Natural Operations, what are the Kinds of secret and subtile Actors, and what the abstruse and hidden Instruments and Engines there made use of, may be; It seems not, to me, as yet at all adapted and wholly deficient."

Hooke contended that to overcome these deficiencies natural philosophy needed a new method—as he put it, a "Philosophical Algebra, or an Art of directing the Mind in the search after Philosophical Truths," which would make it possible "for the meanest Capacity acting by that Method to compleat and perfect it." Hooke's "philosophical algebra" would consist of two main parts: helps to the senses and new rules of reasoning. . . . Hooke proposed making a detailed examination of the sensual faculties so that natural philosophers would have a better understanding of how empirical knowledge was limited and how these limitations might be corrected. He then outlined a method for collecting empirical data, arranging them into tables and histories, and preparing them for the induction of axioms. Not only are the unaided senses inadequate, Hooke observed, but nature itself is deceptive. Hence even when our perceptions are accurate, they cannot always be taken at face value. Experiments would help surmount this problem. . . . The experimental methodology Hooke proposed was essentially the same as Bacon's learned experience, although his explication of the method was informed by an intimate familiarity with the nuances and hazards of experimentation.

In addition to proper experimental methods, Hooke maintained that the senses had to be armed with instruments to enhance their powers of perception. Foremost among such instruments were the telescope and the microscope. . . .

Hooke was optimistic that the microscope would reveal the mechanical causes of phenomena, enabling natural philosophers to "discern all the secret workings of Nature, almost in the same manner as we do those that are the productions of Art, and are manag'd by Wheels, and Engines, and Springs, that were devised by humane Wit." By exposing the interior "machinery" of nature, the microscope would also confirm the principles of the mechanical philosophy. This, he believed, would go a long way toward resolving the ancient problem of occult qualities. . . .

Like Bacon, Hooke attempted to elucidate a method whereby discovery would not have to depend upon the genius or cunning of a few investigators, but would rely instead upon the dedicated work of teams of researchers. . . . In order to overcome the danger of such dogmatism, the new philosophers insisted upon basing natural philosophy upon experimental "matters of fact." . . .

The repeated references to the "secrets of nature" in seventeenth-century scientific literature should not be dismissed as mere rhetoric. Far from being a mere hackneyed metaphor, the continual appearance of that well-worn phrase indicates a fundamental shift in the direction of natural philosophy. The concept of nature's "secrets"—that is, the idea that the mechanisms of nature were hidden beneath the exterior appearances of things—was the foundation of the new philosophy's skeptical outlook, and of its insistence upon getting to the bottom of things through active experimentation and disciplined observation. The Scholastics had been too trusting of their senses, the new philosophers asserted. Their naive empiricism was responsible for the erroneous belief that nature exhibits her true character on the outside. Moreover, scholastic philosophy's inclination to accept at face value whatever the unaided senses revealed had given rise to the sterile science of elements and qualities. In reality, the new philosophers declared, nature's workings are hidden. The unaided, undisciplined senses do not reveal reliable information about what makes nature tick any more than observing the hands of a clock reveals how the clock works. All the dogmatic pronouncements of scholastic philosophy were but chimeras based upon unreliable empirical foundations.

The rejection of Aristotelian natural philosophy's naive empiricism—its assumption that nature could be immediately observed—was an essential precondition of the Scientific Revolution. The concept of the "secrets of nature" was one of the premises underlying the "Baconian sciences," which according to Thomas Kuhn emerged simultaneously with the revolution in the classical sciences. This new cluster of scientific interests, Kuhn argued, was characterized by the accumulation of observations and experiments rather than the revolutionary overthrow of existing paradigms. To the extent that these sciences existed at all prior to the Scientific Revolution, he maintained, they were little more than interesting classes of phenomena. There was no governing paradigm to explain them or to give them cohesion. Thus Kuhn argued that the Baconian sciences emerged essentially without precedents during the period of the Scientific Revolution. In contrast to the traditional, mathematical disciplines of the university curriculum, whose paradigms were completely overthrown, the Baconian sciences emerged from a "preparadigm" condition. . . .

Paula Findlen

Possessing Nature: Museums, Collecting and Scientific Culture in Early Modern Italy, 1994

Paula Findlen describes the collecting activities of early modern naturalists, who sought to display the strange and familiar objects of natural history in their museums. These collectors were not usually advocates of the new science, but they were at the heart of the scientific culture of the sixteenth and early seventeenth centuries. They sought to incorporate Aristotelian ideas about the natural world with the thought of the Roman natural historian Pliny and the Greek medical philosophers. The space they operated in was the museum, which became a "paradigmatic space" for the investigation of nature. Although their inclusive attitudes towards ancient knowledge ultimately were abandoned, their belief that nature could be known and catalogued influenced the later Scientific Revolution.

Introduction

This book recounts two overlapping histories. The first details the appearance of museums in early modern Europe, particularly collections whose purpose was to bring all of nature into one space. The second offers a reading of the development of natural history as a discipline. Both stories take Italy as their case study. There collecting first became a widespread practice, among an elite desirous to know the past, in all its forms, through the possession of its remnants. The collecting of antiquities and the passion for natural objects appeared in Italy before any other part of Western Europe; in both instances, a strong historicizing impulse on the part of Italian Renaissance humanists precipitated these activities. Simultaneously, at the universities of Pisa, Padua, and Bologna, and in the Italian courts, academies, and pharmacies, nature was subjected to an intensive inquiry in ways that she had not been since the time of Pliny and the great encyclopedic work of Albertus Magnus. These two activities—collecting and the interrogation of nature—met in the studies of naturalists such as Ulisse Aldrovandi (1522–1605) and Athanasius Kircher (1602–1680), resulting in new attitudes toward nature, as a collectible entity, and generating new techniques of investigation that subsequently transformed natural history.

Contemporaries were well aware of Italy's primacy in the renaissance of natural history. . . .

Possessing nature was part of a more widespread delight in collecting objects of scientific worth. During the sixteenth and seventeenth centuries, the first science museums appeared—repositories of technology, ethnographic curiosities, and natural wonders. They emerged at a time when all of Europe seemed to be collecting; museums, libraries, intricate gardens, grottos, and galleries of art filled the landscape of late Renaissance and Baroque Europe. . . .

. . . Collecting, in short, had become an activity of choice among the social and educated elite. It filled their leisure hours and for some seemed to encompass every waking moment of their lives. Through the possession of objects, one physically acquired knowledge, and through their display, one symbolically acquired the honor and reputation that all men of learning cultivated.

Within the wider matrix of collecting, the possession of nature figured prominently. Along with art, antiquities, and exotica, nature was deemed a desirable object to own. Building upon Pliny's encyclopedic definition of nature as everything in the world worthy of memory and the narrower view of such writers as Dioscorides and Galen, who defined natural history as the study of objects useful in medicine, collectors brought ordinary and exotic nature into their museums. The alleged remains of legendary creatures—giants, unicorns, satyrs, basilisks—took their place next to real but puzzling phenomena such as fossils, loadstones, and zoophytes; previously unknown creatures such as the armadillo and the bird of paradise; and a plethora of ordinary artifacts that filled in the gaps between one paradox and the next. From the imaginary to the exotic to the ordinary, the museum was designed to represent nature as a continuum.

Why did so many Europeans envision collecting as the key to understanding their world? In a sense, the creation of the museum was an attempt to manage the empirical explosion of materials that wider dissemination of ancient texts, increased travel, voyages of discovery, and more systematic forms of communication and exchange had produced. While all of these factors contributed to the increased curiosity of the Europeans toward other cultures, and ultimately redefined the European world view as a relative rather than an absolute measure of "civilization," they also produced new attitudes toward nature and the discipline of natural history. "It is not to be esteemed a small matter that by the voyages & travels of these later times, so much more of nature has been discovered than was known at any former period," wrote Francis Bacon, who made natural history the paradigm for a new philosophy of nature in the seventeenth century:

> *It would, indeed, be disgraceful to mankind, if, after such tracts of the material world have been laid open which were unknown in former times—so many seas traversed—so many countries explored—so many stars discovered—philosophy, or the intelligible world, should be circumscribed by the same boundaries as before.*

Natural history, as Bacon observed, was a form of inquiry designed to record the knowledge of the world for the use and betterment of mankind. As Europeans traveled farther with greater frequency, this knowledge expanded, yielding new and unexpected results. Collecting was one way of maintaining some degree of control over the natural world and taking its measure. If knowledge of the world could no longer be contained in a set of canonical texts, then perhaps it could be displayed in a museum. Thus, philosophers at the vanguard of the intellectual community, most significantly Bacon, urged fellow investigators of nature to establish storehouses to monitor the flow of objects and information. From these activities, a new philosophy of nature would emerge based on experience rather than erudition.

Despite Bacon's admonitions, none of the collectors whom I discuss dissolved the boundaries of their world. While the Italian naturalists would have agreed with Bacon that experience was a necessary and often under-valued part of knowledge, they would not have appreciated his dismissal of ancient authority. Collectors such as Aldrovandi and Kircher understood their activities to be the fulfillment of the work of Aristotle and those who had followed him; for them, experience did not compete with authority but rather complemented and enhanced it. The novelties they encountered did not lead them to discard their philosophical framework but instead to modify it. As a paradigm of knowledge, collecting stretched the parameters of the known to incorporate an expanding material culture. From the sixteenth-century naturalist's including of New World plants in Old World categories, to the seventeenth-century Jesuit's Christian synthesis of all cultures and their artifacts, the museum "saved appearances" rather than unsettling ancient systems. By the mid-seventeenth century, it would become a symbol of the "new" science, incorporated into scientific organizations such as the Royal Society in England, the Paris Academy of Sciences, and later the Institute for Sciences in Bologna. In the preceding century, however, the museum emblematized the revitalization of Aristotelian natural philosophy and Plinian natural history; it was about the reinvention of the old rather than the formation of the new.

While collecting did not immediately usher in a new philosophical definition of and structure for *scientia*, it certainly constituted a significant addition to the practice of philosophizing in early modern Europe. Organizing ideas around objects, naturalists increasingly saw philosophical inquiry as the product of a continuous engagement with material culture. The decision to display the fruits of collection led naturalists gradually to define knowledge as consensual, shaped in relation to the audience that entered the museum and therefore participated in the peculiar discursive practices that emerged within that context. Tactile as well as sociable, the philosophizing done in and around the museum enhanced the Aristotelian definition of knowledge as a product of sensory engagement with nature. Ultimately the value placed upon the experience of the senses would result in its uncoupling from this traditional philosophical framework. But at this point, naturalists perceived their museums to be a tangible sign of their commitment to the ancient study of nature. In the sixteenth century, this entailed little more than subsuming everything collected within a proper philosophical framework, as determined by the traditional classification of the sciences. By the seventeenth century, in the wake of the new experimental philosophies of Bacon, Descartes, and Galileo, naturalists still committed to the preservation of ancient views of nature now faced the challenge of responding to the hostile critics. Putting the techniques of the "new" philosophy in the service of the old, Aristotelian naturalists designated the museum as a site of critical synthesis. With hindsight, it is easy for us to predict their failure. At the time, they had the weight of more than 2000 years of authority on their side.

Telling this tale of failed encyclopedic dreams is a fairly complicated endeavor. In this study, I have used the rich font of materials available on this subject to sketch a broad portrait of naturalistic and collecting activities in the sixteenth and seventeenth centuries. Between Aldrovandi and Kircher lie a host of other patrons and collectors of nature who merit equal attention. Some — Pier Andrea Mattioli (1500–1577), Giovan Battista della Porta (1535–1615), Federico Cesi (1585–1630), Manfredo Settala (1600–1680), and Francesco Redi (1626–1697) — are well known, at least by name. Others have receded into obscurity over the course of time, as their publications have grown dusty and their museums have vanished. While many contemporaries knew of the famed apothecaries Francesco Calzolari (1521–1600) and Ferrante Imperato (1550–1625), only the latter merits a brief entry in the *Dictionary of Scientific Biography*. Similarly, the humanist broker Giovan Vincenzo Pinelli (1535–1601), the papal physician Michele Mercati (1541–1593), the grandducal botanist Paolo Boccone (1633–1704), and the Jesuit naturalist Filippo Bonanni (1638–1725) grace modern histories of science briefly, if at all. Their contributions have not, by our standards, merited a retrospective assessment. Perhaps it is worth asking ourselves why we remember the most prolific, measuring importance by the number of weighty tomes, when a different kind of documentation — one that takes into account the teaching and training of students and the collaborative process at work behind any publication — reveals that others, who published less, contributed as much if not more. If other instances, we might query why one form of copiousness — that of Galileo or Newton, to offer contemporaneous examples — merits attention, while another — that of Aldrovandi, Redi, or Kircher — goes relatively unremarked. In the process of writing the sort of history that speaks to our present image of "science," we often find it preferable to neglect those who do not fit comfortably into this category. One of the primary goals of this study is to bring to life individuals who, while marginal to our own science, were central to the early modern definition of scientific culture. . . .

In shaping this project, I have implicitly defined the formation of a *scientific culture* as the broadening of the activities that we subsume under the category of science into new arenas: the court, the academy, the pharmacy, the piazza, the marketplace, the museum. By doing this, I hoped to avoid the pitfall of describing what these naturalists did as "science," a category that had no relevance for them. Most naturalists aspired to be "natural philosophers," an appellate that allowed them to traverse the boundaries between medicine, natural history, and natural philosophy, in short, to be qualified to comment on all domains of scientific knowledge. They would have been puzzled by and indeed disparaging of our own attempts to reduce their expansive, encyclopedic activities by labeling them "scientists." Our own conception of science has discarded many of the practices that they saw as essential to the definition of *scientia*. While we perceive the museum of natural history to be alternately a research laboratory or a place of public education, they understood it to be a repository of the collective imagination of their society.

At the same time, the museum also publicized a scientific culture formerly confined to scholastic discourse. It was the centerpiece of the humanist vision of knowledge. Collecting provided an important mechanism to facilitate the transition of natural philosophy from a largely textual and bookish culture, difficult for all but the most learned to access, to a tactile, theatrical culture that spoke to a multiplicity of different audiences. It was circumscribed by a variety of newly reconstituted practices, among them experimenting, observing, and translating. The proliferation of words, images, and objects accompanying the formation of museums gives testimony to the fact that late Renaissance natural history was defined by its audience as well as by the books that outlined its shifting parameters. The new visibility of natural history was as much an act of cultural production as intellectual orchestration or institutional resolution; the centrality of collecting to the reformulation of this discipline had much to do with its ability to rearrange the boundaries of the scientific community.

The success of natural history as a profession for numerous doctors, apothecaries, and natural philosophers, in conjunction with its popularity as a learned pastime for patricians, points to a common problem in the history of science, where neat divisions between "scientists" and "amateurs" have often prevailed. Rather than perpetuating these cleavages, I wish to encourage the notion that old and new, sacred and secular, occult and scientific, professional and amateur systems of knowledge could and did coexist in the sixteenth and seventeenth centuries. While something we might approximately designate as the precursor to modern science was in the process of formation, it was assisted by, in fact derived from, a most "unscientific" world of philosophizing that did not privilege "science" because it had not yet identified it as a better, truer form of knowledge. The intellectual problem of understanding what Renaissance naturalists meant when they "did science" also has social consequences. The indistinguishability of natural history from other aspects of learned and courtly culture certainly calls into question the notion of a scientific community, as historians of science have commonly understood it. The museum was simultaneously a harbinger of new experimental attitudes and sociological formations, and the dominion of Aristotelian dicta and the magus who fabricated secrets in his laboratory. Standing at the cross-roads between these two seemingly diverse scientific cultures, the museum provided a space common to all.

My purpose throughout has been to reconstruct the discipline of natural history as a whole, at least in the form that it took in Italy. I am interested in knowing not only *why* the study of nature was revived—the intellectual question most commonly asked in shaping such a study—but also *how* and *where*. What conditions allowed it to emerge from relative obscurity and neglect to become a practice lauded by scholars, promoted by academies and universities, and accepted at court? How did the formation of "theaters of nature" facilitate this transition? Natural history was a vibrant and multifaceted enterprise during this period. Despite the relative lack of attention that it has received in the historiography of the scientific revolution, it attracted scholars as well as courtiers, those with a professional interest in nature as well as virtuosi who delighted in the intricacy, subtlety, and copiousness of her parts; in short, the learned and the curious. While naturalists came to the study of nature for a variety of different reasons, all found common grounds for interaction in the museum, a microcosm of elite society as well as nature herself. It is to this intersection of patrician values, scientific aspirations, and collecting practices that we now turn. . . .

By the mid-sixteenth century, natural philosophers had a variety of different approaches to knowledge from which to choose. Most traditional and canonical was the Aristotelian view of nature that favored the collecting of particular data only when directly pertinent to the universal axioms they created and reinforced. Aristotle also offered clear procedures by which knowledge would be disseminated, emphasizing the importance of deductive logic as the cornerstone of good scientific method. With the exception of the Linceans and possibly Redi, all the naturalists discussed here were avowed Aristotelians, to some degree. But the qualification is important. Aristotelian philosophy underwent numerous transformations in the thirteenth and fourteenth centuries at the hands of Albertus Magnus and his pupil Thomas Aquinas. This dynamic approach to the words of the Philosopher continued in the sixteenth and seventeenth centuries, creating an even greater profusion of what Charles Schmitt aptly had dubbed "Aristotelianisms." Just as Aristotelian philosophy was modified to meet the needs of late medieval Christianity, it underwent a similar metamorphosis in the context of late Renaissance humanism and Catholic Reformation culture. While Aldrovandi opened up Aristotelianism to a world of heightened sensory experience, Kircher used it as a point of departure for his Baroque meditations on the hidden meaning of the universe. They reflected a trajectory that began with the reedition and retranslation of the Aristotelian corpus at the end of the fifteenth century and ended with works such as Emanuele Tesauro's *Aristotelian Telescope* (1654).

Neither Aldrovandi nor Kircher confined themselves to one philosophical framework. Instead they combined different approaches to nature, reflecting the syncretist tendencies of the age. While maintaining a healthy respect for ancient authority, they eagerly embraced new philosophies of nature, secure in the knowledge that their openness would only enhance the traditions they upheld. Like many of the contemporaries, their novelty lay less in the creation of something radically new than in the reinvention of older forms of knowledge. Reconstituting Aristotle, they also reinvented Pliny, altering the philosophy of the former and giving the work of the latter greater centrality to the study of nature. Their expansive attitude toward the ancient canon also allowed them to include a variety of other authors who had not previously merited canonical status as philosophers of nature—Aristotle's pupil Theophrastus, the Greek physician Dioscorides, the Roman writers Ovid and Pliny, the mythical Hermes, and so on. . . . New forms of intellectual communication and exchange—the printing press and the editorial and epistolary activities that surrounded it—revitalized the time-honored enterprise of learning with the ancients as one's guide. Eventually this newfound intimacy would lead scholars to question the transcendent status of ancient authorities, casting them down from the Olympian heights to mortal ground. The rejection of the ancients was a slow and painful process, resisted by many of the people who, ironically, made it possible. In different ways, Renaissance and Baroque naturalists chose to extend the ancient paradigm of natural history rather than to dismantle it. Yet their decision to allow new influences to impinge upon this structure made it a precarious edifice indeed.

Beyond the classical framework defining the scope of natural history, other philosophies of nature, more specific to the early modern period, beckoned collectors. The fifteenth-century discovery of the Hermetic corpus, a body of allegedly pre-Christian writings attributed to the Egyptian God Hermes Trismegistus, greatly enhanced the symbolic study of nature. Translated into Latin by Marsilio Ficino, it soon became a standard text for the humanists, particularly adherents of neo-Platonic and occultist natural philosophies. The hermetic view of nature, which presented it as a divinely encoded structure, held little attraction for most Renaissance naturalists who reveled more in the openness than in the secrecy of the universe. A century later, Kircher made it a central feature of the Jesuit system of knowledge. . . . mnemonics as philosophical guides to the construction of his museum and his view of nature, he nonetheless benefited from the expanded role of symbolic discourse. As William Ashworth notes, Aldrovandi participated fully in the culture of emblematics that reached its height in the late sixteenth century. His desire for *complete knowledge of every natural creation* led Aldrovandi to incorporate adages, morals, emblems, proverbs, sympathies, and antipathies alongside discussions of anatomy, physiology, and the various uses of the object under inspection. Thus, the Bolognese naturalist was not interested in symbolic discourse per se but rather he studied and deployed it as a necessary part of the humanist definition of knowledge. He evidenced a common tendency among Renaissance encyclopedists to define inquiry not according to any *one* set of principles but as the interweaving of numerous and diverse philosophical systems.

If we turn to Kircher's treatises, for instance, his *Loadstone or Three Books on the Magnetic Art* (1641), *Great Art of Light and Shadow* (1646), or *Subterranean World* (1664), we find none of the subdivisions that characterized Aldrovandi's classification schemes. Kircher perceived the world as an organic, self-replicating entity. The structures that he sought lay not in Renaissance humanist categories of knowledge but in universal philosophical principles. Hermeticism, the most ancient of ancient wisdoms — Kircher apparently was undaunted by Isaac Casaubon's announcement in 1614 that the Hermetic corpus was a late antique rather than pre-Christian invention — offered one such framework. As close to the origins of mankind as any text could be, allegedly predating the Bible, it offered readers divine knowledge. For a natural philosopher who found communion with God in the study of nature, this represented priceless wisdom. In contrast to Aldrovandi's natural history, organized around the formal categories of humanist inquiry, Kircher's encyclopedia represented the culmination of the more mystical and allegorical strands of humanistic culture. Concerned with divine order and harmony, he had more affinities with neo-Platonists such as Ficino and Kepler than with the Renaissance Aristotelian Aldrovandi.

Hermeticism offered a new philosophical framework for natural philosophy, one particularly attractive to naturalists intent on making nature a moral object lesson for their contemporaries. Natural magic allowed the same individuals the opportunity to define their own role in explicating the operations of nature. Aldrovandi certainly knew something of this tradition. . . .

. . . For seventeenth-century naturalists, knowledge of nature increasingly signified *power over nature*. Constantly critiquing Renaissance natural magic for being overly speculative in its claims to perform extravagant and unheralded experiments, they nonetheless drew inspiration from these activities. Their own attempts to replicate the operations of the natural world—volcanoes erupting, Atlantis submerging, light refracting and reflecting, sound dispersing, not to mention the standard array of perpetual motion machines, air pumps, telescopes, and microscopes that filled their galleries—created the bizarre technologies that we associate with Baroque museums. While hermeticism defined the collector as a magus, natural magic made the philosopher a true master of nature. . . .

As the previous examples illustrate, naturalists followed many different trajectories during this period, from the traditional to the esoteric to the experimental. Despite the divergent paths they took, all shared the common trait of curiosity. Curiosity led naturalists out into the world. It led them to define knowledge in terms of wonder and experience. "Wonder" encompassed the emotions that confrontation with the unexpected aroused; "experience" defined the knowledge gained from the repetition of such encounters. Aldrovandi, a product of the first wave of travel and exploration, linked curiosity to his encyclopedism, allowing both to define the quest for total knowledge. Kircher, nurtured in the missionary culture of the Jesuit order, expressed his curiosity through the desire to master the most ancient and exotic forms of knowledge. Aldrovandi hoped to know something of the Americas; Kircher made it his goal to become the leading expert on China and ancient Egypt. Aldrovandi struggled with the standard humanist languages: Latin, Greek, some Arabic, and Hebrew; Kircher added Chinese, Sanskrit, Aramaic, and Etruscan to the list and attempted to unlock the mysteries of the hieroglyphs. Both allowed curiosity to guide them in their endeavors. Museums were fabricated out of the emerging dialectic between authority and curiosity, reverence for the wisdom of the past and excitement about the possibilities of the present. In his *Advancement of Learning* (1605), Francis Bacon defined knowledge as "a couch, whereupon to rest a searching and restless spirit." The museum was the place in which the majority of "searching and restless spirits" congregated from the late sixteenth century onward. In the museum, naturalists could imagine nothing less than complete mastery of all the things of the world, and it was to this end that they strove.

Sixteenth- and seventeenth-century naturalists shared several common tendencies. They revered authority and subsumed their philosophical speculations within a highly Christianized framework. In contrast to their medieval predecessors, they perceived the encyclopedia of knowledge to be infinitely permeable, open rather than closed to multiple influences, discontinuous rather than continuous. They also perceived nature to be a text. Reading the "book of nature" was one of the primary activities for early modern naturalists. Collecting was an activity that contributed to the reactivation and redefinition of the metaphor of the book. Possessing nature was a process that paralleled the humanists' possession of the wisdom of the ancients. In the late fifteenth century, Nicholas of Cusa compared the possession of nature to Petrarch's possession of certain Greek codices. While ignorance of Greek prevented Petrarch from deciphering their meaning, his sympathy toward their content gave his ownership a certain value. Similarly, naturalists hoped that their possession of nature eventually would precipitate an understanding of her contents.

By the late sixteenth century, the timidness of the first humanists toward the paired books of nature and learning had been replaced with a new confidence. Emboldened by their ability to reactivate the languages of ancient philosophy, solving Petrarch's philological problem, naturalists used their humanist training to decipher the language of nature. . . .

. . . Nature was no longer a text for obdurate Aristotelians such as Aldrovandi, Kircher, and Bonanni, but instead revealed herself to naturalists who had absorbed the lessons of Bacon and Galileo. The possession of nature no longer refined and amplified the Aristotelian program. It could only undermine and ultimately destroy it.

While differing greatly on the nature and meaning of the contents, sixteenth- and seventeenth-century naturalists imagined the "book of nature" to be a text whose significance did not exceed their grasp. Possessing nature materially grounded this metaphor, just as it made many other aspects of natural philosophy visibly apparent. Searching for ways to come to terms with a shifting and unstable field of knowledge, the study of nature, collectors made the museum a "paradigmatic" space in which to philosophize. . . .

Sara Schechner Genuth

Comets, Popular Culture, and the Birth of Modern Cosmology, 1997

Sara Genuth's encyclopedic study of ideas about comets during the Middle Ages and early modern times includes excursions into the beliefs of both the lower and upper classes. In this selection, she argues that although Newton and the astronomer Edmond Halley may have denied that the appearance of comets could be used to predict earthly events, they retained the view that comets were both signs and causes of terrestrial and celestial happenings. Newton believed that comets had a teleological function. They were agents used by God to restore vital moisture to the heavens, and they were witnesses to God's benevolence towards humanity.

Chapter VII: Comets, Transmutations, and World Reform in Newton's Thought

In the late 1650s, a Lincolnshire schoolboy played a "philosophical" joke on his neighbors in Grantham:

> *He first made lanterns of paper crimpled, which he used to go to school by, in winter mornings, with a candle, and tied them to the tails of the kites in a dark night, which at first affrighted the country people exceedingly, thinking they were comets.*

That boy was Isaac Newton (1642–1727), and his artificial comet "caus'd not a little discourse on market days, among the country people, when over their mugs of ale."

Sara Schechner Genuth, *Comets, Popular Culture, and the Birth of Modern Cosmology* (Princeton: Princeton University Press, 1997). © 1997 Princeton University Press. Reprinted by permission of Princeton University Press. Excerpt from "Ode to Newton," trans. Leon J. Richardson, in *Isaac Newton, Mathematical Principles of Natural Philosophy and his System of the World,* Florian Cajori, ed. Edited/translated by Andrew Motte. (Berkeley and Los Angeles: University of California Press, 1962). Copyright © 1934 and 1962 Regents of the University of California. Reprinted with permission.

We tend to think of Newton as living a life beyond the grasp of popular culture, but his kite-flying escapades tell us otherwise. Newton was a provincial boy, but his upbringing enabled him to engage in high and low activities. On one hand, he came from yeoman stock. His father was a prosperous husbandman who inherited the manor of Woolsthorpe, which had been purchased by Newton's grandfather. Although lord of the manor, Newton's father could not sign his own name, and his relatives were all illiterate. Their lives revolved around their sheep, cattle, and corn. Newton's mother, on the other hand, was the daughter of a gentleman and sister to an Anglican clergyman educated at Cambridge. She was barely literate. As it turned out, Newton's father died before he was born, and he was raised by his mother's family, who expected him to have at least a basic education. At age twelve, he was sent to grammar school in Grantham, where he lodged with an apothecary. During this period, he read books, built sundials and mechanical contrivances, and learned about the composition of medicines. The apothecary's house stood on the High Street, next to an inn, exposing Newton to the popular culture of the village. He took advantage of popular beliefs when he used his artificial comets to tease his neighbors. . . .

Newton, therefore, was no stranger to popular culture or comet lore, even though his kite prank suggests that he viewed certain folk beliefs with detached interest. Although it would be presumptuous to say that Newton consciously rehabilitated folk beliefs in his physical studies of comets, they were nevertheless principal players. . . .

Celestial Mechanics of Comets

In the field of cometography, Newton is best known for showing that comets were members of the solar system. "I am out in my judgment," he wrote, "if they are not a sort of planets revolving in orbits returning into themselves with a continual motion." This remark led off Newton's masterful analysis of comets at the close of Book III of the *Principia*. This discussion was no mere afterthought. Newton's fascination with comets was lifelong. As a Cambridge scholar, Newton "sate up so often long in the year 1664 to observe a comet that appeared then, that he found himself much disordered," he later remembered. . . . Sixty years later, comets still held his interest when he had a famous fireside chat with John Conduitt, his nephew-in-law. . . .

In early November of 1680, a comet appeared before sunrise and was sighted heading toward the sun until the end of the month. In mid-December, another comet appeared in the evening sky, heading away from the sun. Its tail was immense, growing to be over seventy degrees long. . . .[T]his comet stunned the common folk, who were showered with dire predictions about its political import. In England, it arrived on the heels of the Popish Plot and during the Exclusion Crisis, when paranoia about Catholics' coming to power reached a peak.

The comet not only interested radical pamphleteers but also commanded the attention of astronomers. Newton observed it from December until March; kept a log of its tail; read works by Robert Hooke, Johann Hevelius, and Pierre Petit; and corresponded with John Flamsteed, the astronomer royal. . . . Flamsteed proposed that the comets observed in November and December of 1680 were not two comets but rather one comet traveling in a highly bent line. . . . Newton . . . opposed Flamsteed's claim that the comet had turned in front of the sun. "To make ye Comets of November & December but one is to make that one paradoxical," he told Flamsteed as late as April 1681.

Although Newton had already solved the dynamical problem of a planet circling the sun, in 1681 he did not apply the same method to these comets. He had not yet formulated his theory of universal gravitation. Like most astronomers, he saw comets as bodies foreign to the solar system and not governed by its laws. Comets were transient bodies. They moved in straight lines. In 1681, he attempted to find a rectilinear path for each comet moving at a uniform velocity. The results were not convincing. . . . Newton began to question the standard theory. . . . In the spring of 1681, Newton began a letter to Flamsteed in which he discussed the nonlinear path a comet would describe under the influence of a magnetic force seated in the sun. The sun would pull the comet toward itself, but the comet's centrifugal force would overpower the attraction, carry the comet around the sun, and enable it to escape. Clearly, Newton had not yet fully articulated the theory that celestial motions were due to the combination of centripetal force and inertial motion in a straight line, but we see that he had privately begun to treat comets like the planets. It apparently was his first inclination to use the familiar if outmoded model that he had abandoned only recently for the planets, but it was a planetary model nonetheless. Newton had taken a step toward his mature cosmological theory. But he suppressed this passage from the letter he eventually sent to Flamsteed. Publicly, he dug in his heels, insisting that the comets of November and December were distinct.

Sometime between the spring of 1681 and the autumn of 1684, Newton changed his mind. As stubbornly as he had opposed Flamsteed's premise, he was now convinced that a single comet in November and December 1680 had rounded the sun in a tight, hairpin turn. Gravity, not magnetism, was the attractive force that had turned this comet from its rectilinear path. In a set of propositions composed before 1683, Newton remarked that all comets moved in curved paths, and some, like the planets, moved in closed orbits. . . . In *De motu*, a tract concerned with orbital mechanics, he outlined his theory of universal gravitation, asserting that the motions of comets and planets were governed by the same laws. *De motu* laid the groundwork for the *Principia*, which was published three years later. As the revolutionary theory took shape, the comet of 1680–1681 became an important test case. . . . [By 1685 Newton planned] "to determin ye lines described by ye Comets of 1664 & 1680 according to ye principles of motion observed by ye Planets." . . .

Much was invested in the comet theory. Not only did Newton wish to prove his comet theory by phenomena—that is, by showing that observations agreed with computed orbital positions—but he also took pride in the fact that the success of the comet theory was seen to confirm his theory of universal gravitation. . . .

But even more was at stake. In arguments from design, comet orbits were called upon to testify. Comets traveled about the sun in highly eccentric orbits inclined every which way to the ecliptic. This arrangement was not due to blind fate. Comets were carried quickly through the planetary regions with little time to disturb the motions of planets or other comets. At aphelion, where a comet's slow velocity and weak attraction to the sun might render it easily disturbed by other comets, the vast distance separating all comets from one another prevented disruptive interactions between them. "Thus we always find, that what has, at first sight, the appearance of irregularity and confusion in nature, is discovered, on further enquiry, to be the best contrivance and the most wise conduct," reported Colin Maclaurin. Wise conduct, indeed, for Newton perceived the behavior of comets to be goal-directed. During the course of his career, Newton observed again and again that comets were divine agents working to restore order in the cosmos. This chapter will spell out the manifold ways that celestial mechanics and natural philosophy reinforced and developed this belief. The bottom line, however, was Newton's faith in his theory's role in reestablishing true religion in an age of dangerous politics; and the first inkling appeared in a draft of the *Principia*.

Pristine Truths and Political Corruption

By showing comets to be a sort of planet, Newton felt that he was returning comets to their rightful place in the heavens in accordance with ancient religion and Chaldaean astronomy. Although Newton never went public with this view, the strength of his conviction is apparent in the many surviving philosophical manuscripts in which he expressed it. Of note is a suppressed draft for the third book of the *Principia*, written in the autumn of 1685 and known as "The System of the World." Here Newton argued that ancient philosophers had understood: (1) the universe to be heliocentric; (2) comets to be a sort of planet traveling in eccentric orbits; and (3) celestial space to be devoid of matter (just as Newton's own system required). According to Newton, the ancients had encoded these doctrines in the design of their temples, at whose hearts perpetual fires burned. Within these buildings, sacred rites were meant to teach people that the natural world was the true temple of God. Unfortunately, true religion had been corrupted, and with it natural philosophy. "When the ancient philosophy began to decline," Newton wrote, Eudoxus and others had introduced the "whim of solid orbs." Comets were "thrust down below the Moon," where they epistemologically remained until recent work shattered the fictitious orbs and restored comets to their rightful place among the planets. . . . Newton's allegation that his doctrine had been anticipated by ancient mystical philosophers had theological and political ramifications.

To understand these ramifications, we must first recognize that the ideas in these philosophical extracts were connected to those in unpublished theological manuscripts: most notably, the "Philosophical Origins of Gentile Theology," begun by Newton in 1683–1684 and revised until the second decade of the eighteenth century. In this text, Newton argued for the existence of a pristine natural-philosophical religion, which long ago had degenerated and spawned erroneous astronomical precepts and polytheistic customs. One of the early perversions had been the assignment of a soul to each solid heavenly sphere and the identification of the soul with the spirit of a dead hero or monarch. Newton reasoned that "the old heathens first commemorated their dead men then admired them, afterwards adored them as Gods then praised them . . . so as to make them Gods celestial." This was an idolatrous practice, for it attributed false powers to natural objects; it led to the worship of heavenly bodies and the veneration of relics associated with the deceased. Newton had already begun to develop this theme at the time of the Popish Plot, when he attacked "monstrous Legends, fals miracles, veneration of reliques, charmes, ye doctrine of Ghosts or Daemons, & their intercession invocation & worship & such other heathen superstitions" that were brought into the Catholic Church by "that crafty politician Athanasius." These idolatrous superstitions were particularly heinous insofar as corrupt individuals exploited natural signs in order to win allegiance or secure power. Newton explained that when the ancients mistook stars for deities, astrology and gentile theology reinforced each other. Cunning philosopher-priests promoted the study of the stars as a way to enhance their prestige. By claiming the right to interpret celestial signs, they had the means to control the lives of their followers. Monarchs joined diviners in basing their power on this corrupt view of nature. Kings "called ye stars & elements by their names & caused them to be honoured with such solemnities & pompous ceremonies as soon created in the people a superstition towards them as Gods & by consequence a veneration of ye whole race of kings as descended from these Deities." Princes then claimed to rule by divine right, and they "erect[ed] such a worship & such a priesthood as might awe the blinded & seduced people into such an obedience as they desired." For Newton, divine-right monarchy and Catholicism were both to be condemned for institutionalizing distorted views of nature as a means to grab and keep power. Astrology, the handmaiden to idolatrous politicking, was to be condemned along with them. The cure for these corruptions, Newton implied, was to restore Chaldaean cosmology. If comets were given free reign, they would sweep away all vestiges of the theory of solid spheres and with it the cult of priestcraft and divine-right politics.

These manuscripts . . . suggest Newton's frame of mind as he developed his comet theory. Newton wrote many of these papers during the period of the Popish Plot, the Exclusion Crisis, and the accession of the Catholic James II (1685), and the intensity of his writing suggests that he was worried about the Catholic "threat" and the doctrine of divine right. This view is supported by Newton's actions on two occasions. First, in the spring of 1687, Newton was upset about the king's efforts to catholicize Cambridge University; and he was among those to appear before the Court of Ecclesiastical Commission in order to defend the university's noncompliance with a royal mandate that would have admitted a Benedictine monk to the degree of master of arts. Second, in January 1689, after William had landed and James had fled, Newton was elected to represent the university in the parliamentary assembly convened to settle the terms of the Glorious Revolution.

In their interconnectedness, Newton's political activities and astronomical projects likely brought him into contact with popular beliefs about comets. I have already mentioned Newton's direct contact with popular culture. Here we have further evidence—albeit circumstantial—of his contact with comet lore. Newton's political concerns reinforced his cometary work in a way that suggests his familiarity with English propaganda capitalizing on recent comets and viewing them as portents of the Stuart Restoration, the Popish Plot, the accession of James II, or the Second Coming. Such propaganda was disseminated by both the court and its adversaries, by both high and low members of society. Although Newton did not directly refer to the modern tracts, his interpretation of ancient texts shows that he was sensitive to the existence of this sort of astrological politicking, especially when carried out from the top down. Indeed, his criticism of rulers' deifying their ancestors in order to aggrandize themselves brings to mind a well-known case of comet lore used for political gain: the case of Augustus and the comet of 44 B.C. Since Augustus was the chief symbol of the restored Stuart monarchy, this historical episode had immediate relevance for Newton and deserves a closer look.

Roman emperors encouraged the belief that the souls of their dead predecessors had become stars in the heavens. They gave the title "divus" (meaning "divine") to the deceased emperors and had them worshiped in temples. In this way, the political power of the current emperor was strengthened by the apotheosis of the former. Augustus appreciated this when a comet appeared soon after the death of Julius Caesar (44 B.C.). As Caesar's successor, Augustus exploited the common view that Caesar's soul had been received among the gods, and used the comet to legitimate the power of the Julian line.

This famous story—undoubtedly known to Newton—was not simply of antiquarian interest, for Augustan politics were alive and well in Restoration England. Just as Augustus had laid claim to the Julian comet, which appeared at the start of his rule, so Charles II took advantage of a star or comet that purportedly had blazed at midday on the occasion of his birth. It was a sign, royalists said, that Charles ruled by divine right. The Augustan message was reinforced in the pageantry of the coronation

(1661), where allusions to ancient Rome abounded. Triumphal arches greeted the king's cavalcade as it traveled from the Tower to Whitehall. On the first arch were the words "ADVENTUS AUG[USTI]," identifying Charles II as a new Augustus. Statues of James I and Charles I flanked a tableau of Charles II driving Usurpation into the jaws of Hell. The monarchs were given the epithets "DIVO JACOBO" and "DIVO CAROLO" in emulation of the Roman practice and in affirmation of the view that Charles II ruled Britain by the grace of his divine ancestors. When Charles II died in 1685, staunch supporters of the Stuart line in turn apotheosized him in order to legitimate his brother's reign. The dead monarch now ruled in the kingdom of heaven, they said, but his godlike perfection had been passed on to his successor, James II. It was time to "pay Religious Worship" to Charles by giving political allegiance to James.

Newton did not support the rule of James II, and he opposed Anglo-Augustan politics. Such politicking had its roots in ancient Rome and in Augustus's exploitation of the comet of 44 B.C. Newton knew of this comet; he referred to it in the *Principia* and praised Halley for showing it to be the same as the 1680 comet. In carrying out his program to re-instate comets in the heavens, Newton felt that he was rescuing comets from the hands of priests, astrologers, and rulers like Augustus, Charles, or James, who wrongly attributed God's powers to these bodies and con-nivingly used the apparitions to legitimate their own authority. . . .

In professing this view, Newton, . . . revealed how much he scorned vulgar astrology, but this does not mean that Newton was uninfluenced by popular tenets concerning comets. This is apparent even in "The System of the World," where after his appeal for the restoration of Chaldaean cosmology, Newton described the splendor of comet tails in language that would have done any prodigy book proud. . . . "In the year 1527, Aug. 11. about four in the morning," he wrote, "*there was seen almost throughout Europe*, a terrible Comet in *Leo*, which continued flaming an hour and a quarter every day. It rose from the east, and ascended to the south and west to a *prodigious length*. It was most conspicuous to the north, and *its cloud (that is its tail) was very terrible; having, according to the fancies of the vulgar, the form of an arm a little bent, holding a sword of a vast magnitude.*" Newton confided "*a rumour, that there appeared about Sun rising a bright beam*" in 1618; and he took note of a wondrous comet in 1668, whose "head was small, and scarcely discernible, but its tail extremely bright and refulgent, so that *the reflexion of it from the sea was easily seen by those who stood upon the shore.*" These are the kinds of phrases one finds in prognosticative pamphlets, prodigy books, folk-tales, and broadsides. To find them in the 1685 draft of Book III of the *Principia* is most fascinating. To learn that this language is excised from the published version (even though some references remain) is revealing. It tells us that between 1685 and 1687, Newton was in the process of submerging comet lore into his astrophysics.

I say submerge, because Newton did not eradicate comet lore. Newton's analysis of cometary orbits repeatedly drew his attention to their divine offices. According to David Gregory, Newton remarked that "the great eccentricity in Comets in directions both different from and contrary to the planets indicates a divine hand: and implies that Comets are destined for a use other than that of the planets." What was this special use? Or, as Newton himself raised the question, 'To what end were comets framed?" I shall argue that the ends Newton proposed differed little from the popular opinions retailed in vulgar street literature or the traditional beliefs codified in learned texts.

Transmutations and Perpetual Interchange

While comet lore guided Newton in developing a teleological framework, matter theory explained how comets could fulfill their divine ends. Therefore, my account begins with Newton's views on the transmutation of matter. In the 1687 *Principia,* Newton stated that any body could be transformed into another, and he held this doctrine throughout his career. . . .

A premise of this chemical philosophy was the unity of matter, the existence of one universal substrate that could be wrought by nature into a plurality of forms. In 1675, Newton believed this catholic matter to be an aether, and he confided to Henry Oldenburg that "perhaps the whole frame of Nature may be nothing but aether condensed by a fermental principle." This aether was extremely rarefied, subtle, and elastic. . . . [It contained] a vital aerial spirit requisite for conserving flame and vital motions. In Newton's aethereal cosmology, matter naturally circulated between the heavens and earth. . . .

By 1687, however, Newton had cleared this aether from the heavenly spaces, fearful that it would impede the planets in their revolutions. He began to envision a cosmos filled with forces but devoid of much matter. To fill the aether's chemical role, Newton endorsed a watery fluid as a universal substrate. . . .

The transmutation of water into manifold forms of gross matter was apparently a unidirectional process. Water transmuted was water lost. . . . Without an extraterrestrial source of fluid, all planetary activity would cease. The magnificent earth would decay. This was not the case with the aethereal transmutations in Newton's earlier essays. Those transmutations were reversible, cyclical, and perpetual. Since Newton still believed that a cosmic circulation and transmutation of primal matter was requisite for the well-being of the cosmos, he looked for a new source of celestial nourishment. In the early 1680s, he had made extracts of Flamsteed's letters concerning the watery surfaces of comets, and as he prepared his *Principia*, he became impressed by the tenuous vapor tails of comets, which pointed away from the sun. . . . If comet tails did mix with the atmosphere, then they could supply the vital fluid the system required.

> . . . *For as seas are absolutely necessary to the constitution of our earth, . . . for watering of the earth, and for the production and nourishment of vegetables; . . . so for the conservation of the seas, and fluids of the planets, comets seem to be required, that, from their exhalations and vapors condensed, the wastes of the planetary fluids spent upon vegetation and putrefaction, and converted into dry earth, may be continually supplied and made up.*

Moreover, Newton suspected "that it is chiefly from the comets that spirit comes, which is indeed the smallest but the most subtle and useful part of our air, and so much required to sustain the life of all things with us." . . .

In this way, a transmutation chain that began with comet tails ended in the concoction of animals, vegetables, and minerals. "Thus comes about the perpetual interchange of all things," Newton concluded, "and the Lord of all alone remains immutable, who by his own counsel and will disposes (through Ministers) all things in the best order."

In fact, the "interchange of all things" described in the 1687 *Principia* was far from perpetual and complete. Nothing refueled the sun or stars. As these bodies wasted away, comet tails increased the solid bulk of the planets. Consequently, the solar system would gradually become unbalanced. In the 1706 *Optice*, Newton further stressed that the mutual attraction of planets and comets would cause increasing perturbations in their respective orbits. Moreover, the quantity of motion in the world was evidently decreasing. Nature was unwinding and decaying without divine intervention. God's providence was essential to conserve motion and reform the cosmic system.

For many years, Newton turned this problem of the unbalanced world over in his mind. . . .

Newton informed readers of the 1713 edition of the *Principia* that God used comets to conserve the stellar bodies. Orbital calculations positioned the 1680 comet exceedingly close to the sun at perihelion. Indeed, the comet seemed to have passed through the solar atmosphere, where its motion would have been resisted and retarded. Every subsequent passage through the solar atmosphere would slow it further. Attractions by other comets would retard it also. Eventually, it would descend into the sun and would then rekindle that wasting star.

> *So fixed stars, that have been gradually wasted by the light and vapors emitted from them for a long time, may be recruited by comets that fall upon them; and from this fresh supply of new fuel those old stars, acquiring new splendor, may pass for new stars.*

In 1713, Newton thus made public his belief that comets replenished the sun and stars, as well as the planets. Following the laws of universal gravitation, comets swept through the solar system with their beneficent supplies of a watery vapor and vital spirit. In this way, blazing stars helped to renovate the cosmos and preserve world order. . . .

"Revolutions in the Heavenly Bodies"

. . . From biblical sources, Newton was convinced that the physical state of the world paralleled the moral history of mankind. This conviction opened the door to cosmogonic speculations premised on Scripture and natural philosophy. Like Burnet, Newton attempted to provide physical accounts of the Creation, the Deluge, the Conflagration, and the rise of the newly purged earth after the Apocalypse; but as he warned Richard Bentley in 1693, "Ye growth of new systems out of old ones without ye mediation of a divine power seems to me apparently absurd." What Newton's theory needed was a physical agent that operated routinely and nonmiraculously yet was capable of causing catastrophic change by divine design. In comets, he found what he required. . . .

Moreover, Newton suggested a mechanism that made possible the succession of worlds predicted in Scripture. Thirty years earlier, Gregory had reported Newton's disclosure that "the Satellites of Jupiter and Saturn can take the places of the Earth, Venus, Mars if they are destroyed, and be held in reserve for a new Creation." Newton's conversation with Conduitt clarified how a satellite could become a planet fit for a new creation. Indeed, in this transformation, comets had dual roles. By naturally amassing the vapors from comet tails, the sun, stars, and even planets, a satellite grew to planetary proportions. Moreover, as Gregory explained, a close-approaching comet not only could alter the orbit and period of a planet but "may also by its Attraction so disturb the Satellite, as to make it leave its Primary Planet, and itself become a Primary Planet about the Sun." With the creation of new worlds explained, Newton explored how the present world would end. At first, he considered the impact of a comet. In 1703, Gregory noted, "The Comet whose Orbit Mr Newton determins may sometime impinge on the Earth. Origen relates the manner of destroying the Worlds by one falling on another." . . . But in the end, Newton found destruction by fire to be more in line with Scripture. In 1725, he told Conduitt that when a comet fell into the sun, the newly stoked flames would sear the earth. In fact, Newton determined that the sun-grazing comet of 1680 was designed for that very end. . . .

Newton regarded "these revolutions in the heavenly bodies" to be effected at the discretion of God. "He seemed to doubt whether there were not [i.e., suspect that there were] intelligent beings superior to us, who superintended these revolutions of the heavenly bodies, by the direction of the Supreme Being." The earth and its inhabitants testified that the world had previously undergone dramatic reformations wrought by providentially directed comets for divine ends. No doubt it would undergo reformations in the future. . . .

Comets, Teleology, and Newton's Appropriation of Comet Lore

. . . Newton's views on the teleological design of comets has much in common with the traditional comet lore his celestial mechanics has been said to undermine. On the most general level, folk wisdom held that comets augured good as well as bad. For Newton, comets sustained life as well as destroyed worlds. The popular press depicted comets as monsters. For Newton, comets continued to demonstrate God's will. Religious traditions held comets to be signs of Noah's Flood, the birth of Jesus, the Protestant Reformation, and the Day of Judgment. Newton agreed that God sent comets to herald the punishment of the wicked, vindication of the elect, and reform of the world. Comets initiated the mutations recorded or prophesied in Scripture. They were key players in the beginning, deluge, and end of the world. In comparing Newton's comet theory to comet lore, we find parallels on more specific tenets too: Folklore taught that comets announced the deaths of princes, plague, poor weather, and bad crops. For Newton, comets affected health, weather, and agriculture, but in a positive way, being "absolutely necessary for [the] watering of the earth, and for the production and nourishment of vegetables." Broadsides and pamphlets linked comets to civil disorder, social upheaval, and rebellion. Newton hinted that there was "a sort of revolution in the heavenly bodies" in which comets overturned the order of the solar system and set up new planetary hierarchies. Throughout Europe, clergymen preached that comets were sent by God to urge sinners to awake and repent; and in England, they said that comets presaged the downfall of Catholicism. For Newton, an understanding of the true nature of comets would lead people back to the principles of true religion and away from priestcraft.

By now it should be abundantly clear that Newton did not strip away the religious, political, and agricultural associations of comets but rather appropriated popular beliefs. Although comets were depicted as natural bodies following routine courses throughout the heavens, they remained apparitions of God's design. God used comets as a natural means to constitute, conserve, and renovate the cosmos. Even though Newton believed that his comet theory would overturn the kind of predictions found in street literature, there were only two tenets of his theory that truly differentiated it from the traditional lore: (1) that comets acted exclusively in a global theater; and (2) that laws of motion could be used to determine which comets were likely to wreck the earth. But this information was to be reserved for the scientific elite, rather than the pamphlet prognosticators, even though both desired to see the moral order reflected in the natural world. . . .

We will never know if Newton consciously appropriated these ideas. We do know, however, that folklore was perceived by some early modern scholars to consist of degraded ancient knowledge. Newton mined ancient philosophical texts for veins of pristine wisdom compatible with Scripture. It may be that he thought he had found kernels of truth to be preserved in popular culture as well. If that is the case, Book III of the *Principia* can be read as a text in the tradition of books of errors, for here Newton subtly separated the wheat from the chaff and so corrected popular beliefs about comets. . . .

Margaret Cavendish. The writer is dressed in neo-classical style to emphasize her connection with ancient philosophy. (*Private Collection/Bridgeman Art Library*)

V Did Women Have a Scientific Revolution?

The History of Science has broadened to include craftsmen, magicians, university professors, Puritans and Catholics, and even the common people, but many of the historians analyzing the broader context of the Scientific Revolution still cling to one tenet of the subject's traditional narrative: There are no women. Modern feminist historians refuse to accept this exclusion. They recognize that women in the sixteenth and seventeenth centuries were relegated to a largely subservient position in a patriarchal society, but nevertheless argue that women played a role in both the production of knowledge and its content.

The relationship of gender to science during the Scientific Revolution has been explored most vividly and controversially by Carolyn Merchant. The Merchant Thesis argues that the Scientific Revolution drove the female out of nature, which had long been associated with that sex. Increasingly in the seventeenth century, women and nature were viewed as disorderly, and in need of control. Nature, like women, had to be compelled to obey male rational rule; culture (male) had to triumph over nature (female). The mechanistic natural philosophy eliminated all living and female forces from nature, rendering it inert and exploitable. Hence, Merchant argues, science in its maxims and epistemology expressed the misogyny of early modern society. The progressiveness of science thereby becomes problematic—at least from the point of view of those sensitive to gender issues.

Other recent attempts to understand the relationship of gender to the history of science concentrate on reintroducing women into the historical story. This kind of historiographical account traces the role particular women have played in the development of science. Thus, while most traditional historians of science, perhaps blinded by their own preconceptions, do not recognize women scientists or natural philosophers, that does not mean such women did not exist. Margaret Alic's *Hypatia's Heritage: A History of Women in Science from Antiquity through the Nineteenth Century* (1986) is emblematic of this approach, shared by and large in the work of Londa Schiebinger—although Schiebinger's account broadens the participation of women by broadening the definition of scientist.

My article also seeks to include women—or at least one woman, Margaret Cavendish, Duchess of Newcastle—in the cast of characters belonging to the Scientific Revolution. Indeed, Cavendish's most important natural philosophical work has recently been published in the Cambridge Texts in the History of Philosophy series, a sign that she has been added to the traditional canon. Like Merchant, I am interested in the role of gender in the articulation of natural philosophical ideas. I examine the question of whether Cavendish's science reflected "female" sensibilities, which gave a female Nature a larger role in her system, and I argue that the skepticism towards authority in early modern science could be used to justify a critique of traditional gender roles.

Even in the traditional historiography of the History of Science, the role of aristocratic women as patrons of learning—if not producers of knowledge—has been recognized, as well as their increasing importance as audiences and disseminators of the new science in the salons of the seventeenth and eighteenth centuries. Schiebinger reflects the new interest in the sites of intellectual activity, arguing that it was not inevitable that women would be excluded from the formal scientific institutions created in the seventeenth century. Nevertheless, women were, and so Schiebinger—reflecting historiographical traditions from Zilsel to Findlen—broadens the arena of scientific activity in order to reconceptualize women's roles in science. She shows that women of the lower classes played an important role not only in the social space of the craft guilds, but also as participants in the technical culture of artisans. Once the History of Science broadens its parameters, women are seen to play a more important role. As much as men may have wanted to eliminate the female from their science and their associations, they still lived in a world with women.

Carolyn Merchant

The Death of Nature: Women, Ecology and the Scientific Revolution, 1980

Carolyn Merchant draws on an abundance of literary and nonliterary sources to support her argument that nature and the female were connected in the worldview of medieval and early modern Europeans. The disorder in the heavens revealed by the telescope, and the disorder in the world revealed by the discoveries of the new world, resulted in an effort to control the physical world, just as disorderly women, personified by the witch, needed to be controlled in the social world. Both needed to be rendered passive and inert. Merchant argues that Francis Bacon elaborated an epistemology that implicitly transferred the inquisitional techniques used in the interrogation of witches to the discovery of nature's secrets.

Dominion over Nature

Disorderly, active nature was soon forced to submit to the questions and experimental techniques of the new science. Francis Bacon (1561–1626), a celebrated "father of modern science," transformed tendencies already extant in his own society into a total program advocating the control of

Carolyn Merchant, *The Death of Nature: Women, Ecology and the Scientific Revolution* (San Francisco: HarperSanFrancisco, 1980). Pages 164–172 from Chapter 7, Dominion over Nature. Copyright © 1980 by Carolyn Merchant. Reprinted by permission of HarperCollins Publishers, Inc.

nature for human benefit. Melding together a new philosophy based on natural magic as a technique for manipulating nature, the technologies of mining and metallurgy, the emerging concept of progress and a patriarchal structure of family and state, Bacon fashioned a new ethic sanctioning the exploitation of nature.

Bacon has been eulogized as the originator of the concept of the modern research institute, a philosopher of industrial science, the inspiration behind the Royal Society (1660), and as the founder of the inductive method by which all people can verify for themselves the truths of science by the reading of nature's book. But from the perspective of nature, women, and the lower orders of society emerges a less favorable image of Bacon and a critique of his program as ultimately benefiting the middle-class male entrepreneur. Bacon, of course, was not responsible for subsequent uses of his philosophy. But, because he was in an extremely influential social position and in touch with the important developments of his time, his language, style, nuance, and metaphor become a mirror reflecting his class perspective.

Sensitive to the same social transformations that had already begun to reduce women to psychic and reproductive resources, Bacon developed the power of language as political instrument in reducing female nature to a resource for economic production. Female imagery became a tool in adapting scientific knowledge and method to a new form of human power over nature. The "controversy over women" and the inquisition of witches—both present in Bacon's social milieu—permeated his description of nature and his metaphorical style and were instrumental in his transformation of the earth as a nurturing mother and womb of life into a source of secrets to be extracted for economic advance.

Bacon's roots can be found in middle-class economic development and its progressive interests and values. His father was a middle-class employee of the queen, his mother a Calvinist whose Protestant values permeated his early home life. Bacon took steps to gain the favor of James I soon after the latter's ascent to the throne in 1603. He moved from "learned counsel" in 1603 to attorney general in 1613, privy councillor in 1616, lord keeper in 1617, and, finally, lord chancellor and Baron Verulam in 1618. His political objectives were to gain support for his program of the advancement of science and human learning and to upgrade his own status through an ambitious public career.

Bacon's mentor, James I, supported antifeminist and antiwitchcraft legislation. During the "controversy over women," females had challenged traditional modes of dress considered as appropriate to their place in society. In Holland, for example, young women were criticized for wearing men's hats with high crowns. In England, the title page of a work called *Hic-Mulier or The Man–Woman* (1620) showed a woman in a barber's chair having her hair clipped short, while her companion outfitted herself in a man's plumed hat. In an attempt to keep women in their place in the world's order, King James in that same year enlisted the aid of the clergy in preventing females from looking and dressing in masculine fashions: "The Bishop of London had express commandment from the king to will [the clergy] to inveigh vehemently against the insolence of our women, and their wearing of broad-brimmed hats, pointed doublets, their hair cut short or shorn, and some of them [with] stilettos or poinards . . . *the truth is the world is very much out of order.*" (Italics added.)

In 1616, Mrs. Turner, accomplice in the murder of Sir Thomas Overbury, had been sent to the gallows by James wearing the yellow, starched ruffs she had brought into vogue and that he detested. As the king's attorney general, Bacon participated in the controversy, since it was his role to bring charges for the poisoning of Overbury against the Countess of Somerset. Overbury had publicly (through a poem, "The Wife") opposed the romance between his close friend, subsequently Earl of Somerset, and the countess. The perfect wife, he said, was one who combined goodness, virtue, intelligence, and common sense but not too much "learning and pregnant wit," for "Books are a part of man's prerogative." Angered by his insults, and fearful of his influence, the countess contrived to poison Overbury through the help of a physician's widow, Mrs. Turner, and an apothecary named Franklin.

Bacon prepared two versions of his charge against the countess, one should she confess, the other should she plead not guilty. At the packed trial, at which some places sold for £10–50, the countess confessed, but was spared. Mrs. Turner, however, was convicted and sent to the gallows, and "as she was the person who had brought yellow starched ruffs into vogue, [it was decreed that] she should be hanged in that dress, that the same might end in shame and detestation."

The Overbury case increased interest in the popular controversy over women and resulted in the publication of several editions of Overbury's poem and a number of reactions to the murder; for example, "A Secret Second Husband for Sir Thomas Overburies' Wife, Now a Matchless Widow" (1616) and Thomas Tuke's "A Treatise Against Painting and

Tincturing of Men and Women: Against Murder and Poysoning: Pride and Ambition" (1616).

Bacon was also well aware of the witch trials taking place all over Europe and in particular in England during the early seventeenth century. His sovereign, while still James VI of Scotland, had written a book entitled *Daemonologie* (1597). In 1603, the first year of his English reign, James I replaced the milder witch laws of Elizabeth I, which evoked the death penalty only for killing by witchcraft, with a law that condemned to death all practitioners.

It was in the 1612 trials of the Lancashire witches of the Pendle Forest that the sexual aspects of witch trials first appeared in England. The source of the women's confessions of fornication with the devil was a Roman Catholic priest who had emigrated from the Continent and planted the story in the mouths of accused women who had recently rejected Catholicism.

These social events influenced Bacon's philosophy and literary style. Much of the imagery he used in delineating his new scientific objectives and methods derives from the courtroom, and, because it treats nature as a female to be tortured through mechanical inventions, strongly suggests the interrogations of the witch trials and the mechanical devices used to torture witches. In a relevant passage, Bacon stated that the method by which nature's secrets might be discovered consisted in investigating the secrets of witchcraft by inquisition, referring to the example of James I:

> *For you have but to follow and as it were hound nature in her wanderings, and you will be able when you like to lead and drive her afterward to the same place again.* Neither am I of opinion in this history of marvels that superstitious narrative of *sorceries, witchcrafts, charms,* dreams, divinations, and the like, where there is an assurance and clear evidence of the fact, should be altogether excluded. . . . howsoever the use and practice of such arts is to be condemned, yet from the speculation and consideration of them . . . a useful light may be gained, not only for a true judgment of the offenses of persons charged with such practices, *but likewise for the further disclosing of the secrets of nature. Neither ought a man to make scruple of entering and penetrating into these holes and corners, when the inquisition of truth is his whole object — as your majesty has shown in your own example.* (Italics added.)

The strong sexual implications of the last sentence can be interpreted in the light of the investigation of the supposed sexual crimes and practices of witches. In another example, he compared the interrogation of courtroom witnesses to the inquisition of nature: "I mean (according to the practice in civil causes) in this great plea or suit granted by the divine favor and providence (whereby the human race seeks to recover its right over nature) to *examine nature herself* and the arts upon interrogatories." Bacon pressed the idea further with an analogy to the torture chamber: "For like as a man's disposition is never well known or proved till he be crossed, nor Proteus ever changed shapes till he was *straitened* and *held fast*, so nature exhibits herself more clearly under the *trials* and *vexations* of art [mechanical devices] than when left to herself."

The new man of science must not think that the "inquisition of nature is in any part interdicted or forbidden." Nature must be "bound into service" and made a "slave," put "in constraint" and "molded" by the mechanical arts. The "searchers and spies of nature" are to discover her plots and secrets.

This method, so readily applicable when nature is denoted by the female gender, degraded and made possible the exploitation of the natural environment. As woman's womb had symbolically yielded to the forceps, so nature's womb harbored secrets that through technology could be wrested from her grasp for use in the improvement of the human condition:

> *There is therefore much ground for hoping that there are still laid up in the womb of nature many secrets of excellent use having no affinity or parallelism with anything that is now known . . . only by the method which we are now treating can they be speedily and suddenly and simultaneously presented and anticipated.*

Bacon transformed the magical tradition by calling on the need to dominate nature not for the sole benefit of the individual magician but for the good of the entire human race. Through vivid metaphor, he transformed the magus from nature's servant to its exploiter, and nature from a teacher to a slave. Bacon argued that it was the magician's error to consider art (technology) a mere "assistant to nature having the power to finish what nature has begun" and therefore to despair of ever "changing, transmuting, or fundamentally altering nature."

The natural magician saw himself as operating within the organic order of nature—he was a manipulator of parts within that system, bringing down the heavenly powers to the earthly shrine. Agrippa, however, had begun to explore the possibility of ascending the hierarchy to the point of cohabiting with God. Bacon extended this idea to include the recovery of the power over nature lost when Adam and Eve were expelled from paradise.

Due to the Fall from the Garden of Eden (caused by the temptation of a woman), the human race lost its "dominion over creation." Before the Fall, there was no need for power or dominion, because Adam and Eve had been made sovereign over all other creatures. In this state of dominion, mankind was "like unto God." While some, accepting God's punishment, had obeyed the medieval strictures against searching too deeply into God's secrets, Bacon turned the constraints into sanctions. Only by "digging further and further into the mine of natural knowledge" could mankind recover that lost dominion. In this way, "the narrow limits of man's dominion over the universe" could be stretched "to their promised bounds."

Although a female's inquisitiveness may have caused man's fall from his God-given dominion, the relentless interrogation of another female, nature, could be used to regain it. As he argued in *The Masculine Birth of Time*, "I am come in very truth leading to you nature with all her children to bind her to your service and make her your slave." "We have no right," he asserted, "to expect nature to come to us." Instead, "Nature must be taken by the fore-lock, being bald behind." Delay and subtle argument "permit one only to clutch at nature, never to lay hold of her and capture her."

Nature existed in three states—at liberty, in error, or in bondage:

> *She is either free and follows her ordinary course of development as in the heavens, in the animal and vegetable creation, and in the general array of the universe; or she is driven out of her ordinary course by the perverseness, insolence, and forwardness of matter and violence of impediments, as in the case of monsters; or lastly, she is put in constraint, molded, and made as it were new by art and the hand of man; as in things artificial.*

The first instance was the view of nature as immanent self-development, the nature naturing herself of the Aristotelians. This was the organic view of nature as a living, growing, self-actualizing being. The second state was necessary to explain the malfunctions and monstrosities that frequently appeared and that could not have been caused by God or another higher power acting on his instruction. Since monstrosities could not be explained by the action of form or spirit, they had to be the result of matter acting perversely. Matter in Plato's *Timaeus* was recalcitrant and had to be forcefully shaped by the demiurge. Bacon frequently described matter in female imagery, as a "common harlot." Matter is not devoid of an appetite and inclination to dissolve the world and fall back into the old Chaos." It therefore must be "restrained and kept in order by the prevailing concord of things." "The vexations of art are certainly as the bonds and handcuffs of Proteus, which betray the ultimate struggles and efforts of matter."

The third instance was the case of art (techné)—man operating on nature to create something new and artificial. Here "nature takes orders from man and works under his authority." Miners and smiths should become the model for the new class of natural philosophers who would interrogate and alter nature. They had developed the two most important methods of wresting nature's secrets from her, "the one searching into the bowels of nature, the other shaping nature as on an anvil." "Why should we not divide natural philosophy into two parts, the mine and the furnace?" For "the truth of nature lies hid in certain deep mines and caves," within the earth's bosom. Bacon, like some of the practically minded alchemists, would "advise the studious to sell their books and build furnaces" and, "forsaking Minerva and the Muses as barren virgins, to rely upon Vulcan."

The new method of interrogation was not through abstract notions, but through the instruction of the understanding "that it may in very truth dissect nature." The instruments of the mind supply suggestions, those of the hand give motion and aid the work. "By art and the hand of man," nature can then be "forced out of her natural state and squeezed and molded." In this way, "human knowledge and human power meet as one."

Here, in bold sexual imagery, is the key feature of the modern experimental method—constraint of nature in the laboratory, dissection by hand and mind, and the penetration of hidden secrets—language still used today in praising a scientist's "hard facts," "penetrating mind," or the "thrust of his argument." The constraints against penetration in Natura's lament over her torn garments of modesty have been turned into sanctions in language that legitimates the exploitation and "rape" of nature for human good. The seventeenth-century experimenters of the Accademia del Cimento of Florence (i.e., The Academy of Experiment, 1657–1667) and the Royal Society of London who placed mice and plants in the artificial vacuum of the barometer or bell jar were vexing nature and forcing her out of her natural state in true Baconian fashion.

Scientific method, combined with mechanical technology, would create a "new organon," a new system of investigation, that unified knowledge with material power. The technological discoveries of printing, gunpowder, and the magnet in the fields of learning, warfare, and navigation "help us to think about the secrets still locked in nature's bosom." "They do not, like the old, merely exert a gentle guidance over nature's course; they have the power to conquer and subdue her, to shake her to her foundations." Under the mechanical arts, "nature betrays her secrets more fully . . . than when in enjoyment of her natural liberty."

Mechanics, which gave man power over nature, consisted in motion; that is, in "the uniting or disuniting of natural bodies." Most useful were the arts that altered the materials of things—"agriculture, cookery, chemistry, dying, the manufacture of glass, enamel, sugar, gunpowder, artificial fires, paper, and the like." But in performing these operations, one was constrained to operate within the chain of causal connections; nature could "not be commanded except by being obeyed." Only by the study, interpretation, and observation of nature could these possibilities be uncovered; only by acting as the interpreter of nature could knowledge be turned into power. Of the three grades of human ambition, the most wholesome and noble was "to endeavor to establish and extend the power and dominion of the human race itself over the universe." In this way "the human race [could] recover that right over nature which belongs to it by divine bequest."

The interrogation of witches as symbol for the interrogation of nature, the courtroom as model for its inquisition, and torture through mechanical devices as a tool for the subjugation of disorder were fundamental to the scientific method as power. For Bacon, as for Harvey, sexual politics helped to structure the nature of the empirical method that would produce a new form of knowledge and a new ideology of objectivity seemingly devoid of cultural and political assumptions.

Lisa T. Sarasohn

A Science Turned Upside Down: Feminism and the Natural Philosophy of Margaret Cavendish, 1984

In a 1984 article, I examined the natural philosophical thought of the first women to publish on scientific subjects in English, Margaret Cavendish. I argued that Cavendish's vitalistic materialism, a product of her exposure to the scientific ideas of mechanistic and Renaissance natural philosophers, was an attack on traditional authority in science and society. Cavendish's ideas were no more radical than those of many of her contemporaries, who were members of the Royal Society, but although she made a famous visit to the institution in 1667, she was never asked to join, perhaps because it was feared her notoriety would bring dishonor on the Society.

In Margaret Cavendish's play *Love's Adventures*, the heroine dons male clothes, saves her intended and the Republic of Venice from the Turks, and lectures the College of Cardinals on theology to universal acclaim. This literary echo of the famous "world turned upside down" topos of early modern European culture reverberates often in the work of the wife of the "arch-conservative" duke of Newcastle. It is a potent symbol. As Natalie Davis has shown, the reversal of male-female roles in early modern culture, during those strange times in either fiction or fact when women were on top, not only represented a safety value for releasing the tensions and preserving the order of hierarchical society, but also provided a tool for criticizing, challenging, and sometimes even changing the dominant values and powers of society. Margaret Cavendish believed that the social order

Lisa T. Sarasohn, "A Science Turned Upside Down: Feminism and the Natural Philosophy of Margaret Cavendish," *Huntington Library Quarterly* 47 (1984): 289–307. © 1984 by the Henry E. Huntington Library and Art Gallery. Reprinted from the *Huntington Library Quarterly*, Vol. 47, by permission of the University of California Press.

could expand to accommodate the intellectual equality of women, without its structure fragmenting from this innovation. Thus, it comes as no surprise to see her embrace the ambiguity of a world turned upside down.

In the seventeenth century, the traditional intellectual values of society also were being challenged by the revolutionary findings of the new science. When Copernicus reversed the places of the sun and the earth, and Galileo and Descartes substituted motion for rest as the basic fact of physics, the universe itself was turned upside down. Margaret Cavendish's work unites the dual assaults on traditional authority implicit in both feminism and the new science.

Joan Kelly has argued that "every learned tradition was subject to feminist critique, since all were dominated by men and justified male subjection of women." In this paper it will become clear that Cavendish used the skeptical methodology of the new science not only to attack traditional natural philosophy, but also as a weapon in her battle for the recognition of female intellectual equality. We shall see, however, that this skepticism became a two-edged sword, both damning and justifying female subservience.

Cavendish fused revolutionary scientific ideas and an underlying feminist ideology in her conception of a living universe, infused with motion, and ordered by a female spirit, which could best be understood from the empathetic viewpoint of a female scientist. Thus, both the substance of her philosophy and its exposition justified a revolution in the interpretation of the traditional female role. Cavendish's work shows how the radical implications of one area of thought can reinforce and strengthen the subversive tendencies of another, quite different attack on authority.

Cavendish urged "learned professors to free their minds from the prejudice that nothing coming from the pen of a woman could be worth serious attention." She realized that women were kept in "a hell of subjection" because of the suppression of their natural faculties and intelligence by men. Thus, for Cavendish, the exposition of natural philosophy became a conduit for a reappraisal of the position of women, in which her actions spoke as loudly as her words. Her husband, who was her staunchest ally, wrote in the preface to one of her books of philosophical opinions, "but here's the crime, a lady wrote them, and to entrench so much on the male prerogative is not to be forgiven."

The duchess met the philosophic and scientific geniuses of the age — René Descartes, Thomas Hobbes, and Pierre Gassendi — while in exile in France in the mid-1640s. Her husband had been Hobbes's patron for many years, and both Descartes and Gassendi dined with the Newcastles.

It is likely that the duke's enthusiasm for the Scientific Revolution and its proponents originally awakened Cavendish's interest in natural philosophy. The duchess incorporated several themes of the new science into her own enormous corpus of literary works: poems, plays, essays, orations, and disquisitions on natural philosophy. . . .

Cavendish first elaborated her scientific theories in a book of poetry, *Poems and Fancies,* published in 1653. . . .

In *Poems and Fancies* the duchess advocated an atomistic cosmology which Robert Kargon, the historian of English atomism, characterizes as "so extreme and so fanciful that she shocked the enemies of atomism, and embarrassed its friends." Her atomism was indeed very extreme and reflects her rejection of all kinds of intellectual authority. According to Cavendish, the world is composed of four differently shaped kinds of atoms: square atoms which constitute earth, round atoms which make up water, long atoms which compose air, and sharp atoms which compose fire. The various concatenations and motions of these different atoms, and the void, make up all the variety of forms and change we find in nature; their motion in the brain constitutes our understanding and emotions as well; their harmony produces health, their disharmony sickness.

To this extent, the duchess's system, although it may sound strange to modern ears, is not very different from the corpuscular philosophies advocated by Descartes, Hobbes, and Gassendi. The shocking element of Cavendish's atomism was the almost complete lack of theological qualifiers necessary to dissociate mechanism from the charge of atheistic materialism, a complaint often made against Hobbes himself. The duchess's atoms are eternal and infinite, two attributes which the proponents of corpuscular philosophy were careful to separate from their doctrines of matter, because in a Christian cosmology only God can be eternal and infinite. Furthermore the atoms, as the duchess described them, seem to act out of their own volition; whether they are ordered by God is left a very open question:

> *Small atoms of themselves a World may make*
> *As being subtle, and of every shape:*
> *And as they dance about, fit places find,*
> *Such forms as best agree, make every kinde. . . .*
> *And thus, by chance, may a new world create;*
> *Or else predestined to worke my Fate. . . .*

The underlying methodological premise of Cavendish's natural philosophy is a form of extreme skepticism about the possibility of absolute knowledge of nature, which she shared with her husband and brother-in-law, who in turn were influenced by the natural philosophers they associated with in France. . . .

Cavendish's skepticism was, in part, the consequence of her sex and upbringing. Like most women in the Stuart period, she was relatively uneducated. Although she had tutors in "reading, writing, working, and the like," she was not "kept strictly thereto, they were rather for formality than benefit," since her mother preferred that her daughters be virtuous rather than cultivated. The duchess never learned any foreign language, and her command of English grammar and spelling was at best rudimentary, even given seventeenth-century conditions. Because of these factors, Cavendish was unable to develop a systematic understanding of the work of others. She was very aware of these shortcomings, and on several occasions complained that university education was denied to women, and their minds consequently were underdeveloped: "I will not say, but many of our sex may have as much wit, and be capable of learning as well as men; but since they want instructions, it is not possible they should attain to it. . . ."

Just as the old learning had denied educational opportunities to women, likewise the new learning was largely a male prerogative. Although the duchess was the only woman in the period ever to be invited to a session of the Royal Society, she was invited only to observe a few experiments; it was inconceivable that she could ever become a member. Pepys was afraid that even this small courtesy would cause scandal for the Society. Not surprisingly, Cavendish treated the empirical methodology of the Royal Society with great scorn, claiming that the microscopes and telescopes of experimental science could never discover the interior secrets of nature. . . .

While the duchess may have borrowed many of her ideas and preconceptions from the general intellectual climate of her day, she believed that her system was entirely unique. The desire for originality was the driving force of her creativity and the impetus for the development of her own unique natural philosophy. . . .

In *Observations upon Experimental Philosophy*, the duchess argued defensively that her philosophy was different than anything taught before, and indeed,

> *were it allowable for our sex, I might set up a sect or school for my self. . . . But I, being a woman, do fear they would soon cast me out of their schools, for though the Muses, Graces, and Sciences are all of the female gender, yet they were most esteemed in former ages, then they are now;*

nay could it be done handsomely, they would now turn them all from females into males; so great is grown the self-conceit of the masculine, and the disregard of the female sex.

The only option left to the duchess, since she could not be admitted into the male preserves of learning, was to develop her own speculative philosophy, rejecting not only the teachings of the ancients, but the system of the moderns as well, at least in theory. If the Scientific Revolution can be considered an attack on the authority of Aristotle and the medieval world-view, the natural philosophy of Margaret Cavendish was a further attack on the authority of a male-dominated science, and, by implication, an attack on all male authoritarianism. In adopting the role of the female scientist, Cavendish implicitly turned the world upside down.

Thus Cavendish abandoned atomism by 1661, instead developing a scientific theory where a hierarchy of matter, integrated into an organic whole, composed the entire natural world. According to her theory the universe is composed of matter and motion, which are inseparable. There are three kinds of matter, differing in figure and type of motion, but inextricably integrated in composed forms of matter: rational matter, the most excellent, which is self-moving, the seat of conception, and the director of the rest of matter; sensible matter, which carries out the commands of rational matter, and is the vehicle for sensual perception; and inanimate matter, which is the least excellent because it lacks perception, although it is self-conscious and the material substratum of all being. All of matter is to some degree animate, but this does not cause divisive or natural anarchy because all types of matter are essentially one; diversity is resolved in unity. Self-moving matter is the principle of the world. This materialism is no less extreme than the duchess's atomism, because in it matter remains eternal and infinite, and the soul is considered material.

Did Cavendish's gender affect the content of her science itself? We have seen that the roles which women filled in the seventeenth century circumscribed the duchess's education and influenced the development of her epistemology and methodology. In addition, Cavendish's gender may have acted as an heuristic device, causing her to be sympathetic toward those ideas which substantiated and supported a fuller role for women in the social and natural cosmos. Thus, whenever there is a choice, Cavendish chose the more organic and nurturing view of nature, not necessarily because these ideas are inherently attractive to women, but perhaps because the psychological presuppositions of the early seventeenth century associated the roles of women and nature.

Many of Cavendish's male contemporaries were equally attracted to the notion of an organic universe, which had been a dominant world-view for centuries, but most of the proponents of the new science had rejected organicism for the mechanistic model of the universe. The duchess was unusual in her attempt to integrate some of the basic axioms of the new science, for example the pervasiveness of matter in motion, within an organic and vitalistic universe.

Thus matter is animistic, eternal, and a unity in the most far-reaching sense: "Nature is a body of a continued infiniteness, without holes or vacuities." The conservation of matter, the empathy of its parts for one another, and the transformation of constantly changing forms, results in an ordered, harmonious universe: "And since Nature is but one body, it is entirely wise and knowing, ordering her self-moving parts with all facility and ease, without any disturbance, living in pleasure and delight, with infinite varieties and curiosities, such as no single part or creature can ever attain to."

While Cavendish sometimes treats nature as the totality of matter, which is immanently self-ordering, in other parts of her work nature is considered as an ordering principle, somehow transcendent as well as immanent in matter. She considered this principle to be female. Since the duchess had abstracted God so thoroughly from her metaphysics, nature was left with an extraordinarily large sphere of action:

> *Tis true, God is the first Author of motion, as well as he is of Nature; but I cannot believe, that God should be the prime actual movent of all natural creatures, and put all things into local motion, like as one wheel turns all the rest; for God's power is sufficient enough to rule and govern all things by absolute will and command, or by a Let it be done, and to impart self-motion to Nature to move according to his order and degree, although in a natural way.*

Once God has infused nature with the power of regulating motion, nature operates in an almost entirely autonomous manner, "Nature is neither absolutely necessitated, nor has absolute free-will . . . and yet hath so much liberty, that in her particulars she works as she pleaseth. . . ." This autonomous and almost independent nature is functionally equivalent to a seventeenth-century housewife:

> *Nature, being a wise and provident lady, governs her parts very wisely, methodically and orderly; also she is very industrious, and hates to be idle, which makes her employ her time as a good huswife doth, in brewing, baking, churning, spinning, sewing, etc. . . . for she has numerous employments,*

and being infinitely self-moving, never wants work but her artificial works are her works of delight. . . .

By the end of this disquisition, the duchess tied her robust concept of nature directly to her own feminism: women may be particularly apt as experimental philosophers because they are experienced in the creation of artificial constructs, like "sweetmeats, possets, . . . pyes, and puddings." Moreover, if women became experimental philosophers, they could release men from the burden of "useless experiments," thus enabling them to devote their time to fundamental studies. In this case, Cavendish revealed an ambivalent attitude toward women; they are intellectually equal to men, but nevertheless should be socially subservient to men. Paradoxically, they are good only for those tasks Cavendish most despises. She concluded, "woman was given to man not onely to delight, but to help and assist him." . . .

The organic and vitalistic quality of Margaret Cavendish's natural philosophy distinguished it from the mechanistic systems of Hobbes and Descartes. While the duchess shared their fascination with matter and motion, she denied that insensible matter, without self-movement, could produce an ordered universe. Likewise, she rejected the argument of the Cambridge Platonists who claimed that the universe was animated and moved by an immaterial spirit. It was impossible in her view that an immaterial spirit could affect and cause alteration in material being. Cavendish's natural philosophy is more closely related to the organic theories of the Renaissance natural magicians and the vitalistic thought of the chemists of the sixteenth and seventeenth century, and to some aspects of the thought of Pierre Gassendi, with whose works she was probably familiar through the intermediacy of Charles Cavendish and Walter Charleton.

As a scientific philosophy, Margaret Cavendish's materialism is an interesting, but unimportant by-product of the Scientific Revolution. Many of her ideas, like vitalistic matter, the great chain of being, or a female and fecund nature, were part of the intellectual currency of her day, even if they were not usually associated with the new science. Thus, her philosophy had no influence in her own time, and most scholars who study Cavendish's work, such as Virginia Woolf, deplore the stultifying effect natural philosophy had on her poetic genius: "Under the pressure of such vast structures, her natural gift, the fresh and delicate fancy, which had led her in her first volume to write so charmingly of Queen Mab and fairyland, were crushed out of existence." While this may be the case from a literary point of view, her natural philosophy is significant in what it reveals about the female, or at least one female, attitude toward nature and cosmology. Repeatedly in her work, in the least metaphorical way possible, Cavendish claims that her philosophy is her child. Not surprisingly, she envisions a universe that lives. . . .

Cavendish realized that the principle of hierarchy which she so eagerly embraced in her natural and political philosophies, had dire implications for the status of women. Thus, in *The World's Olio*, the duchess proclaimed,

> *True it is, our sex makes great complaints, that men from the first creation usurped a supremacy to themselves, although we were made equal by nature: which tyrannical government they have kept ever since; so that we could never come to be free, but rather more and more enslaved. . . . Which slavery hath so dejected our spirits, that we are become so stupid, that beasts being but a degree below us, men use us but a degree above beasts. Whereas in nature we have as clear an understanding as men, if we are bred in schools to mature our brains. . . .*

This strong statement of radical feminism arose from Cavendish's despair at her own position and that of her sex. In fact, this despair paradoxically often resulted in long diatribes against women interspersed in her work, perhaps reflecting her own insecurity. Although the duchess realized the condition of her sex was due to historical circumstances, she sometimes lost sight of this perception and blamed women for their own innate inferiority. . . .

Cavendish believed that the current unenlightened state of most of her female contemporaries made them incapable of intelligent political action or even rational thought: "neither doth our sex delight or understand philosophy, for as for natural philosophy, they study no more of Nature's works than their own faces . . . and for moral philosophy, they think that too tedious to learn, and too rigid to practice." On some level, Cavendish realized that this female incapacity was the result of the traditional roles women filled in marriage. Although her opinion sometimes wavered, Cavendish often denounced marriage as a vehicle for male immortality, in which women lost all identity and independence. She even went so far as to attack motherhood, which she believed benefited only the husband and his family, while only endangering the health and life of the wife. While Cavendish did not explicitly recommend the destruction of traditional social norms as the vehicle for female emancipation, as did her peers in the French salons, she realized that equality could only be found when women rejected marriage as the totality of life, and sought to develop their intellectual capabilities. For most women of her age, however, Cavendish seemed to realize this was an impossible ideal. Thus, Cavendish's radicalism sometimes splinters into social conservatism: the unenlightened woman can only improve herself by virtuous behavior within the traditional framework of home and family. . . .

Cavendish's ultimate answer to the ambivalent position she found herself in was recourse to fantasy to express her ideas, to assert her equality with men, and to receive the adulation and fame she believed she deserved. Attached to *Observations upon Experimental Philosophy*, her most mature and sophisticated scientific work, is a strange romantic fantasy, *The Description of a New Blazing World*. Douglas Grant, the duchess's most recent biographer, accounts for its presence because Cavendish "had become restive under the discipline increasingly imposed on her by natural philosophy." *The Blazing World* is not the result of restlessness. Rather, it is a prime example of a world turned upside down, where Cavendish could fulfill her wishes on the grand scale.

According to the story, a beautiful young maiden is kidnapped by a lascivious merchant, but after he and his crew have died in the polar wastes, she escapes by transversing the poles between her world and the "Blazing World," so-called because of the brightness of its stars. There she meets its strange inhabitants, all sorts of anthropomorphic beasts and many-colored humans, and eventually marries the emperor of the Blazing World. He gives her an absolute dominion over his realm and his subjects worship her as if she were a divinity. This is a classical reversal of male-female roles, and an expression of Cavendish's desire for dominance within a traditional hierarchy.

However, the story does not end there. The first thing the empress does is to call a meeting of all the natural philosophers in the land: fish-men, worm-men, ape-men, bird-men, fox-men, etc. Then ensues a wonderful satire of seventeenth-century science with all the various beings arguing abstruse points of both ancient and modern science. The worm-men largely reiterate Cavendish's own natural philosophy, which the empress emends and approves. The discussion ends by "the Empress having thus declared her mind . . . and given them better instructions than perhaps they expected, not knowing that her Majesty had such great and able judgment in natural philosophy." In the Blazing World, at least, the duchess's science has triumphed as she triumphs over all other natural philosophers.

Moreover, Cavendish was not content in her Blazing World merely to overawe mythical scientists. Later in the story, the empress decides to write a "caball," and wants to use either the soul of Galileo, Descartes, Gassendi, Helmont, or Hobbes as her scribe. The immaterial spirits, who are her advisors in this enterprise inform her "that they were fine ingenious writers, but yet so self-conceited, that they would scorn to be scribes to a woman." Instead, they suggest she use the soul of the duchess of Newcastle, who, "although she is not one of the most learned, eloquent, witty, and ingenious, yet she is a plain and rational writer; for the principle of her writings is sense and reason. . . ." Thus, by the curious device of introducing herself as a character in her own fiction, Cavendish not only castigates the prejudice male philosophers feel for women, but repudiates them in taking refuge with herself. Nothing could speak more eloquently of the duchess's sense of isolation and forced reliance on herself. . . .

Londa Schiebinger

The Mind Has No Sex? Women and the Origins of Modern Science, 1989

In this selection, Londa Schiebinger examines the role of upper and middle class women in the late seventeenth and eighteenth centuries. She argues that while aristocratic women were increasingly barred from participation in the scientific culture of the age, except through the mediation of husbands, brothers, or fathers, craftswomen continued to play an important role in the more technological sciences. She examines the career of the German entomologist, Maria Merian, who ran her own business and published many works on insects.

Londa Schiebinger, *The Mind Has No Sex? Women and the Origins of Modern Science* (Cambridge: Harvard University Press, 1989), pp. 20–21, 23–26, 36, 66–68, 70, 71, 72, 79. Copyright © 1989 by Londa Schiebinger.

Scientific Academies

Historians of science have focused on the founding of scientific academies as a key step in the emergence of modern science. The major European academies of science were founded in the seventeenth century—the Royal Society of London in 1662, the Parisian Académie Royale des Sciences in 1666 (after 1816, the Académie des Sciences), the Societas Regia Scientiarum in Berlin in 1700 (later called the Akademie der Wissenschaften). By the end of the eighteenth century, a network of academies stretching from Saint Petersburg to Dublin, Stockholm to Palermo had consolidated Europe's intelligentsia in what one historian has called a "unified Republic of Letters." As the scepter of learning passed from courtly circles to learned academies, science took a first step toward losing its amateur status and ultimately becoming a profession. These state institutions, founded or protected by kings, provided social prestige and political protection for the fledgling science.

This first legitimation of the new science also coincides with the formal exclusion of women from science. With the founding of the academy system in Europe, a general pattern for women's place in science begins to emerge: as the prestige of an activity increases, the participation of women in that activity decreases. The exclusion of women from these academies was not a foregone conclusion, however. Women had been active participants in the aristocratic learned circles which these academies recognized as their forebears. There were, in fact, a significant number of women trained in the arts and sciences (and in the crafts).

The exclusion of women at this particular juncture in the history of science, then, needs explanation. The seventeenth-century scientific academy had its roots in two distinct traditions—the medieval university and the Renaissance court. Insofar as academies were rooted in universities, the exclusion of women is easily explained: women were unlikely candidates for admission to institutions deriving their membership largely from the universities, which since their founding had generally proscribed women. It is also possible, however, to argue that scientific societies arose more directly from courtly traditions. Frances Yates has identified the Platonic academy founded in mid-fifteenth-century Florence under the auspices of the great prince Lorenzo de' Medici as the root of the whole academy movement. If we emphasize the continuities between scientific academies and Renaissance courtly culture—where women were active participants in intellectual circles—it becomes more difficult to explain the exclusion of women from the academies.

The founding of the Académie Française—an academy devoted generally to the promotion of the French language and literature—initiated the academy system in France. Incorporated by the king in 1635, the Académie Française was the first of the modern state academies to be founded outside Italy, predating the Royal Society of London by some twenty-five years and the more specialized Académie Royale des Sciences in Paris by some thirty years. The founding of the Académie Française is a particularly important moment for our analysis of women's place in intellectual culture, for—although this was not an academy devoted to science—it was here that women were first excluded from the modern institutions of learning.

In its early years, it was not clear that women would be excluded from membership in the Académie Française. Noblewomen had been active *académiciennes* at several of the courtly academies out of which the Académie Française developed. . . .

Women faced similar problems in the early Académie Royale des Sciences. As was the case with the Académie Française, women were an integral part of the informal *réunions,* salons, and scientific circles that grew up in opposition to the tyranny of old methods in the French university system. Women gathered among the curious every Monday at Théophraste Renaudot's Bureau d'Adresse to watch his experiments. Women were especially strong among the Cartesians, who sought refuge from hostile academics in the salons of Paris. . . .

Despite their prominence in informal scientific circles, women were not to become members of the Académie Royale des Sciences. Why not? Certain aspects of the French academic system could have encouraged the election of gentlewomen. Seventeenth-century academies perpetuated Renaissance traditions of mixing learning with elegance, adding grace to life and beauty to the soul. The Académie Royale des Sciences retained a conviviality in its program, with rules of etiquette and a routine of dinners and musical entertainment, all of which tended to blur the boundaries that would later separate the scientific academy from the salon. This was an atmosphere in which the *salonnière* would have been at home. At the same time, the Académie was monarchial and hierarchical. At the head of the Académie sat twelve honorary nobles whose presence was largely ornamental; working scientists—the new aristocracy of talent—found themselves on a lowlier rung. Yet noble birth was not enough to secure women a place in the academic system. The closed and formal character of the academy discouraged the election of women. Membership in the academy was a public, salaried position with royal protection and privileges. A salaried position in itself would not preclude the admission of women (Marie de Gournay, for example, received a modest *pension* from Richelieu until her death in 1645); with membership of the Académie limited to forty, however, the election of a women would have displaced a man.

The exclusion of women from the Royal Society of London is also difficult to explain but for different reasons. At least ideologically, the Royal Society was supposed to be open to a wide range of people. Thomas Sprat, the first historian of the society, emphasized that its philosophy was not to be a parochial one restricted to the tenets of a particular religion, nation, or profession, but rather was to be "a Philosophy of *Mankind.*" According to Sprat, valuable contributions were to come from both learned and vulgar hands: "from the Shops of *Mechanicks*; from the Voyages of *Merchants*; from the Ploughs of *Husbandmen*; from the Sports, the Fishponds, the Parks, the Gardens of *Gentlemen.*" In addition, no special study or extraordinary preparations of learning were required: "Here is enough business for *Minds* of all sizes: And so boundless is the variety of these *Studies*, that here is also enough delight to recompence the Labors of them all, from the most ordinary capacities, to the highest and most searching *Wits.*"

In fact the Royal Society never made good its claim to welcome men of all classes. Merchants and tradesmen comprised only 4 percent of the society's membership; the vast majority of the members (at least 50 percent in the 1660s) came from the ranks of gentlemen *virtuosi*, or wellborn connoisseurs of the new science. Considering that the society relied for its monies on dues paid by members, the absence of noblewomen from the ranks of enthusiastic patrons is puzzling.

One woman in particular—Margaret Cavendish, duchess of Newcastle—was a qualified candidate, having written some six books about natural philosophy, along with several other plays and books of poetry. She had long been a generous patron of Cambridge University and would have been a financial asset to the impoverished society. One should recall that fellows of noble birth bestowed prestige upon the new society; men above the ranks of baron could become members without the scrutiny given other applicants. When the duchess asked for nothing more than to be allowed to visit a working session of the society, however, her request aroused a flood of controversy. Although never invited to join the Royal Society, Cavendish was allowed to attend one session after some discussion among society fellows. The famous visit took place in 1667. Robert Boyle prepared his "experiments of . . . weighing of air in an exhausted receiver, [and] . . . dissolving of flesh with a certain liquor." The duchess, accompanied by her ladies, was much impressed by the demonstrations and left (according to one observer) "full of admiration."

Although no official record of the discussion of Cavendish's visit remains, Samuel Pepys tells us that there was "much debate, *pro* and *con*, it seems many being against it, and we do believe the town will be full of ballads of it." When no other ballads appeared, Royal Society member John Evelyn was moved to write one of his own. From Pepys's report it seems many fellows felt that Cavendish's membership would bring ridicule rather than honor. Evelyn's wife, probably reflecting the attitudes of many in the society, described the duchess's writings as "airy, empty, whimsical and rambling . . . aiming at science, difficulties, high notions, terminating commonly in nonsense, oaths, and obscenity.

Margaret Cavendish's visit indeed appears to have set a precedent—a negative one. No woman was elected to full membership in the Royal Society until 1945. For nearly three hundred years, the only permanent female presence at the Royal Society was a skeleton preserved in the society's anatomical collection. . . .

The unformed state of intellectual culture in the seventeenth century left much room for innovation. Yet women did not fare well in the new institutions of science established in seventeenth-century Europe. Where science emerged as part of the public domain in established academies, women might be found on the periphery, as anatomical demonstrators or prizewinners, but they were not to be found participating in mainstream academic life as recognized members.

Exclusion from the academies, while it distanced women from the centers of scientific endeavor, did not end their participation in science. In the seventeenth and eighteenth centuries, as we shall see, there were a number of women working in natural history and natural philosophy, as well as the experimental sciences. Though few in number, women made real contributions. It is important to understand how these and other women, though barred from universities and scientific societies, could nonetheless acquire the training required for work in the sciences. . . .

Scientific Women in the Craft Tradition

. . . It may be surprising that between 1650 and 1710 a significant proportion—some 14 percent—of all German astronomers were women. These women came not from the aristocracy but from the workaday world of the artisanal workshop, where women as well as men were active in family businesses. Craft traditions, central to working life in early modern Europe, also contributed to the development of modern science. This route to science was more open for women in Germany, where craft traditions remained especially strong. To be sure, Germany had its outstanding royal women—Caroline of Ansbach, Princess Elizabeth, and Sophie Charlotte, the founder of the Academy of Sciences in Berlin—but it was working women who made steady contributions to the empirical base of science. As Alphonse des Vignoles, vice-president of the Berlin academy, observed there were more women astronomers in Germany at the turn of the eighteenth century than in any other European country.

Edgar Zilsel was among the first historians to point to the importance of craft skills for the development of modern science in the West. Zilsel located the origin of modern science in the fusion of three traditions: the tradition of letters provided by the literary humanists; the tradition of logic and mathematics provided by the Aristotelian scholastics; and the tradition of practical experiment and application provided by the artist-engineers.

What Zilsel does not point out, however, is that the new value attached to the traditional skills of the artisan also allowed for the participation of women in the sciences. Of the various institutional homes of the sciences, only the artisanal workshop welcomed women. Women were not newcomers to the workshop: it was in craft traditions that the fifteenth-century writer, Christine de Pizan, had located women's greatest innovations in the arts and sciences—the spinning of wool, silk, linen, and "creating the general means of civilized existence." In the workshop, women's (like men's) contributions depended less on book learning and more on practical innovations in illustrating, calculating, or observing.

Women's position in the crafts was stronger than has generally been appreciated. . . .

Astronomers and entomologists were never, of course, officially organized into guilds. Yet craft traditions were very much alive in the practice of these sciences. This was especially true in Germany, where stirrings of industrialization came late. . . .

Women's work in household workshops differed widely from trade to trade, from town to town. Yet it is possible to sketch general patterns. Women participated in craft production as: (1) daughters and apprentices; (2) wives who assisted their husbands as paid or unpaid artisans;

(3) independent artisans; or (4) widows who inherited the family business. As we shall see, these categories were also important for defining women's place in scientific production.

Maria Sibylla Merian and the Business of Bugs

Maria Sibylla Merian was a leading entomologist of the eighteenth century. At a time when travel was difficult for women (as for men), she sailed to the Dutch colony of Surinam, where she undertook a series of studies that broadened significantly the empirical base of European entomology. In the seventeenth and early eighteenth centuries, the apprentice system was the key to women's training in science. Maria Sibylla Merian was born in Frankfurt am Main in 1647, daughter of the well-known artist and engraver, Matthäus Merian the elder. In her father's workshop she learned the techniques of illustrating—drawing, mixing paints, etching copperplates. From the age of thirteen, Maria Merian served as informal apprenticeship with her stepfather, guild painter Jacob Marell (her own father died when she was three), and with her stepfather's apprentice, Abraham Mignon. . . .

Interestingly, it was this training in art that gave Merian her entrée to science; the primary value of her studies of insects derived from her ability to capture in fine detail what she observed. In early modern science women commonly served as observers and illustrators. A woman's success as an illustrator rested, in part, on her ability to adapt to a new field skills in which women excelled (nuns had long illuminated manuscripts; other women were active members of painters' guilds). The recognized need for exact observation in astronomy, botany, zoology, and anatomy in this period made the work of accomplished illustrators particularly valuable. . . .

Merian began her scientific career with the publication of her *Wonderful Metamorphosis and Special Nourishment of Caterpillars* in 1679, a book that captured in pictures the transformation of caterpillars. As Merian told later in life, this study emerged from years of observation and research:

> *Since my youth, I have studied insects. In my place of birth, Frankfurt am Main, I began studying silkworms. When I realized that butterflies and moths develop more quickly than other caterpillars, I collected all the caterpillars that I could find, in order to observe their metamorphosis. . . .*

In fifty copperplates she drew the life cycle of each insect—from egg to caterpillar to cocoon to butterfly—attempting to capture each change of skin and hair and the whole of their life "as much as possible in black and white." Merian undertook her study of caterpillars in an attempt to find other varieties that, like the silkworm, could be used to produce fine thread. Others in Germany shared Merian's interest in the silk business. Leibniz, as president of the Berlin Academy of Sciences, imported mulberry trees from China for the new academy. Though the king had granted the academy a monopoly on silk making in 1700, the trees did not flourish and silk was not as profitable as Leibniz had hoped. Maria Merian continued her research, over a period of five years searching out and collecting various caterpillars along with enough of their particular food to sustain them for the days or months of observation and drawing. After much earnest and wearisome study, she found many caterpillars that change into moths or flies, but none that spin a useful thread similar to that of the silkworm. . . .

In Maria Merian we find a confident and independent woman directing her own business interests, training young women in her trade, experimenting with technique, and following her own scientific interests. In the prefaces to her publications she never apologized for her achievements (as did so many women of this period) nor spoke, as did Margaret Cavendish, of the "softness" of the female brain. Yet even Merian found it necessary to profess a certain modesty. She had been persuaded, she wrote, to publish her work by "learned and well respected people." This she did "not for my own glory, but for the glory of God alone, who created such wonders." Craftswomen were also required to keep well-regulated households. Joachim von Sandrart made a point of saying that Merian's business did not interfere with her household duties. . . .

It would be a mistake to think that Maria Merian was merely an exceptional woman who, defying convention, made her mark on science. Merian's life and career may have been exceptional but it was not unusual; Merian did not forge a new path for women as much as take advantage of routes already open to women. She emerged from the artisanal workshop, where it was not uncommon for women to engage in various aspects of production, and her ties to craft traditions facilitated her contribution to science. Few women followed Merian's lead into the science of entomology. The more usual craft-based science for women in this period was a different science altogether: astronomy. . . .

Isaac Newton. This heroic eighteenth-century engraving of Newton adds a compass and a map to show his mastery of the universe. (© *Bettmann/CORBIS*)

PART

VI Was There a Scientific Revolution?

Francis Bacon—claimed as both hero and villain of the Scientific Revolution—wrote, "The human understanding is of its own nature prone to suppose the existence of more order and regularity in the world than it finds. And though there be many things in nature which are singular and unmatched, yet it devises for them parallels and conjugates and relatives which do not exist." The quest for a way to order history, as well as the natural world, has resulted in the categorizing of historical eras: antiquity, the Classical Age, the Renaissance. But this may simply be what Bacon calls "Idols of the Theatre," ways of thinking that impose order where none really exists. The Scientific Revolution particularly, as specialized studies have increasingly revealed, seems amorphous and a product of categories imposed on the past in a way that the past does not justify.

The most recent historiography in the History of Science seeks to historicize the past and understand it in terms of its own contexts, rather than to impose presentist attitudes on the sixteenth and seventeenth centuries. Earlier histories of the Scientific Revolution stressed physics and astronomy, because they were the most important scientific disciplines in the twentieth century. Now, historians recognize that emphasizing these disciplines masks the complexity of natural

175

philosophy in early modern times, when current disciplinary borders did not yet exist. Likewise, emphasizing those figures in the past who are most important to modern science disguises the importance of other figures in the development of science. And situating science only in formalized settings misses the many spaces where scientific culture existed.

But when all these elements are introduced into the study of the history of science in the sixteenth and seventeenth centuries, the period seems to lose all coherence. Steven Shapin, in his survey of the Scientific Revolution, proclaims, "There was no such thing as the Scientific Revolution, and this is a book about it." The eminent historian of science, Roy Porter announces, "Explorers once believed in the great Southern Continent, though they couldn't agree where it was or what it was like. The same goes for the Scientific Revolution. Look closely, and, like the Cheshire cat, its features dissolve before the eyes."

Can historians study science without an ordering principle? Even as historians argue about the relevance of the term "Scientific Revolution" and how it distorts historical understanding, they nevertheless continue to use it. Some try to avoid the problem by abandoning the investigation of metaphysics and methodology, which so occupied the traditional history of science. Others refer to the period only chronologically as the sixteenth and seventeenth centuries, without necessarily saying why the sixteenth and seventeenth centuries should be separated from the fifteen and eighteenth centuries. It becomes a time period in need of a name.

This problem did not bother the historian Betty Jo Dobbs, who analyzed Newton's alchemical studies. In her address to the 1993 meeting of the History of Science Society, she announced, "I intend to undermine one of our most hallowed explanatory frameworks, that of the Scientific Revolution—almost entirely written with capital letters, of course." Reflecting historical criticism that had already been directed at the concept of the Renaissance, she argued that the Scientific Revolution lacked all the characteristics of a real political revolution. It was not "sudden, radical, and complete." Instead of elucidating the past, the imposition of the category of Scientific Revolution distorts the past, especially when it comes to understanding canonical figures such as Newton.

Richard S. Westfall takes issue with Dobbs's argument in Margaret J. Osler's collection, *Rethinking the Scientific Revolution*. Arguing that before 1500 Christianity dominated thought and culture and after 1700, science took its place, he concluded, "I am convinced that there has been no more fundamental change in the history of European Civilization. Dispense with the concept of Scientific Revolution? How can we dream of it?"

The shadow of Herbert Butterfield's depiction of the Scientific Revolution, which "outshines everything since the rise of Christianity and reduces the Renaissance and Reformation to the rank of mere episodes within the system of medieval Christendom" still haunts the History of Science. Historians still seek to understand just what happened in the sixteenth and seventeenth centuries and what it meant, in its own context and in ours.

The first two selections in this chapter reveal the power the metaphor of revolution retains for some historians of science. I. Bernard Cohen and Roy Porter both reformulate definitions of "revolution" in science, but they continue to conceptualize the seventeenth century as a period of scientific revolution. Cohen states, "I take it as a given that revolutions occur in the sciences, although I am aware there are disbelievers and that among believers there is no consensus concerning which events in the development of science constitute revolutions." Nevertheless, Cohen not only identifies the characteristics of the Scientific Revolution, but of all scientific revolutions. Porter, who is very sensitive to the changing historiography of the Scientific Revolution and shares its antipathy for the intellectualist approach, still insists that there was fundamental change in the seventeenth century, culminating in the work of Isaac Newton. Although Dobbs had lamented the role Newton plays in the history of science, a "final cause," which implies the inevitability of his physics, Porter is happy to argue that "Newton set the seal" for science and thought, even if it did not emerge as a unitary burst of genius.

Today, the attempt to redefine the Scientific Revolution continues in the work of both philosophers and historians of science. Peter Dear, one of the most important, suggests a new way of approaching it. He shares with Cohen and Porter the belief in a dramatic change in the seventeenth century, and points out that while specialized studies may deny the validity of the concept of Scientific Revolution, they nevertheless implicitly rely on it to emphasize the importance of their own work. Dear suggests another way of understanding this period. He returns to the distinction, made by several authors in this volume, between the disciplines of natural philosophy and mathematics, and argues that it can be used in creating a new "master heuristic," a new approach to understanding the changes that occurred during the Scientific Revolution. Dear argues that a new "physico-mathematics" characterized this period, and was embedded in social behavior. A history of the Scientific Revolution becomes the story of the rise in status of mathematics, which was increasingly thought to reveal the real physical universe.

With Dear, we might say the story of the Scientific Revolution has revolved to its beginnings. Once more, intellectual factors take preeminence in the definition—but as Dear acknowledges, there are other ways to tell this story.

I. Bernard Cohen

Revolution in Science, 1985

I. Bernard Cohen's discussion of the nature of scientific revolutions is in the tradition of Thomas S. Kuhn's *Structure of Scientific Revolutions*, although he redraws the requirements for what constitutes a scientific revolution. According to Cohen's analysis, a scientific revolution consists of four stages: an individual act of genius; a commitment to the new theory by its discoverer; a "revolution on paper," where the new theory is disseminated; and the adoption of the new theories in scientists' conceptions and practices. Cohen identifies the Scientific Revolution as an ideological change, when the practitioners of the new science discarded the traditional authorities and replaced them with experimentation. The Scientific Revolution was democratic in its rejection of hierarchy, and similar to modern political revolutions.

[T]here can be no debate concerning the overall historical record: it shows that for some three hundred years, ever since the first coming-of-age of modern science, great events in the development of science have been seen as revolutions in thought and practice. The main burden of this book is to delineate and to analyze those events and the interpretation of them as revolutions.

It is a matter of record that the word "revolution" first gained general currency as a technical term in the exact sciences, where it long had (and still has) a meaning very different from that of a sudden dramatic shift. Revolution means to return again, to go through a cyclical succession, as in the seasons of the year, or to ebb and flow, as in the motion of the tides. In the sciences, revolution thus implies a constancy within all change, an endless repetition, an end that is a beginning all over again. This is the meaning we have in mind in such a phrase as "the revolutions of the planets in their orbits." The expression "scientific revolution" or "revolution in science," however, conveys no such sense of continuity and permanence; rather, it implies a break in continuity, the establishment of a new order that has served its links with the past, a sharply defined plane of cleavage between what is old and familiar and what is new and different. It is the historian's task to find out how and when an innocent scientific term that implies permanence and recurrence became transformed into an expression for radical change in political and socioeconomic affairs, and then to discover the way in which this altered concept was applied to science itself. This set of transformations embodies more than a mere shift in terminology. It suggests that there has been a profound conceptual change in our analysis of human and social action and in our image of the scientist and of scientific activity.

From the eighteenth century to our own, many scientists have written of their own scientific creations as revolutionary, but neither Copernicus nor Newton did so. Newton and his predecessors did not conceive of themselves as revolutionaries in part because their work was produced before the term "revolution" had become generally applied to the sciences. But there is a deeper reason; we shall see that during the first century or so of modern science, many of the great creative scientists tended to think of themselves (and even to be viewed by their contemporaries) as revivers or rediscoverers of ancient knowledge, even as innovators who improved or extended knowledge, but not as revolutionaries in the sense in which we would commonly use this expression today. . . .

Comparison of Political and Scientific Revolutions

Political theories and events that involve rapid change in the social structure have had a pervasive influence on concepts of scientific revolution since the seventeenth century. Therefore we might profitably ask which specific features of political revolutions (and theories about them) have been incorporated into the concept of scientific revolution that most of us recognize today, and which other ones have proved to be inapplicable. A comparison of the two types of revolution reveals a closer degree of concordance than might at first be imagined.

One of the features that all political revolutions have in common is the element of "newness."

Anyone who studies revolutions in science will quickly find that these events—like social, political, and economic revolutions—can have different orders of magnitude ranging from maxirevolutions to minirevolutions. . . .

In addition to newness, another feature that revolutions in science share with political and social revolutions is the phenomenon of conversion. One example will suffice to indicate the revolutionary zeal of the scientific convert. In 1596, in the original preface to *The Secret of the Universe* (1981, 63), Kepler described the stages of his conversion to the Copernican astronomy, a topic which he enlarged upon in the first two chapters. He believed that God had shown him how and why the Copernican system was put together, why there were six planets and "not twenty or a hundred," and why the planets were situated in their respective orbits with the speeds that they there exhibited. His solution was later expressed in what we now call Kepler's third (or harmonic) law, but in 1596 he undertook to prove that God, in creating the universe and regulating the order of the cosmos, had in view "the five regular bodies of geometry, known since the days of Pythagoras and Plato." He later wrote that he owed the Copernican heliostatic system "this duty: that since I have attested it as true in my deepest soul, and since I contemplate its beauty with incredible and ravishing delight, I should also publicly defend it to my readers with all the force at my command." . . .

Scientific change through a political kind of power is not limited to twentieth-century totalitarianism in the Soviet Union and Nazi Germany, however. . . .

When the new revolutionary science of Isaac Newton was set forth in 1687, it was obvious that the real enemies to be routed were not the Aristotelians and scholastics but the Cartesians and their physical cosmology based on vortices. Newton showed, in the conclusion to book 2 of his *Principia*, that the Cartesian hypothesis "is completely in conflict with the phenomena of astronomy" and leads to a "confusion rather than an understanding of the celestial motions." But it was not enough to confute the Cartesians and others; an active campaign had to be mounted on a number of fronts simultaneously. First, there was a definite courting of the forces of the State, initiated when Newton dedicated the first edition of his *Principia* to the Royal Society and its patron, King James II. Edmund Halley, knowing of the King's interest in naval affairs, wrote for him a special account of the portion of the *Principia* dealing with the tides. Because the church was such a powerful force in all intellectual matters, the Newtonians wanted control of the new Boyle Lectures (founded under the terms of the will of the chemist and natural philosopher Robert Boyle), which consisted of eight sermons in London churches on the evidences of Christianity. These at once became a major vehicle for expounding the Newtonian science. . . .

A final point of difference between political or social revolutions and scientific revolutions is the goal. In one sense, both types of revolution have a specific, narrowly defined goal. For instance, the goal of the Newtonian revolution was to produce a new system of rational mechanics on the basis of which one could retrodict and predict the phenomena observed on earth and in the heavens. It was postulated on concepts of mass, space, time, force, and inertia, and it embraced the status quo *in science*, but not usually in the society at large. . . .

. . . This aspect of scientific revolutions—their effect on the thinking of men and women outside the strict domain of science—has been called the ideological component.

A dramatic example of the ideological component of a revolutionary scientific idea is found in the implications of the Copernican doctrine: the displacement of man and his earthly abode from a central place in the universe. It must have seemed a real blow to man's pride to be told that his planet had been shifted from a fixed place at the center, only to become just "another planet," as Copernicus called it, and physically a rather insignificant planet at that. John Donne (who probably could not have followed the simplest technical astronomical argument for and against the new system) wrote that without a fixed position the earth is lost and no man even knows where to look for it: "all cohaerence [is] gone." Martin Luther, who did not know much (if any) technical astronomy, reacted violently to the Copernican idea before even reading anything Copernicus wrote.

The Newtonian revolution also affected the way in which philosophers, theologians, political and social scientists, and educated men and women thought about the physical universe at large and about nature, "nature's laws," the basis of religion or religious belief, the nature of God, even the forms of government. But perhaps the ideas of Copernicus ultimately had a greater effect beyond the strict limits of the sciences than did those of Newton, since Copernicus's ideas shook the old anthropocentric notions of man's privileged position in the universe and, by implication, his uniqueness. In this respect Copernicus's impact would be more closely akin to Darwin's than Newton's. . . .

From Intellectual Revolution to Revolution on Paper

In the course of studying a large number of revolutions, I have found four major and clearly distinguishable and successive stages in all revolutions in science. The first stage I call the "intellectual revolution," the "revolution-in-itself." This revolution occurs whenever a scientist (or a group of scientists) devises a radical solution to some major problem or problems, finds a new method of using information (sometimes extending the range of information far beyond existing boundaries), sets forth a new framework for knowledge into which existing information can be put in a wholly new way (thus leading to predictions of a kind that no one would have expected), introduces a set of concepts that change the character of existing knowledge, or proposes a revolutionary new theory. In short, this first stage of revolution is what one or more scientists are always found to accomplish at the beginning of all revolutions in science. It consists of an individual or group creative act that is usually independent of interactions with the community of other scientists. It is complete in itself. Of course such an innovation arises from the matrix of existing science and is generally a fundamental transformation of current scientific ideas. Furthermore, it tends to be closely related to certain canons of the received philosophy and modes and standards of the science of the time. But the creative act that expresses itself in new science with a revolutionary potential is apt to be a private or individual experience.

Almost always, the new rules or findings are recorded or written up in the form of an entry in a diary or notebook, a letter, a set of notes, a report, or the draft of a full account which might eventually be published as an article or book. This is the second stage of a revolution—a commitment to the new method, concept, or theory. Very often, this stage consists of writing out a program of research. . . .

Every revolution in science begins as a purely intellectual exercise on the part of a scientist or a group of scientists, but a successful revolution—one that influences other scientists and affects the future course of science—must be communicated to colleagues either orally or through the written word. For a revolution in science to occur, the initial intellectual and commitment stages, which are private, must lead to a public stage: dissemination of the ideas to friends, associates, and colleagues and then to the world of science at large. Today this third stage may start with telephone calls, correspondence, conversations with friends and immediate colleagues, or group discussion within one's department or laboratory, followed by more formal presentation at the traditional departmental colloquium or a scientific meeting. If there are no severe adverse reactions of colleagues and if no basic flaws are found by critics or by the author himself, this preliminary communication may lead to a privately circulated preprint or a scientific paper or book submitted for formal publication. The phrase "revolution on paper" accurately describes this third stage, in which an idea or set of ideas has been entered into general circulation among members of the scientific community.

Very often the intellectual revolution is not completed until the scientist fully works out his ideas on paper. A notable example is Newton's radical construction of celestial dynamics. In 1679, in correspondence with Robert Hooke, Newton learned of a new way of analyzing planetary motion, which he then used to solve the outstanding problem of the cause of planetary motions in ellipses according to the law of areas. He next put his preliminary findings on paper, but he did not (so far as we know) fully write up his ideas and their consequences. He did not even admit publicly that he had made such a breakthrough until Halley's visit (in August 1684) to ask him about the problem of forces and planetary orbits. Then Newton composed a full report of his results and sent them on to be registered at the Royal Society in November

1684 at Halley's suggestion, so that his priority of invention might be secured. As Halley well knew, no one had advanced as far as Newton in the radically new and revolution-making analysis of the forces producing planetary motion. But only after preparing the paper for Halley and the Royal Society, that is, after transforming his private intellectual revolution into a public revolution on paper in the first months of 1685, did Newton go beyond even this extraordinary level of achievement to find that the sun and each planet must act on each other gravitationally and that consequently each planet also acts on and is acted on by every other planet—the essential step that would open the way to the invention of the concept of universal gravity, the basis of the Newtonian revolution in science.

A revolution in science can fail at any one of these first three stages. . . . [G]reat scientific advances could not realize their revolutionary potentialities simply because they were not made known until the efforts of scholarly research in our own time, some three centuries or more later. . . .

From Revolution on Paper to Revolution in Science

Even after publication, no revolution in science will occur until a sufficient number of other scientists become convinced of the theories or findings and begin to do their science in the revolutionary new way. At that time, what had been merely a public communication of an intellectual achievement on the part of a scientist or group of scientists becomes a scientific revolution. This is the fourth or final stage of every revolution in science.

The history of science records the fate of many revolutionary ideas that never got beyond the public paper stage. . . .

Given these many obstacles in the path to a revolution in science, it is somewhat surprising that any new theory or finding succeeds. In fact, many revolutionary ideas do not survive in a form that would be recognized and accepted by their first proponents; instead, they become transformed in the hands of later revolutionaries. To take an example, the system of the world that was fully elaborated by Copernicus in his *De Revolutionibus* in 1543 had no fundamental impact on astronomy until after 1609, when Kepler published his own radical reconstruction of Copernican astronomy. From that time on we can begin to discern a revolution in astronomy, culminating in the work of Newton. But this revolution was not merely the Copernican revolution delayed by half a century. Rather, the new astronomy was in a real sense not Copernican at all (though it is often still called "the Copernican revolution"). Kepler's reconstruction essentially rejected almost all of Copernicus's postulates and methods; what remained was primarily the central idea that the sun is immobile, while the earth moves in an annual circumsolar orbit and has a daily rotation. But this concept was not original with Copernicus, as he was well aware; it came from his ancient predecessor, Aristarchus of Samos. . . .

. . . Newton's *Principia*—the most significant and influential book of the Scientific Revolution—appeared in 1687, one year before the Glorious Revolution; it was, in fact, dedicated to James II and the Royal Society. In many ways the Scientific Revolution was more radical and innovative than any of the political revolutions of the seventeenth century and its effects have proved to be more profound and lasting. But so far as I know, no one has linked the Scientific Revolution to the other revolutions that occurred in that same century, or speculated that the revolutionary spirit which moved in the realm of politics might have been the same as that which caused upheavals in the sciences.

The best way to assess the depth and scope of the Scientific Revolution is to compare and contrast the science that came into fruition in the seventeenth century with its nearest equivalent in the late Middle Ages. Consider the central problem of motion (since "to be ignorant of motion is to be ignorant of nature"). . . . When scholars considered specifically local motion, in the fourteenth century, they became well aware that motion could be uniformly accelerated or nonuniformly accelerated, and they were able to prove mathematically that the effect of a uniformly accelerated motion in a given time is exactly equivalent to a uniform motion during that same time if the magnitude of the uniform motion is the mean of the accelerated motion. But the mathematical philosophers of the fourteenth century and those who discussed their work in the fifteenth century never put these mathematical principles to the test by applying them to physical events, say falling bodies. Galileo's approach to this same problem, on the other hand, was to view these principles, and others, not as pure mathematical abstractions but as laws that governed actual physical processes and occurrences in the world of experience. . . .

This example shows us how novel and revolutionary it was to discover principles by experiment combined with mathematical analysis, to set scientific laws in the context of experience, and to test the validity of knowledge by making an experimental test. Traditionally, knowledge had been based on faith and insight, on reason and revelation. The new science discarded all of these as ways of understanding nature and set up experience—experiment and critical observation—as the foundation and ultimate test of knowledge. The consequences were as revolutionary as the doctrine itself. For not only did the new method found knowledge on a wholly new basis, but it implied that men and women no longer had to believe what was said by eminent authorities; they could put any statement and theory to the test of controlled experience. What counted, therefore, in the new science of the seventeenth century was not the qualifications or learning of any author or reporter but rather his veracity in reporting, his true understanding of the method of science, and his skills in experiment and observation. The simplest and humblest student could now test (and even show the errors in) the theory or laws put forth by the greatest scientists. Knowledge thus took on a democratic rather than a hierarchical character and no longer depended so much on the insight of a chosen few as on the application of a proper method, accessible to anyone with sufficient wit to grasp the new principles of experiment and observation and the way to draw proper conclusions from the data. It is not surprising, therefore, that so much attention should be given during the Scientific Revolution to codifiers of the method—men like Bacon, Descartes, Galileo, Harvey, and Newton, who wrote about the way to proceed in scientific inquiry.

The scientists of the seventeenth century and of the late sixteenth century were fully aware of the newness of their approach in directly appealing to nature. . . .

The Scientific Revolution, which produced a new kind of knowledge and a new method of obtaining it, also produced new institutions for the advancement, recording, and dissemination of that knowledge. These were societies or academies of like-minded scientists (and some others who were just interested in science) who met to do experiments in concert, to see performances and tests of experiments done elsewhere, to hear reports on scientific work done by members, and to learn what was going on in other scientific groups and in other countries. The emergence of a scientific community is one of the distinguishing marks of the Scientific Revolution. By the 1660s permanent national academies arose in France and England, and both had official journals for the publication of research done by their members. . . .

Roy Porter

The Scientific Revolution: A Spoke in the Wheel?, 1986

In this selection, Roy Porter considers the challenges to the traditional historiography of the Scientific Revolution. Although he agrees that the many contextualized and specialized studies of this period necessitate a reformulation of the concept of Scientific Revolution, he nevertheless believes the concept is valid.

Porter's new definition of revolution in science includes the following attributes: a vigorous attack on the established order, the substitution of a self-consciously new understanding of the universe, and a sense of grandeur and urgency. For Porter, most of the canonical figures of the Scientific Revolution exhibited these characteristics.

. . . Historians write about scientific revolutions as automatically as of political, economic or social revolutions: the "French revolution" in chemistry led by Lavoisier is almost as familiar as the political revolution which cut off his head. Indeed, the idea that science advances by revolutionary leaps has long been with us, ever since the eighteenth century in fact. For, as Bernard Cohen has shown, it was Enlightenment propagandists for science from Fontenelle and the *Encyclopédistes* to Condorcet who first began to depict the transformations in astronomy and physics wrought by Copernicus, Newton and others as revolutionary breaks with the past, creating new eras in thought.

And significantly it was through being applied in this way to epochs in *science* that the term "revolution" itself took on its present meaning. Traditionally, when used to describe political fortunes, "revolution" had, of course, denoted change (the fall of one prince, the rise of a rival); but it was change within an essentially cyclical system in which all dynas-ties and empires had their rise and fall, their waxings, wanings and eclipses, for human affairs were governed by the endless "revolutions" of Fortune's Wheel. In the traditional metaphor, in other words, it was the orbits of the planets, so gravid with astrological influence, which had defined and governed revolutions in sublunary affairs. But, from the early eighteenth century, the old equation of revolution with cycles began to yield to a secular, directional myth of human destiny. "Revo-lution" kept its massiveness—a mundane event as portentous as one in the heavens, far grander than a mere revolt; but it came to signal not endless repetition but a break with the past, a fresh start, or what the Enlightenment called an "epoch." Hence from the *philosophes* onwards, scientific breakthroughs actually became normative for general usage, underpinning modern views of revolution as constructive and progres-sive, rather than as tainted by fatalism and hubris. Condorcet's faith in human perfectibility was buoyed up on hopes of scientific revolutions yet to come, programmed into the march of mind.

Such a reading of science's development, not as cumulative but as punctuated by creative discontinuities, has long appealed to historians, philosophers and prophets. And scientists have endorsed it too. . . .

The upshot of all this is that our dominant image of the history of science is bursting at the seams with revolutions. Browse book titles, or scan their chapter headings, and the truth of that remark strikes the eye. Revolutions, historians assume, have been so ubiquitous in science that, where they seem absent even that absence needs to be explained. . . . Or, to take another example, when Butterfield pondered the mys-terious lack of a seventeenth-century chemical revolution, he felt the need to label Lavoisier's new chemistry of a century later "the post-poned revolution." . . .

. . . And so to guide us, we now have atlases provided by the philoso-phy of science, which itself, according to Hesse, has recently undergone a "revolution," and where Kuhn's ultra-influential *The Structure of Scien-tific Revolutions* conjured up a quasi-Trotskian scenario of permanent revolution. All this may be deplored as a sad devaluation of the currency, but this grumble is not unique to historians of science: inflation of "revo-lution" has long been the bane of historians of all stripes.

Yet the practice of historians of science does differ in one key respect, as there is something quite singular in their use of the term. For, while making free with such localized labels as "chemical revolu-tion," "Darwinian revolution," "quantum revolution," and so forth, they also write about The Scientific Revolution, in the singular, as a unique phenomenon. . . .

The stamp of The Scientific Revolution (that is, roughly, the totality of those transformations taking place in the early modern era) is watermarked into today's scholarship. . . . Few challenge its validity. Even radical scholars such as Carolyn Merchant and Brian Easlea, who deny the standard eupeptic readings of The Scientific Revolution, do not question its existence. . . .

Explorers once believed in the great Southern Continent (*nondum cognita*), though they couldn't agree where it was or what it was like. The same goes for The Scientific Revolution. Look closely and, like the Cheshire cat, its features dissolve before the eyes. Take, for instance, the question of its timing. Most historians see it stretching broadly over the sixteenth and seventeenth centuries (say, from Vesalius and Copernicus through to Newton). Some, however, would abbreviate it. Thus Cohen restricts it to the seventeenth century, roughly from Kepler and Galileo to Newton (and here it might be significant that Rupert Hall has recently dubbed the sixteenth century, scientifically speaking, "a century of confusion"). By contrast, Ronan confines it to an earlier era entirely, seeing it as having "begun in the fifteenth century and carried on to end of the sixteenth." Ronan's periodization—stopping the Revolution where others start—is eccentric, yet he isn't the only scholar who would drive The Scientific Revolution right back in time. Butterfield reckoned that The Scientific Revolution, "popularly associated with the sixteenth and seventeenth centuries," in fact reached "back in an unmistakable line to a period much earlier still"; and in a similar vein, Crombie has argued that, though "from the end of the 16th century the Scientific Revolution began to gather a breathtaking speed," it should in fact be traced "as far back as the 13th century." Doesn't the extraordinary leisureliness of this unique Scientific Revolution smack of paradox? In his 1954 survey, Rupert Hall wrote of *The Scientific Revolution 1500–1800*. This three-hundred-year revolution has been pared down by half a century in his later *The Revolution in Science 1500–1750* (1983); but compared with *Ten Days that Shook the World*, this view of the shaking of the scientific foundations risks confusing continuity with cataclysm and creating a Shandeian muddle between evolution and revolution.

Its contents as well as dating also pose interpretative problems. Most scholars argue that the astrophysical sciences form the core of the Revolution (though doubts remain, for example, whether the astronomical revolution centres on Copernicus, Kepler, Galileo, or whoever). But should the life-sciences also be included? And indeed is the *sine qua non* a question of transformations in facts and theories, in scientific method, or in a man's relations to Nature? And historians remain at odds as to how The Scientific Revolution related to total history. Some regard it as integral to other contemporary revolutions (e.g., as Bernal claimed, the Commercial and the Bourgeois Revolutions) during what Christopher Hill has called the *Century of Revolution*; others, such as Rupert Hall, by contrast, have contended that scientific change was essentially independent of such socio-economic pressures. Faced with these confusions, small wonder that Thackray has recently concluded that, though the notion of The Scientific Revolution remains "a central heuristic device . . . and subject of myriad textbooks and courses," it explains little: "with each passing year it becomes more difficult to believe in the existence or coherence of a single, unique Scientific Revolution." . . .

The idea of The Scientific Revolution is not, then, part of the intellectual commons which historians have grazed time out of mind. Rather it was initially the brain-child and shibboleth of a specific cluster of scholars emerging during the 1940s, including the Russian émigré Alexandre Koyré, Butterfield, whose outline history popularized Koyré's work, Rupert Hall, who was Butterfield's pupil, and, a little later, Marie Boas [Hall]. Their scrupulous scholarship and prolific works of synthesis animated an emergent discipline, and laid down a coherent framework for future research. In their vision of the epochal nature of The Scientific Revolution—one embroidered by other scholars such as Gillispie and popularized in such works as Koestler's *The Sleepwalkers*—they not only claimed that science was revolutionized in the early modern period. They also made no secret of their "Whiggish" view that The Scientific Revolution was a good thing. For it marked a triumph of mind, free and fearless, underscoring the essential link between liberty of thought and intellectual advance, a lesson not to be lost on Western democracies just freeing themselves from Hitler's and Stalin's brain-washings and from the utopian Marxism that had been the opium of the thirties intelligentsia.

As analyzed by these scholars, what The Scientific Revolution proved was that science was not battery farming. Great ideas could not be hatched by mechanized husbandry—Baconian data-gathering, systematic experimentation, better instrumentation, institutionalization, funding and so forth. Science had not chugged forward following Five Year Plans, but had been transformed in stupendous, unpredictable leaps of reason. Such leaps were revolutions in *thought*. And so, as Koyré,

Butterfield, the Halls and their followers saw it (advancing what I shall label the "classical interpretation"), the business of the historian of science was first to grasp the *Weltanschauungen* of entrenched science, and then show how these had been turned upside-down by the thought-revolutions of science's giants. To depict such strokes of genius, Butterfield hit upon happy metaphors such as "picking up the other end of the stick," or "putting on a new pair of spectacles," rather as Kuhn was later to speak of "Gestalt-switches." This "classical interpretation" focused as never before on explicating the stunning conceptual displacements involved in moving from the Ptolemaic geocentric universe to Copernicus's heliocentrism, or in Kepler's courageous imaginative leap in abandoning circular planetary orbits—*de rigueur* for centuries—and embracing elliptical ones. How the bounds of the thinkable were changed by Galileo's New Science of motion, Descartes's mechanics of inertia and momentum, Boyle's corpuscular chemistry, and finally by Newton's synthesis of the laws of motion and the laws of gravity! Such triumphs—the mechanization of the world-picture, the shift from the "closed world" to the "infinite universe"—needed more than tireless empirical bricklaying. Copernicus's achievement did not consist in adding to Ptolemy, but in viewing old data through new spectacles. Science was revolutionized by new ways of seeing. . . .

Thus idealism has been pervasive, and its implications run even to the interpretation of detailed episodes. For instance, Koyré argued that Galileo didn't actually dirty his hands performing his kinetic experiments; or at least, if he did, he did so not with a view to making discoveries, but only after his conceptual breakthroughs, merely for the purpose of elegant demonstration. . . . But *was* the real Galileo a performer not of experiments but only of thought-experiments? Or are Koyré's and Hall's portraits merely ideal-types, themselves thought-experiments about the *beau idéal* of science? Recent archival research by Stillman Drake and others suggest that Galileo did indeed perform his experiments on inclined planes as *explorations* of the phenomena of motion, and that the results of these trials may well have guided him to his theories. Clearly, driving wedges between experimentation and conceptualization is fatuous, but the bias towards "purely intellectual factors" in the "classical interpretation" must be kept in mind.

Overall, this idealist reading of The Scientific Revolution as disembodied thought sustained a heroic, even romantic, image of the scientist, typified by Newton, "with silent face, Voyaging through strange seas of thought alone." For Gillispie and Koestler in particular, the scientist is dramatized as truth-seeker, dicing with the "cruel edge of objectivity," duty-bound to confront reality regardless of psychic cost, to "peer into a nature deprived of sympathy and all humane associations," stripped of the mythopoeic comforts of traditional cosmology. The imperative of truth demanded that the just-so stories of metaphysics and theology, with their teleology, providences and miracles, had to be swept away. The old, man-centered, anthropomorphic cosmos was now exposed as a fairy-tale, the charming correspondences of macro- and microcosm and the personification of Nature were banished and left to the poets. As Gillispie stressed, the universe as laid bare by Descartes or Hobbes was now dead, determinist, infinite, and, for Pascal, terrifying. The cosy fictions of will, value and purpose had been dissolved. With the "disenchantment of the world," man was left a stranger, an alien. In daring to face these truths, The Scientific Revolution was thus the triumph of honesty as well as of genius, and its hero was the iconoclast, pledged to discover Nature as it really was. For some historians this was glorious. Gillispie saluted the scientist as the new Prometheus, just as more recently Ronan has celebrated the "adventure" of his "unprecedented voyage of conquest." For others, by contrast, new knowledge spelt a new Fall. Koestler's *Sleepwalkers* charted the new alienation of man from Nature, fact from value, head from heart, mechanism from meaning, all as new mind-forged manacles from which the West has never escaped. . . .

. . . Seventeenth-century scientists claimed to abandon words for realities, values for facts, and some historians of The Scientific Revolution have taken them at their word. But even a superficial glance at the fabric of the new science in the seventeenth century and beyond shows that it remained permeated by precisely the kinds of human values and rhetoric—the Baconian idols—it claimed to have expunged. Indeed, much of the most stimulating scholarship from the 1970s onwards has been uncovering just how important was the continuing imput into science from metaphysics, theology and human interests, long after the New Science had proclaimed its independence from these influences. And it is worth remembering that the New Science's self-image of its own "new dispensation" was clearly taken over wholesale from Biblical eschatology. Ironically the "classical interpretation," which casts the Scientific Revolution as a watershed in the transition from primitive thought to rationality, reproduces such myths, generates new ones about progress and modernity, and runs closely parallel to the pre-history/history teleology of scientistic Marxism.

Just because its historiography embodies myths, the notion of scientific revolution need not however be summarily dismissed. The question remains: is it helpful to picture the course of the history of science as revolutionary? Or might it not make better sense to stress its "evolutionary" aspects, its continuities and accommodation to the wider socio-intellectual environment? These large questions matter, not least because, with the irresistible rise of specialization, scholarship becomes myopic and fragmented, and, though philosophers continue to dogmatize, historians may be in danger of defaulting on the task of assessing the overall patterns of science.

To judge whether science has had its revolutions, we need a working idea of revolution, one compatible with common historical usage in other contexts. For my purposes, I propose that a revolution in science requires the overthrow of an entrenched orthodoxy; challenge, resistance, struggle and conquest are essentials. The mere formulation of new theories doesn't constitute a revolution; neither is it a revolution if the scientific community leaps to applaud an innovation, saluting its superiority. Moreover, revolution requires not just the battering of old theories but the triumph of the new. A new order must be established, a break visible. Furthermore, revolutions presuppose both grandeur of scale and urgency of tempo. Mini-revolutions, partial revolutions, and long revolutions are terminological abuses; why dilute the word when "change" will do stout service? Lastly, I suggest that, though it may not be indispensable that the protagonists should intend from the outset to make a revolution (revolutionaries often begin as reformers), it is vital that, at some stage, consciousness should dawn of revolution afoot. The notion of silent or unconscious revolution is next door to nonsense.

Following these guide-lines, it does seem helpful to characterize the transformations in science occurring in the seventeenth century—though not the sixteenth—as revolutionary. There is no room here, and perhaps little need, to argue this contention chapter and verse. But certain key elements are worth stressing. First, many of the protagonists clearly cast themselves as crusaders for a radically New Science, engaged in life-and-death struggles against the hidebound dogma of the schools: the very titles of Bacon's *New Atlantis*, Kepler's *New Astronomy*, and Galileo's *Two*

New Sciences catch this tone of embattled innovation. Bacon and Galileo amongst others were witheringly dismissive of the dead hand and dead mind of orthodoxy to a degree that finds no parallel, for instance, in Copernicus or Vesalius. Doubtless, much of this was rhetoric; doubtless, it was largely straw schoolmen who were being slain and slain again; doubtless, seventeenth-century natural philosophers tapped the scholastic legacy more than they admitted. Yet the seventeenth century really saw intense struggle between rival natural philosophies, and the call for liberation from die-hard orthodoxy runs right through the century, culminating in the Ancients versus Moderns debate and the Battle of the Books, won in science by the Moderns (according to the Enlightenment, by a knockout). . . .

Moreover, many sciences did undergo fundamental reorientations both in their conceptual foundations and their fine texture. A few examples will surely suffice. In astronomy, geostatic and geocentric systems still predominated in 1600; but by 1700 all members of the scientific elite espoused heliocentricity. In 1600, versions of the Aristotelian physics of finitude, local motion and the four elements still held the floor, in many cases, in newly refined and reinvigorated forms; by 1700, one mode or other of the mechanical philosophy had swept them away amongst leading scientists. Matter theory had come to hinge not on the traditional four elements and on qualities but on particles and short-range forces incorporating new laws of motion and principles of dynamics. The traditional divide between science celestial and terrestrial was challenged by Galileo, and bridged by Newton's universal gravitation. Methodologically, observation was set at a premium and so stimulated, and was in turn reinforced by, the development of new scientific instruments such as the telescope and microscope. This opened up both the macro- and micro-worlds, both visible and conceptual, and contributed to the general development of instrumentation which is so important a factor in modern science. Going hand in hand with this, experimentation led to a new way of doing science and a new way of promoting science's claims to "objective truth." Moreover, mathematical advances—preeminently Descartes's coordinate geometry and Newton's and Leibniz's infinitesimals—empowered science to calculate and control areas which had been impressionistic before. Such a list could be greatly extended.

These changes, it must be stressed, were not just pious hopes for a great instauration; they were substantial and permanent achievements which were built upon. Taken singly, it is true, the work of Kepler or

Descartes, Galileo or Boyle, created as much chaos as it resolved. But collectively, their investigations amounted to a progression of fruitful reformulations of fundamentals until, with Newton above all, a synthesis was reached widely saluted as coherent, dazzling in scope and potential, ripe both for solving workaday problems (Kuhn's "normal science") and for generating future investigations. Newton set the seal. . . .

In other words, the transformations in science were revolutionary not just in techniques and concepts, but in forging an unparalleled place for science in European culture and consciousness. Above all, new conceptions of Nature and man's relation to it became dominant. . . . Traditional beliefs about Nature handed down via the intertwining systems of Christian theology, Humanistic philosophy and occult wisdom now seemed all too confused, difficult, anarchic, dangerous. The proliferation and ubiquity of spiritual forces, magical resonances, and providential infiltrations had confused God, man and Nature in ways that increasingly seemed scandalous and enervating to powerful intellectual currents, engaged (as Rabb has put it) in a search for stability.

Seventeenth-century scientific ideologues embarked upon their task of conceptual clarification with a will. Not without fierce controversy, new formulations of the fundamentals were hammered out. The true divide between God and Nature had to be insisted upon; typically, in the mechanical philosophy, all activity was attributed to God, but a God who was increasingly distant, and Nature was reduced to a machine, inert and passive. Similarly, man and Nature were also demarcated, most extremely in Cartesian dualism in which Nature became merely extension (matter in motion) and man alone possessed consciousness. Such programmatic segregation of the divine, the natural and the human had gigantic consequences in terms of franchising man's right, through science and technological intervention, to act upon Nature. For, once Nature was thus "disenchanted," the New Scientists increasingly claimed man's right, as Bacon put it, to "conquer and subdue her." If Nature were not after all alive but just an object, it could be taken to pieces, anatomized, resolved into atoms. Passive and uniform, Nature was open to experiment, or, in Bacon's grim metaphor, to be "tortured" into revealing its truth. The dictum that science should (in Bacon's phrase) "penetrate from Nature's antechambers to her inner closet" became axiomatic.

Within these seventeenth-century reconceptualizations, God became more remote and Nature less sacrosanct. Man's right to progress (even to redeem himself) through the pursuit of knowledge of, and power over, Nature became central to influential visions of human destiny; and the conquest of Nature became a practical, noble and even godly goal. The material transformation of the West over the last three centuries would have been impossible without the technical capacity generated by seventeenth-century science; but it would also have been unthinkable without the sanction and encouragement given by the new visions of science and Nature formulated in Baconianism, Cartesianism and other parallel seventeenth-century philosophies.

Here it is important however, not to confuse causes and consequences. Much of the best scholarship of the last couple of decades has challenged the old view that science advances by individual thought revolutions, by demonstrating the huge range of intellectual traditions which helped fecundate modern science (many of them, such as magic or astrology, conventionally seen as non-scientific). The new science did not spring like Pallas Athene straight from the brains of its giants; indeed it was both "unscientific" in its origins and ideological in its functions. All this amounts to a much-needed iconoclasm. But it would be a mistake to belittle the epochal consequences of scientific change merely because the imputs of that change were "impure." Balance here is important. We may usefully speak of a transition from magic to science, so long as we remain alert to the magic in science and the magic of science at the close of the seventeenth century and beyond. Religion, metaphysics, and ideology continued to play key roles *within* science after Newton. The tendency to place the New Science or the Newtonian synthesis on a pedestal must be resisted, for otherwise it will become a shrine; and attempts to cut the New Science down to size must be welcomed.

Yet, when seventeenth-century science is cut down to size, what remains impressive is indeed its towering magnitude. Recent currents in the sociology of science and the "deconstruction" of scientific knowledge have done sterling service in demythologizing "objective knowledge" and baring science's social relations and ideological freighting. Yet, if we make too much of science's *origins* in other modes of thought, we may lose sight of its extraordinary internal power, and thus render its influence and success mysterious, or intelligible only conspiratorially. Today's fears that (as Peacock's Dr Opimian put it) "it is the ultimate destiny of science to exterminate the human race," shouldn't lead us to forget the deep attractions of the New Science to generations of Europeans disgusted by the *ancien régime* with its suffocating clerical bigotry and arid academicism. Organized science seemed active, liberal, critical, productive, enterprising. Forget this, and we will never have more than a warped understanding of what Harman has called "the dominance of science in contemporary culture." . . .

Betty Jo Teeter Dobbs

Newton as Final Cause and First Mover, 1994

In this selection, Betty Jo Dobbs, the chronicler of Newton's commitment to alchemy, critiques the entire intellectualist historiography of science for inventing scientific heroes in the image of present ideals of scientific excellence. Thus, modern historians have viewed Newton as the necessary end of the Scientific Revolution, the figure to whom all the other canonical heroes had to lead. Newton is like the final cause in Aristotelian physics, without which there can be no change. The concept of Scientific Revolution, Dobbs argues, has so clouded our understanding of the actual historical individuals historians study that it should be dropped as an intellectual framework for understanding the developments in science in the sixteenth and seventeenth centuries.

Friends and colleagues, it is an honor to be asked to speak to you this evening, and I thank you for the occasion. It is, however, entirely possible that you will regret granting me this forum, for I intend to undermine one of our most hallowed explanatory frameworks, that of the Scientific Revolution—almost always written with capital letters, of course.

I am well aware that something happened in the sixteenth and seventeenth centuries that human beings have since come to regard as revolutionary—revolutionary, that is, in the modern sense of that word: in I. B. Cohen's definition of political revolution, "a change that is sudden, radical, and complete." Or, in the words of Arthur Marwick, who has

Selections from Betty Jo Dobbs, "Newton as Final Cause and First Mover," *Isis* 85, No. 4 (December 1994): 633–643. Copyright © 1994 by The History of Science Society. Reprinted by permission of The University of Chicago Press.

scant patience with overuse of the term, "a significant change in political structure carried through within a fairly short space of time." . . . We must keep in mind that the modern meaning of revolution did develop in the political sphere. When we use it for scientific thought, we are in fact using a metaphor.

But as Cohen demonstrated so well in 1985, the word *revolution* hardly began to acquire its modern meaning until the eighteenth century; before then the term had carried the implication of a cyclical turning, a turning around, or even a turning back, a *re*turn to an original position, just as Copernicus used it in the title of his book, *On the Revolutions of the Celestial Spheres.* Cohen was unable to discover a single one of the canonical heroes of the sixteenth and seventeenth centuries who had appropriated the word *revolution* in its modern meaning for his own work. Only in the eighteenth century did Cohen find exemplars: Bernard Le Bovier de Fontenelle termed the invention of the calculus as a revolution in mathematics early in the eighteenth century; one W. Cockburn, M.D., in 1728 treated the work of Paracelsus as a medical revolution; Alexis Claude Clairaut in the 1750s cited Newton for a revolution in rational mechanics. . . .

Such retrospective judgments of the eighteenth century upon the work of the sixteenth and seventeenth centuries received a familiar progressive form in Jean Le Rond d'Alembert's "Preliminary Discourse" for the great Enlightenment encyclopedia project: Bacon, Descartes, Newton, Locke. D'Alembert used the metaphor of political revolution quite explicitly for Descartes: "He can be thought of as a leader of conspirators who, before any one else, had the courage to arise against a despotic and arbitrary power and who, in preparing a resounding revolution, laid the foundations of a more just and happier government, which he himself was not able to see established." Regretting the lack of space, d'Alembert mentioned in passing Kepler, Barrow, Galileo, Harvey, Huygens, Pascal, Malebranche, Boyle, Vesalius, Sydenham, and Boerhaave; he gave a bit more space to Leibniz, despite having little admiration for him apart from his work on the calculus. Except for the rather glaring omission of Copernicus, d'Alembert came close to our modern canonical list of participants in the construction of modern science during the sixteenth, seventeenth, and early eighteenth centuries. We thus see that already at mid-eighteenth century the narrative of the Scientific Revolution had taken shape in d'Alembert's work. Though it has not yet received its dramatic capitalized title, both the story line and the substance were there.

By the time d'Alembert wrote, Enlightenment optimism and belief in progress had achieved notable strength among the philosophes. Although d'Alembert mentioned the great battle between the ancients and the moderns, it is clear that he thought that the battle was essentially over and that the moderns had won. "Progress"—in the sense of the improvement of human life on this earth—had largely supplanted millenarianism among the French philosophers. . . . [T]he scientist was being carefully molded into a new type of cultural hero, as Fontenelle in his *éloges*, and later eulogists also, attributed the moral virtues of the idealized Stoic philosopher to recently deceased natural philosophers. Scientists came to be viewed as a superior breed of men engaged in a high moral venture, objective and selfless, dedicated to the mental and material improvement of humanity. Londa Schiebinger, with her fine sense of historical contingency, has argued that there was even a brief historical moment when women might have been included in the new elect, but negative judgments being forthcoming on that issue, the moment passed. Bringing women into the picture alerts us to the new science as an instrument of political and social power in the heavenly city of the eighteenth-century philosophers, and this point on the political and social significance of the new science is one to which I will return. . . .

As science accumulated more and more social prestige in the later eighteenth, nineteenth, and early twentieth centuries, the image of Newton as principal cultural hero of the new science was handed on and further polished by succeeding generations of scientists and historians, the mathematical sciences taking the *Principia* as their pristine model, the experimental sciences relying on the *Opticks*. The fuller historical record was often reduced to a paragraph or two on Isaac Newton, the canonical "father of modern science." Thus Newton was seen more and more as the First Mover of modern science, the efficient cause in the Aristotelian sense, holding an unassailable primacy in mathematics, enlightened rationality, and experimentation. . . . It is in part this massive apotheosis of Newton that has created problems with the concept of the Scientific Revolution, but of course that is not the only problem with the concept.

The concept of *the* Scientific Revolution of the sixteenth and seventeenth centuries achieved its own historiographic dominance in this century, primarily after World War II. Our own "founding father," George Sarton, was not much enamored of the concept of scientific revolutions, as Cohen observed, preferring to emphasize the cumulative character of "the inquiry concerning nature." But Martha Ornstein in 1913, Alfred North Whitehead in 1923, E. A. Burtt in 1925, John Herman Randall, Jr., in 1926, Preserved Smith in 1930, and J. D. Bernal in 1939 all pressed forward with the concept of *the* Scientific Revolution as an event of major significance for the creation not only of modern science but of the modern world. I. B. Cohen has carefully examined the works of these authors in his fundamental study *Revolution in Science*, but he has gone on to demonstrate that the concept of *the* Scientific Revolution, as a major historiographic concept, was really fully developed in the late 1940s and the 1950s in works of Alexandre Koyré, Herbert Butterfield, and A. Rupert Hall. To Cohen's list I would add *The Copernican Revolution*, published in 1957 by Thomas S. Kuhn. These works are all, I believe, still in print, some in revised editions, and they have probably been utilized in the training of virtually all the historians of science in this room. Their impact has been simply enormous, but, as Cohen observed, it was Kuhn's publication in 1962 of *The Structure of Scientific Revolutions* that gave the concept its widest currency. . . .

But however many scientific revolutions may be described, it is with the first one that I am principally concerned, for it is in the narrative of that first one that the narrative structure itself seems to demand Newton as Final Cause. If he was viewed as the First Mover or efficient cause in nineteenth- and early twentieth-century science, in our accounts of *the* Scientific Revolution we see Newton emerging as the Aristotelian Final Cause. Have you ever stopped to count the number of books that either begin or end with Isaac Newton?

No matter what one chooses to emphasize from the sixteenth and seventeenth centuries in telling the story, one must, it seems, bring the action to a dramatic climax with the work of Isaac Newton. The narrative has assumed all the characteristics of an inevitable progression; we have the sense that Newton must appear on the scene to pull the disparate strands of development into a grand synthesis. It is a teleological story we tell: Newton is the hidden end toward which the whole narrative is inexorably drawn, the Final Clause of the Scientific Revolution. Had he not really existed at the time and in that place, perhaps we would have had to invent him. Perhaps in some sense we did invent him, for the periodization and progressive ideology of the Scientific Revolution created such intractable interpretive problems associated with Newton that one may reasonably argue that our "Newton as Final Cause" is a historical construct bearing little resemblance to the historical record. . . .

. . . Let us consider for a moment the publication of Butterfield's book, *The Origins of Modern Science*, in 1949. World War II had been over for only a few brief years, and, although Britain had been terribly battered, she had emerged on the winning side. The war itself had made the importance of science and science-based technology apparent as never before. Radar—Britain's secret weapon—made it possible for her to survive Hitler's air attack in 1940, in the so-called Battle of Britain. From radar to the development and delivery of atomic bombs by the United States, the most advanced science of the period had generally been deployed by the winners. Small wonder, then, that the British historian Herbert Butterfield would say exuberantly in 1949 that the Scientific Revolution "outshines everything since the rise of Christianity and reduces the Renaissance and Reformation to the rank of mere episodes, mere internal displacements within the system of medieval Christendom." He claimed for his own generation an ability to see the importance of the Scientific Revolution "more clearly than the men who flourished fifty or even twenty years before us." In that latter claim, Butterfield was entirely correct, because of his own precise location in time and space.

But was Butterfield's book good history? Butterfield, you will recall, was one of the persons who first mounted a serious critique of what he called the "Whig interpretation of history." That was a mode of historical interpretation common in nineteenth-century Britain that found in the past a steady progress toward liberal ideas and institutions. Butterfield pointed out that such views omitted vast sectors of human experience and in any case warped the evidence actually considered by imbuing the whole story with an aura of inevitability—it was somehow preordained that liberal ideas and institutions would prevail. Yet Butterfield gave us the most whiggish history of science imaginable. His book is pervaded with the conviction that the "winner" scientific ideas were right and good, and their triumph is made to seem inevitable.

I do not wish to belabor Butterfield's worthwhile book at too great length. It was and is a readable, nontechnical, and useful introduction to the origins of modern science. But I would like to point to a few problems with the concept of the Scientific Revolution it embodied.

One problem turns on the question of time in the use of the revolution metaphor. If a revolution is "a change that is sudden, radical, and complete," then there simply was no Copernican revolution, for by the end of the sixteenth century there were probably only about ten

Copernicans in the whole world. Perhaps partly to avoid that sort of problem, Butterfield expanded the time frame to 500 years, half a millennium, 1300–1800. The time frame for the older narrative of the Scientific Revolution had already been expansive: from publication by Copernicus in 1543 to publication by Newton in 1687, some 144 years. Whether 144 or 500 years, the transfer of the term *revolution* from the political sphere to the scientific sphere has clearly detached the word from its root meaning in politics of a sudden change or one carried through in a fairly short space of time. One suspects, indeed, that we have forgotten we are using a metaphor at all.

In Butterfield's case, this expansiveness led him to develop the remarkable notion of "the postponed scientific revolution in chemistry." "It has often been a matter of surprise," he said, "that the emergence of modern chemistry should come at so late a stage in the story of scientific progress." That statement contains the hidden assumption that the forward motion of "scientific progress" is inevitable, and it also implies that modern chemistry would have come earlier but for some unfortunate obstruction in the path of "scientific progress." . . .

One might suppose that I am here bedeviling a man and a concept that are not only made of straw but are also dead. But I have to tell you that the concept is not dead and that I am not so sure that it is made of straw, because we have rather recently, in 1990, been offered two perfectly fascinating essays on the chemical revolution by prominent historians of chemistry, Allen Debus and Maurice Crosland. . . .

. . . Koyré and Kuhn, in the other most influential books from the 1950s and early 1960s, . . . did think in terms of revolutions, and they have had many followers, including myself. Indeed probably all of us here absorbed elements of the idea that revolutions take place in science, and we use the idea for periodization as well as in reconstructing the origins of the thought patterns of modernity. The concept of *the* Scientific Revolution of the sixteenth and seventeenth centuries and the notion of an entire sequence of revolutions in science since that time have been enormously useful to us in creating the discipline of the history of science. But having said that, I must also say that I think perhaps those ideas are losing some of their utility. Recent trends offer many promising alternatives: local studies of natural philosophy in court, civic, and university cultures; studies like Steven Shapin and Simon Schaffer's *Leviathan and the Air-Pump* and Margaret Jacob's *The Cultural Meaning of the Scientific Revolution,* where the social and political significance and use of ideas are explicated; reconstruction of the contemporary context for the work of Bacon, Kepler, and Boyle. But we are still encumbered with some of the baggage of the metaphor of revolution that obscures so much continuity in the midst of change and produces such improbable interpretations of historical actors, for in many ways we are still most intent upon explicating the changes that led to us. Here we are in the late twentieth century, still privileging the fragments of the past that we recognize as belonging to our own present. In some ways we have continued to act like nineteenth-century whig historians.

It increasingly seems to me that these problems are not new ones. In the seventeenth century many participants in the new natural philosophies railed against Aristotle and against university intellectual culture as arid and barren—like thistles, Francis Bacon said. For three centuries we have accepted and repeated such maxims as fact rather than as part of a political struggle. Only recently, with the work of Charles Schmitt and Mordechai Feingold, for example, can we begin to appreciate the rich variety of university culture, where Aristotle was still at the forefront of the prescribed curriculum but where Bacon, Descartes, Locke, and Newton himself were appropriated and studied almost as soon as they published. The universities reemerge from this new work as nurturing cradles of intellectual life, and it is now possible to reevaluate the major role of Aristotelian thought patterns—and other supposedly outmoded thought patterns—in the new ways of thinking. Similarly, we have carelessly accepted what now begins to look like Protestant propaganda. After Galileo's little problem with the Church of Rome, much was made of the dismal state of natural philosophy in Catholic countries; we only now begin to learn of complex and rigorous Jesuit scientific thought.

But to my mind the issue of the proper interpretation of our scientific heroes has been the most pressing problem of all, a problem that was at least in part generated by the concept of the Scientific Revolution. I think the problem arises somewhat in this fashion: we choose for praise the thinkers that seem to us to have contributed to modernity, but we unconsciously assume that their thought patterns were fundamental just like ours. Then we look at them a little more closely and discover to our astonishment that our intellectual ancestors are not like us at all: they do not see the full implications of their own work; they refuse to believe things that are now so obviously true; they have metaphysical and religious commitments that they should have known were unnecessary for a study of nature; horror of horrors, they take seriously such misbegotten ideas as astrology, alchemy, magic, the music of the spheres, divine providence, and salvation history. We become most uncomfortable and begin to talk about Copernicus as "conservative" or "timid," terms that hardly fit the commonsense concept of a revolutionary. Or we talk about Kepler as a "tortured mystic" or a "sleepwalker" or a "split personality." . . .

Twentieth-century historians have produced . . . wafflings about others in the canonical list. How could Copernicus have taken just that one small step of transposing sun and earth and not have gone further, retaining as he did the primacy of circular motion *and* the closed cosmos *and* Aristotelian physics? How could John Dee—at the forefront of scientific navigation in the sixteenth century—possibly have supposed he could communicate with angels? How could Kepler possibly have maintained his 1595 vision of the Platonic solids as God's architectural plan for the solar system even after he announced the three laws of planetary motion that were subsequently incorporated into *our* science? How could Galileo have ignored Kepler's ellipses even after he proclaimed the Book of Nature to be written in mathematical language? How could Descartes have persisted in believing deductive reasoning to be the way to true knowledge when all about him the experimental method was being pushed forward? How could Newton retain his belief in a sun-centered cosmos after he himself had described an infinite universe? One cannot imagine that, mathematician as he was, he did not know that no center was possible for an infinite space.

But above all, how could Newton, the epitome of austere scientific, mathematical rationality, have pursued alchemy as he did, through exhaustive analysis of alchemical texts and through extensive experimentation? . . .

The problem, as I slowly—very slowly—came to perceive it, was indeed a historiographic one. During the same period that Newton came to be acclaimed as the "father of modern science," alchemy suffered a radical decline, or an eclipse. . . .

Consider, then, the consternation of Sir David Brewster, astronomer royal and the first major biographer of Newton, when he obtained access to Newton's private papers later in the nineteenth century. Brewster "knew" that Newton was correctly placed in "the enlightened part of mankind"—Newtonian celestial physics was Brewster's bread and butter—but Thomson's evaluation of alchemy echoed in his ears. With what horror, then, did he see Newton's alchemical papers: "[We] cannot understand how a mind of such power, and so nobly occupied with the abstractions of geometry, and the study of the material world, could stoop to be even the copyist of the most contemptible alchemical poetry, and the annotator of a work, the obvious production of a fool and a knave." Brewster was shocked, and understandably so. Two totally divergent historical developments had created a chasm he could not span—the apotheosis of Newton as austere mathematician and experimenter who had set the better part of humanity on the right track, and the degradation of alchemy to "delusion and superstition."

Brewster's obvious first mistake was to assume that Newton's whole purpose was to study the material world, which was what he, Brewster, did, as a nineteenth-century scientist. His second mistake was to accept without hesitation the nineteenth-century evaluation of alchemy as delusion and superstition. But I do not know how he could have done otherwise, given those two very powerful historical trends plus several others of which he remained unaware. We in the twentieth century, with much, much more information to bring to bear upon the problem, can surely do better. I hope I have done so, but I regretfully take note that in Rupert Hall's new biography of Newton, the old problems remain.

Hall argues that Newton wanted only "facts" from his alchemical and chemical experiments. Perhaps that is, in a sense, correct, but the word *fact* offers us another problem in historical semantics. Colleagues who know the languages tell me that the ancient Greeks had no word for *fact*, though in the seventeenth century the English word *fact* was acquiring its modern usage of socially validated knowledge of the natural world. Yet alchemy for Newton had more than one ontological level: he supposed he could get from it not just knowledge of the natural world but knowledge of the supernatural world as well. If Newton was looking for "facts" in his alchemical work, I think the sort of facts he hoped to glean from alchemy have very little resonance with the Newton who is perceived only as a student of the natural world. What Newton hoped to gain from alchemy was a precise knowledge of the operations of the Deity in organizing and vivifying the inert particles of matter in the microcosm.

Alchemy never was, and never was intended to be, a study of matter for its own sake or a study of the natural world for its own sake. Alchemists sought perfection or the knowledge thereof, not utility for this life, as chemistry later came to do. They sought the philosopher's stone, an agent of perfection for both nature and humanity—as they said, medicine for both men and metals. The alchemists' philosopher's stone was closely allied with the Christ of Christianity—both were, after all, agents of perfection and redemption. Newton saw an even broader significance: his Arian Christ, God's agent in the creation and governance of the created world, was closely allied with the philosopher's stone, the active principle of alchemy. If he, Newton, could but demonstrate the laws of divine activity in nature, the Christ operating in and governing the microcosm, then he could demonstrate in an irrefutable fashion the existence and providential care of the Deity—a grand goal, though hardly a modern one. Newton indeed hoped to restore the original true religion—to effect a "revolution," a return to a former state, in the earlier meaning of the word *revolution.*

If Newton had succeeded in this aim, and had thereby stemmed the tides of mechanism, materialism, deism, and atheism, as he had hoped, we would of course live in a different world. But I do not much like to play the game of counterfactual history. Perhaps the world would have been better, perhaps not. But of course the tides of mechanism, materialism, deism, and atheism were already quite strong when Newton lived. He was well instructed in the dangers of those tendencies by the Cambridge Platonists, and he fought a valiant holding action against them, but he did not win. His system was very quickly coopted by the very -isms he fought, and adjusted to suit them. He came down to us as coopted, an Enlightenment figure without parallel who could not possibly have been concerned with alchemy or with establishing the existence and activity of a providential God. He did not win in the end, as Koyré knew already in 1957: "The mighty, energetic God of Newton who actually 'ran' the universe . . . became, in quick succession, a conservative power, an *intelligentia supra-mundana,* a 'Dieu fainéant.'" But surely we no longer need play down and make despicable Newton's valiant effort.

In conclusion, I would like to suggest that there may be some historical value in evaluating Newton in a different way: not as one of history's all-time winners, not as the First Mover of modern science, not as the Final Cause of *the* Scientific Revolution, but as one of history's great losers, a loser in a titanic battle between the forces of religion and the forces of irreligion. Perhaps he is no less a hero from that perspective, but a hero of a different sort, rather more like Roland at Ronceval, crushed by overwhelming odds in the rearguard, than like a peerless leader of the vanguard. To reevaluate Newton in that way might also allow us to engage in some fresh and creative rethinking of the many changes taking place in the sixteenth and seventeenth centuries.

Peter Dear

The Mathematical Principles of Natural Philosophy: Toward a Heuristic Narrative for the Scientific Revolution, 1998

Peter Dear endorses the concept of the Scientific Revolution, but he wants to treat it as an intellectual change grounded in actual practice. He admires the work of "visionaries" like E. A. Burtt and Alexandre Koyré, and he believes that "there is still room for large stories" in the history of science, but these stories must consider the ways in which intellectual change was impacted by routine behavioral patterns. Most of Dear's scholarly work has emphasized the importance of mathematics in the cognitive and social practices of the thinkers of the sixteenth and seventeenth centuries. In this selection, he urges scholars to use the rising status of mathematics as a key to understanding the dimensions of change during early modern times.

The "Scientific Revolution" is nowadays, as a category, much less attractive to historians than it once was. It seems to carry overtones of Whiggish triumphalism that are widely seen as out of keeping with a proper scholarly understanding of issues to do with the making of European natural knowledge in the sixteenth and seventeenth centuries. Nonetheless, as our historiographic heritage, it continues to set agendas and direct us to particular problem areas. Given that situation, it is important to know whether we are dealing with nothing but an ideological construct.

An attachment to the "Scientific Revolution" need not be a matter of sentimental attachment to a comfortable historical framework. There

Peter Dear, The Mathematical Principles of Natural Philosophy: Toward a Heuristic Narrative for the Scientific Revolution, *Configurations* 6 (No. 2) (1998) 173–193. © The Johns Hopkins University Press and Society for Literature and Science. Reprinted with permission of The Johns Hopkins University Press.

are grounds for believing that the older, increasingly unfashionable "master narratives" of the Scientific Revolution still have a lot to offer, even though there are important ways in which they can no longer be accepted. In particular, visionaries such as E. A. Burtt and Alexandre Koyré saw things that really are there, and that therefore cannot simply be dismissed. It is possible, I shall argue, to renovate the classic "Scientific Revolution" as a meaningful object in the history of science, even if we might today prefer a different term to designate roughly the same referent.

I

Any "master narrative" is intended by its very nature to subordinate and order the more localized understandings of particular events or themes that are typically the focus of the specialized article literature. But at the same time, that latter kind of scholarship always tends to evade the totalizing ambitions of a master narrative even while implicitly relying on one for its own claims to significance. Historical scholarship thus tends to proceed by a dialectical process wherein ambitious master narratives perennially appear, only to have their pretensions undermined by the objections of smaller-scale detailed research.

Thomas Kuhn's *Structure of Scientific Revolutions* (1962) is a book that in many ways can be seen as the crucial link between the intellectual and the sociocultural approaches to understanding the history of science. Kuhn's starting point was the conceptual analysis of past scientific thought, an attempt to "get inside" an alien way of thought. He acknowledged in this regard the importance of Koyré's work in directing his own approach. . . .

Kuhn's general perspective draws our attention back to the sorts of considerations that made people such as Koyré focus on the sixteenth and seventeenth centuries in the first place. Sociological and anthropological considerations have their appeal in precisely those places where they can help us come to grips with issues of *how people thought*, and how their conceptual frameworks changed. This in turn means that there is still a place for "master narratives" of the period; there is still room for large stories about its importance for understanding modern science.

Koyré's and Burtt's emphasis on "metaphysical frameworks" is no longer historiographically tenable: it disregards local contingency, appears to sideline situated human agency, and talks in zeitgeist-terms about what was "in the air." However, their take on the matter was motivated by a commendable wish to grasp hold of something that seemed to be an authentic feature of the historical landscape. Their problem was very similar to the problems of talking about such large things as national "cultures." A few years ago Dominick LaCapra criticized Robert Darnton's account of the "Great Cat Massacre" on the grounds that it effectively posited some sort of "symbolic system" that hovered in the air, an air that everyone breathed. LaCapra focused on a real difficulty: not the existence of an issue demanding some form of explanation, but the question of finding an adequate idiom in which to understand it. That is, Darnton was onto something, and so were Burtt and Koyré.

The difficulty in the case of the Scientific Revolution is constituted above all by the fact that the relevant overarching cultural constructs have been represented as fundamentally intellectual. If the issues are framed in terms of "intellectual traditions" that affect or determine behavior, a metaphysical problem of intelligibility arises: how could those two radically different categories of object interact causally? By contrast, rather than taking about ideas from high culture as somehow constraining or acting as conditions of possibility for other ideas or actions, we can look at how broad cultural characterizations that may well have intellectual correlates at the phenomenal level are rooted in daily, routine *behavior*. This was what I tried, very experimentally, to do in an article a few years ago called "Miracles, Experiments, and the Ordinary Course of Nature." My idea was to argue that routine patterns of behavior, rather than of ideas, that were expressed in part through theorizing about miracles, were also expressed through behavior relating to the experimental knowledge of nature. On that basis, I tried to make sense of apparent broad distinctions between the French and English cases in the seventeenth century regarding mathematical and physical science.

Such sweeping talk about "national cultures," or any similar large-scale cultural field, is dangerous and difficult to sustain, of course. But if one only allowed recognition and explanation of whatever could be analyzed in terms of local interactions—power, interests, all those elements of the contextualist's armory—then one would lose a great deal of potential explanatory leverage, or would at least render explanation impractical. There have to be different levels of characterization and explanation, rather than a demand for reductionism. For example, one can assert that France today is a country predominantly of French-speakers; and yet to explain *why* in terms of the daily interactions whereby that cultural feature is sustained—or, potentially, subverted (as occurs in every verbal exchange)—would be impossible. It would be necessary to appeal to surrogate explanatory entities, such as the concept of "cultures," or "forms of life," or some such.

The point applies equally to the intellectualist "metaphysical frameworks" used in classic versions of the Scientific Revolution. They are certainly getting at *something*. The problem is in deciding what that something is, which is where approaches that pay attention to sociological or anthropological considerations can be worth considering.

Rather than attempting to get inside other ways of thought by purely intellectual means, we can build a lot of the scaffolding by looking at the ways in which the activities in question were structured at a gross sociological level—which means making use of such materials as those of institutional history. The important thing here is always to be able to translate such considerations back into ideas. The grand narrative that I wish to suggest is one that is aimed at a good Kuhnian target: the academic discipline. The approach in effect uses disciplines as surrogates for "metaphysical frameworks." In particular, it examines a basic disciplinary and cognitive division of the period: the natural philosophy/mathematics division that was first raised up as a significant focus of investigation by Robert S. Westman in specific relation to sixteenth-century astronomy.

In the scholastic curriculum of the sixteenth century, and continuing through most of the seventeenth, natural philosophy (also called "physics") held a prized place in the arts curriculum. It was categorically distinct from the so-called mathematical sciences, descended from the medieval quadrivium, which were themselves divided into "pure" (geometry and arithmetic) and "mixed" (roughly similar to the modern category of "applied" mathematics, including such subjects as positional astronomy, geometrical optics, and mechanics). The mixed mathematical sciences were generally held to be of a lower status because they did not, as natural philosophy did, concern the essences of the things and processes of which they spoke; rather than giving true casual explanations of physical phenomena, rooted in the real natures of the things involved, they just coordinated quantities. Aristotle's four causes, the philosophers generally held, did not apply to mathematical matters. . . .

. . . One of the stories that can be told about the early modern period concerns the increasing status and scope of the classical mathematical sciences vis-à-vis natural philosophy as it was known in the universities and colleges of sixteenth- and seventeenth-century Europe—predominantly (or hegemonically) some kind of Aristotelian natural philosophy. By the beginning of the eighteenth century, the mathematical sciences were becoming the vanguard of an operational science of nature, and Aristotelian natural philosophy was becoming outmoded and unfashionable. . . . And yet the term "natural philosophy" itself remained. The most telling indication of the situation is the title of Isaac Newton's *Mathematical Principles of Natural Philosophy* of 1687. It ought to have been an oxymoron: by definition, natural philosophy could not have *mathematical* principles, as any scholastic philosopher could have explained. Nonetheless, Newton was able to get away with it, and "natural philosophy" lived on, albeit with quite reconstructed connotations, into the last century.

I use the term "natural philosophy" in reference to the seventeenth century fairy loosely, to refer to the wide variety of scholastic-Aristotelian natural philosophy as it existed in the schools and colleges of Latin Europe. Most people talking about "natural philosophy" at this time, even when their own favored kind was non-Aristotelian, nonetheless did so from the basis of an education in Aristotelian physics and an awareness of the sorts of topics and ways of formulating them that it employed. . . .

The story to be told, then, is one of *how* "natural philosophy" became mathematical, of *how* the techniques and ideologies of the mathematical sciences came to subvert or co-opt those of conventional Aristotelian natural philosophy. This construction of the problem is a way of translating the old story of "metaphysical frameworks" into something that deals with the concrete cognitive practices of people in specific social locations, rather than just talking about their "putting on a different kind of thinking-cap," as Herbert Butterfield put it. Such a story still has pretensions to being a "master narrative," by the way that it lays out a research agenda, telling us what sorts of questions to ask and how to know when we have satisfactory answers; perhaps it might better be called a "master heuristic." . . . Consideration of the emergent thinkability of "mathematical principles of natural philosophy" can help to direct our attention toward problems that might otherwise remain invisible. . . .

II

. . . [P]aying attention to the mathematics/physics boundary—and the means adopted for its maintenance or blurring—is, at the very least, a useful heuristic in charting changing approaches to natural knowledge in the sixteenth and seventeenth centuries. In particular, the new seventeenth-century label "physico-mathematics" is a valuable indication that this way of construing the issues reflects real categories of concern to the historical actors themselves.

III

Most grand narratives of the Scientific Revolution present as their culmination the work of Isaac Newton. In the old days (as we historians like to say), he was portrayed as the completer of the project purportedly set in train by the work of Copernicus. Copernicus led to Kepler, and Kepler's laws of planetary motion linked with Galileo's work on a terrestrial mechanics of motion to yield Newtonian mechanics and universal gravitation. Into the bargain, Newton could also be presented as a great empiricist, in keeping with the view that the Scientific Revolution was about the rejection of ancient authority. The framework outlined in earlier sections of this paper seems quite different, but Newton can still be represented as a real emblem of change at the end of the period, and still a useful way of rounding off a story of the Scientific Revolution. Of course, this is no longer because we want to say in an unproblematic way that "Newton was right." Newton—both Newton in himself, and the Newton beloved of the eighteenth and nineteenth centuries—crystallized and rendered uncontroversial for most people (though not all) assumptions that the rhetoric of "physico-mathematics" had encapsulated during the seventeenth century.

The characteristics of what has often been called "Newtonian science" in the eighteenth century involved emphasizing the operational aspects of Newton's mathematical natural philosophy. Not only did the "mathematical" sciences eschew "physical" causes (as with Newton's own occasional agnosticism regarding the cause of gravitational attraction), they also frequently exhibited a pragmatic focus on being able to *do* things, such as navigate from London to Virginia. In a recent book, Christian Licoppe has represented Benjamin Franklin's work on electricity as characteristically "Newtonian" in precisely this sense, and this despite the apparently unmathematized nature of that work. Licoppe's presentation differs from I. Bernard Cohen's classic use of Newton to contextualize Franklin, however; Cohen was concerned to show that Franklin's natural philosophy (involving such things as matter theory) connected to Newton's earlier work in similar areas, whereas Licoppe is interested in the epistemological style whereby Franklin made his knowledge claims through his representations of experimental work. Licoppe stresses the operational dimension of that work: Franklin is always centrally interested in *how to do* things. . . .

    . . . It should be remembered, however, that the present interpretive framework for understanding the Scientific Revolution is by no means the only story that can be told of this time and place. There may be many more untrue stories than true ones in the universe, but there are still many true stories. I would suggest that this conceptualization of the Scientific Revolution is the most useful one for many of the long-recognized aspects of the period that originally encouraged the application of that label; other stories of the period might require a different one.

Suggestions for Further Reading

Many historians have written about the Scientific Revolution for both a general and scholarly audience. The following suggestions are very selective and reflect the themes covered in this volume. Only works in English are included in this bibliography.

The authors whose works have been used in the first section of this book have written other studies of the Scientific Revolution, many of which have become standards in the field. In particular, Alexandre Koyré's *Galileo Studies*, trans. John Mepham (Atlantic Highlands, N.J.: Humanities Press, 1978; orig. publ. 1939) and *Newtonian Studies* (London: Chapman and Hall, 1925) emphasize the importance of rationalism and mathematics in science; A. Rupert Hall's *From Galileo to Newton, 1630–1720* (London: Collins, 1963) complements the study of the Scientific Revolution excerpted in this volume; and Richard S. Westfall's splendid biography of Isaac Newton, *Never at Rest: A Biography of Isaac Newton* (Cambridge: Cambridge University Press, 1980), demonstrates how completely he was able to integrate a traditional and more contemporary approach to this canonical figure. It is worthwhile to look at Herbert Butterfield, *The Origins of Modern Science, 1300–1800,* rev. ed. (New York: Free Press, 1965; orig. publ. 1949) for an eloquent, historically informed and very influential treatment of the Scientific Revolution. Equally important, although often neglected in surveys of the Scientific Revolution, is A. C. Crombie, *Augustine to Galileo: The History of Science, A.D. 400–1650* (London: Falcon, 1952), which traces the roots of the scientific movement to the later Middle Ages. A more comprehensive approach to the development of scientific thought can also be found in E. J. Dijksterhuis, *The Mechanization of the World Picture: Pythagoras to Newton* (Princeton: Princeton University Press, 1986; orig. publ. 1950), which while quite dense, is also extraordinarily informative. An intriguing intellectualist account of a somewhat broader range of canonical figures can be found in Richard H. Popkin, *The History of Scepticism from Erasmus to Descartes*, rev. ed. (New York: Harper & Row, 1964).

The single best place to start reading about the relationship of science and religion in the sixteenth and seventeenth century is David C. Lindberg and Ronald L. Numbers, *God and Nature: Historical Essays of the Encounter between Christianity and Science* (Berkeley: University of California Press, 1986). The introduction is particularly informative in presenting the historiographical tradition, and the essays themselves include revisionist discussions of the role of Catholicism and Protestantism during the Scientific Revolution. John Hedley Brooke, *Science and Religion: Some Historical Perspectives* (Cambridge: Cambridge University Press, 1991) gives a comprehensive account of the historiography on the relationship between science and religion. He also argues for a more complex and nuanced treatment of this subject, which would avoid the generalizations made by historians who are either hostile or sympathetic towards religion. In fact, it would be difficult to find many modern overtly partisan accounts of this subject, although Robert Hooykaas, *Religion and the Rise of Modern Science* (Edinburgh: Scottish Academic Press, 1973) presents a strongly sympathetic account of the relationship between early Protestantism and science. I. Bernard Cohen (ed.), *Puritanism and the Rise of Modern Science: The Merton Thesis* (New Brunswick: Rutgers University Press, 1990) brings together many of the most important commentaries on Merton. Important discussions of the connection between Anglicanism and science include James R. Jacob and Margaret C. Jacob, "The Anglican Origins of Modern Science: The Metaphysical Foundations of the Whig Constitution," *Isis* 71 (1980): 251–267; and Lotte Mulligan, "Civil War Politics, Religion and the Royal Society," in *The Intellectual Revolution of the Seventeenth Century*, ed. Charles Webster (London: Routledge & Kegan Paul, 1974). The important role Catholic theology played in the development of science is emphasized in Amos Funkenstein, *Theology and the Scientific Imagination from the Middle Ages to the Seventeenth Century* (Princeton: Princeton University Press, 1986). The role of the Church in the condemnation of Galileo has been reexamined in William R. Shea and Mariano Artigas, *Galileo in Rome: The Rise and Fall of a Troublesome Genius* (Oxford: Oxford University Press, 2003).

The relationship of science to society continues to be the focus of much of the recent scholarship on the Scientific Revolution. Thomas S. Kuhn developed his theory of scientific revolution in *The Structure of Scientific Revolutions* (Chicago: University of Chicago Press, 1962), and "Mathematical versus Experimental Traditions in the Development of

Science," in *The Essential Tension: Selected Studies in Scientific Tradition and Change* (Chicago: University of Chicago Press, 1977). Kuhn's ideas are sympathetically critiqued in Robert S. Westman, "Two Cultures of One? A Second Look at Kuhn's *The Copernican Revolution*," *Isis* 85 (1994): 79–115. An historiographical account of social constructivism can be found in Jan Golinski, *Making Natural Knowledge: History of Science after Constructivism* (Cambridge: Cambridge University Press, 1998). One of the most developed examples of the social constructivist approach is Steven Shapin, *A Social History of Truth: Civility and Science in Seventeenth-Century England* (Chicago: University of Chicago Press, 1994). A stimulating discussion of the informal sociability of the scientific community in England towards the end of the Scientific Revolution can be found in Anne Goldgar, *Impolite Learning: Conduct and Community in the Republic of Letters, 1680–1750*). There are many studies of the formal scientific institutions that developed in the seventeenth century, including Roger Hahn, *The Anatomy of a Scientific Institution: The Paris Academy of Science 1666-1803* (Berkeley: University of California Press, 1971); Michael Hunter, *Science and Society in Restoration England* (Cambridge: Cambridge University Press, 1981); and W. E. Knowles Middleton, *The Experimentalists: A Study of the Accademia del Cimento* (Baltimore: The Johns Hopkins Press, 1971). A good place to start in examining how patronage affected science is the collection of essays in Bruce T. Moran (ed.), *Patronage and Institutions: Science, Technology and Medicine at the European Court, 1500–1750* (Woodbridge, Suffolk: The Boydell Press, 1991).

As the definition of Scientific Revolution has broadened, the numbers of studies of subjects outside of the traditional approach have increased exponentially. The place to begin is Frances A. Yates, *Giordano Bruno and the Hermetic* Tradition (Chicago: University of Chicago Press, 1964). The relationship of magic and science is examined in Charles Webster, *From Paracelsus to Newton: Magic and the Making of Modern Science* (Cambridge: Cambridge University Press, 1982). Medical and alchemical traditions are explored in Allen G. Debus's comprehensive *The Chemical Philosophy: Paracelsian Science and Medicine in the Sixteenth and Seventeenth* Centuries (New York: Science History Publications, 1977), which should be read in conjunction with Betty Jo Teeter Dobbs's, *The Foundations of Newton's Alchemy or "The Hunting of the Greene Lyon"* (Cambridge: Cambridge University Press, 1975). A classic article reexamining the meaning of occult forces during the Scientific Revolution is

Keith Hutchinson, "What Happened to Occult Qualities in the Scientific Revolution?," *Isis* 73 (1982): 233–253. An excellent collection of essays on the relationship of science and magic in the early Scientific Revolution are included in Brian Vickers (ed.), *Occult and Scientific Mentalities in the Renaissance* (Cambridge: Cambridge University Press, 1984). Astrology's connection to science is examined in Patrick Curry, *Astrology, Science and Society: Historical* Essays (Woodbridge, Suffolk: The Boydell Press, 1987), which contains particularly penetrating discussions of Kepler by J. V. Field and of Newton by Simon Schaffer. The links between popular culture and science are graphically described in Katherine Park and Lorraine Daston, *Wonders and the Order of Nature 1150–1750* (New York: Zone Books, 1998), and in the many fine essays in Stephen Pumfrey, Paolo L. Rossi, and Maurice Slawinski (eds.), *Science, Culture and Popular Belief in Renaissance Europe* (Manchester: Manchester University Press, 1991). The local nature of the development of science is explored in Roy Porter and Mikuláš Teich, *The Scientific Revolution in National Context* (Cambridge: Cambridge University Press, 1992), which includes an excellent essay by Mario Biagioli on differences between Italian, French, and English scientific institutions and practices. The importance of printing for the emergence of the Scientific Revolution is treated in Elizabeth L. Eisenstein's excellent *The Printing Revolution in Early Modern* Europe (Cambridge: Cambridge University Press, 1983). The new focus on material culture during the Scientific Revolution is emphasized in Lisa Jardine's *Ingenious Pursuits: Building the Scientific Revolution* (New York: Nan A. Talese, 1999).

The examination of the role of women during the Scientific Revolution has become a subject of scholarly interest only recently. Two surveys, which include sections on early modern science, are informative, but written for a general audience: Margaret Alic, *Hypatia's Heritage: A History of Women in Science from Antiquity to the Nineteenth Century* (Boston: Beacon Press, 1986), and Patricia Phillips, *The Scientific Lady: A Social History of Women's Scientific Interests, 1520–1918* (New York: St. Martin's Press, 1990). A more specialized volume, Lynette Hunter and Sarah Hutton (eds.), *Women, Science, and Medicine, 1500–1700: Mothers and Sisters of the Royal Society* (Glouchestershire: Sutton Publishing, 1997), contains several excellent essays examining women's role in the domestic sphere, as physicians and midwives, and as aristocratic patrons and participants in the scientific enterprise. Geoffrey V. Sutton, *Science for a Polite Society: Gender, Culture, and the Demonstration of*

Enlightenment (Boulder: Westview Press) writes an eminently readable account of French culture and society, which contains a great deal of material on the role of women in the scientific and philosophical salons of the seventeenth and eighteenth centuries. A recent collection by Sally Gregory Kohlstedt and Mary Terrall, *History of Women in the Sciences: Readings from Isis* (Chicago: University of Chicago Press, 1999), reprints some of the most important articles on women and science published in the last two decades, including articles by Natalie Merchant, Londa Schiebinger, and Paula Findlen. Two new volumes devoted to the work of Margaret Cavendish include sections on her natural philosophy: Stephen Clucas (ed.), *A Princely Brave Woman: Essays on Margaret Cavendish: Duchess of Newcastle* (Aldershot, Hampshire: Ashgate, 2003), and Line Cottegnies and Nancy Weitz, *Essays on Genre in the Writings of Margaret Cavendish* (Cranbury, N.J.: Associated University Presses, 2003). Paula Findlen's interests have turned towards eighteenth century recently, in "Becoming a Scientist: Gender and Knowledge in Eighteenth-Century Italy," *Science in Context* 16 (2003): 59–87, but her work continues to provide insights on the earlier period. Another study of an eighteenth-century woman, Mary Terrall's "Émilie Châtelet and the Gendering of Science," *History of Science* 33 (1995): 307–332, shows how upper-class women were able to participate in the Newtonian Revolution during the Enlightenment. The importance of women in the life of Galileo is portrayed in Dava Sobel's popular *Galileo's Daughter: A Historical Memoir of Science, Faith, and Love* (New York: Penguin Books, 2000).

The contested category of Scientific Revolution is examined by John A. Schuster, "The Scientific Revolution," in *Companion to the History of Modern Science*, ed. R. C. Olby, et al. (London: Routledge, 1990); Andrew Cunningham and Perry Williams, "De-centring the 'Big Picture': the Origins of Modern Science and the Modern Origins of Science," *British Journal for the History of Science* 26 (1993): 407–432; and H. Floris Cohen, *The Scientific Revolution: A Historiographical Inquiry* (Chicago: University of Chicago Press, 1994), which also contains a detailed account of the various historical approaches to the Scientific Revolution. David. C. Lindberg and Robert S. Westman, *Reappraisals of the Scientific Revolution* (Cambridge: Cambridge University Press, 1990), includes many essays on subjects that have been added to the historiographical literature as the definition of Scientific Revolution has changed. Another fine collection of articles which both broaden and question the notion of Scientific Revolution, is Margaret J. Osler (ed.), *Rethinking the Scientific Revolution* (Cambridge: Cambridge University Press, 2000). Osler's introduction to this volume is particularly helpful, and Richard S. Westfall makes a spirited defense of the traditional category of Scientific Revolution in "The Scientific Revolution Reasserted" (41–55). Several new surveys of the Scientific Revolution have appeared recently, all of which deal with the question of whether there actually was a scientific revolution; they include Steven Shapin, *The Scientific Revolution* (Chicago: University of Chicago Press, 1996); John Henry, *The Scientific Revolution and the Origins of Modern Science* (New York: Palgrave, 1997, 2002); and Peter Dear, *Revolutionizing the Sciences: European Knowledge and Its Ambitions, 1500–1700* (Princeton: Princeton University Press, 2001).